CAN VIRTUE BE TAUGHT?

BOSTON UNIVERSITY STUDIES IN PHILOSOPHY AND RELIGION

General Editor: Leroy S. Rouner

Volume Fourteen

Can Virtue Be Taught?

Edited by
Barbara Darling-Smith

UNIVERSITY OF NOTRE DAME PRESS
Notre Dame, Indiana

Library of Congress Cataloging-in-Publication Data

Can virtue be taught? / edited by Barbara Darling-Smith.
      p.   cm. — (Boston University studies in philoso-
phy and religion ; v. 14)
    Includes bibliographical references and index.
    ISBN 0-268-00799-3
    1. Moral education.   2. Virtue — Study and
teaching.   I. Darling-Smith, Barbara, 1954–
II. Series.
LC268.C245   1993
370.11′4 — dc20   93-4578
                                              CIP

Manufactured in the United States of America

FOR SISSELA BOK

Her Institute lectures have advocated personal integrity and perpetual peace. Her work illuminates private and public moral choices with clarity, creativity, and a passion for the right and the good.

Contents

PART III: CONTEMPORARY CONTEXTS
FOR TEACHING VIRTUE

Preface

Boston University Studies in Philosophy and Religion is a joint project of the Boston University Institute for Philosophy and Religion and the University of Notre Dame Press. The essays in each annual volume are edited from the previous year's lecture program and invited papers of the Boston University Institute. The Director of the Institute, who is also the Editor of these Studies, chooses a theme and invites participants to lecture at Boston University in the course of the academic year. The Editor then selects and edits the essays to be included in the volume. Dr. Barbara Darling-Smith, who has been Administrative Assistant to the Director, regularly copy edits the manuscripts. This year she became Assistant Director of the Institute. In celebration of her new appointment, she is Editor of this volume. In preparation is Volume 15, *The Changing Face of Friendship.*

The Boston University Institute for Philosophy and Religion was begun informally in 1970 under the leadership of Professor Peter Bertocci of the Department of Philosophy, with the cooperation of Dean Walter Muelder of the School of Theology, Professor James Purvis, Chair of the Department of Religion, and Professor Marx Wartofsky, Chair of the Department of Philosophy. Professor Bertocci was concerned to institutionalize one of the most creative features of Boston personalism, its interdisciplinary approach to fundamental issues of human life. When Professor Leroy S. Rouner became Director in 1975, and the Institute became a formal Center of the Boston University Graduate School, every effort was made to continue that vision of an ecumenical and interdisciplinary forum.

Within the University the Institute is committed to open interchange on fundamental issues in philosophy and religious study which transcend the narrow specializations of academic curricula. We seek to counter those trends in higher education which emphasize technical expertise in a "multi-versity," and gradually transform undergraduate liberal arts education into preprofessional training.

Our programs are open to the general public, and are regularly broadcast on WBUR-FM, Boston University's National Public Radio affiliate. Outside the University we seek to recover the public tradition of philosophical discourse which was a lively part of American intellectual life in the early years of this century before the professionalization of both philosophy and religious reflection made these two disciplines topics virtually unavailable even to an educated public. We note, for example, that much of William James's work was presented originally as public lectures, and we are grateful to James's present-day successors for the significant public papers which we have been honored to publish. This commitment to a public tradition in American intellectual life has important stylistic implications. At a time when too much academic writing is incomprehensible, or irrelevant, or both, our goal is to present readable essays by acknowledged authorities on critical human issues.

Leroy S. Rouner

Acknowledgments

Gratitude is due first and foremost to the authors of each essay in this volume — for their thoughtful lectures in our series, for their hard work in revising their essays for publication, and for their willingness to accept our editorial suggestions.

Work on this manuscript has been a joint project. Special thanks go to Leroy S. Rouner, who helped with the editorial revisions; Denice K. Carnes, who performed miracles with the scanner and devoted her energy and considerable skill to producing the manuscript; and Sydney Smith III, who provided invaluable last-minute assistance. All three of these friends and colleagues have contributed to the overall effort with intangible support as well, and each has brought good cheer to their vital service.

We cherish our ongoing partnership with the University of Notre Dame Press. Ann Rice, Executive Editor, continues to aid in the publication process with her usual calm and professionalism. Jim Langford, Director, continues to offer suggestions and to work with the Institute on future plans.

The lecture series on which this volume is based — as well as our subsequent three-year program — have been made possible by a generous grant from the Lilly Endowment, Inc. We owe a large debt of gratitude to Jeanne Knoerle, Program Director for Religion, and Craig Dykstra, Vice President for Religion, for their support.

Contributors

BARBARA DARLING-SMITH is Assistant Professor of Religion at Wheaton College and Assistant Director of the Boston University Institute for Philosophy and Religion. She has also taught at Curry College and Bridgewater State College. She received her B.A. from Spring Arbor College, and her M.A. and Ph.D. at Boston University. She has published several articles, and is author of the forthcoming (1994) book: *Lord? Liberator? Friend?: Feminist Understandings of Jesus.*

ELIZABETH KAMARCK MINNICH is a philosopher who has taught at Barnard College, Scripps College, Hollins College, The New School College, and The Graduate School of the Union Institute, where she is presently Professor of Philosophy and Women's Studies. For over twenty years she has been writing, speaking, and consulting on the implications of feminist scholarship for the liberal arts curriculum. Her publications include the books *Transforming Knowledge*, winner of the Frederic W. Ness Prize, and *Reconstructing the Academy: Women's Education and Women's Studies*, edited with O'Barr and Rosenfeld.

ROBERT CUMMINGS NEVILLE received his B.A., M.A., and Ph.D. at Yale University. He is Dean of the School of Theology at Boston University and Professor of Philosophy, Religion, and Theology there. Prior to coming to Boston University in 1987 he taught at the State University of New York at Stony Brook. He has written numerous articles and books, among them *God the Creator, The Highroad around Modernism, Behind the Masks of God, A Theology Primer,* and *Recovery of the Measure.* He has served as president of the American Academy of Religion and of the International Society for Chinese Philosophy.

BHIKHU PAREKH received his B.A. and M.A. in Bombay, India, and his Ph.D. from the London School of Economics. He has taught political theory at Hull University since 1964. In 1981 he returned to India and was Vice-Chancellor (President) of Baroda University until 1984. In Britain he served from 1985 to 1990 as Deputy Chair of the Commission for Racial Equality. His many books include the four-volume *Jeremy Bentham: Critical Assessments, Hannah Arendt and the Search for a New Political Philosophy, Karl Marx's Theory of Ideology, Gandhi's Political Philosophy,* and (as editor) *Bentham's Political Thought.*

SHARON DALOZ PARKS is Senior Research Fellow in Leadership and Ethics at Harvard Business School and the Kennedy School of Government. She is the author of *The Critical Years: Young Adults and the Search for Meaning, Faith, and Commitment;* and coauthor of *Can Ethics Be Taught? Perspectives, Challenges, and Approaches at Harvard Business School,* as well as other books and articles. Her Ph.D. is from Harvard University, her M.A. from Princeton Theological Seminary, and her B.A. from Whitworth College.

KATHERINE PLATT received her Ph.D. in anthropology from the London School of Economics and Political Science after field work in the Kerkennah Islands off the coast of North Africa. She is currently Assistant Professor in Social Sciences in the Boston University College of General Studies and Research Associate at the Center for Middle Eastern Studies at Harvard University. The author of numerous scholarly papers, she has also been Visiting Assistant Professor of Anthropology at Harvard University.

AMELIE OKSENBERG RORTY is Professor of Philosophy at Mount Holyoke College and Visiting Professor in the Harvard Graduate School of Education. She has also taught at a number of other U.S. universities, as well as at the University of Melbourne and at Jilin University in the People's Republic of China. Her B.A. is from the University of Chicago and she received her M.A. and Ph.D. in philosophy from Yale and then studied anthropology (M.S., A.B.D.) at Princeton. Among her books are *Mind in Action, Essays on Aristotle's Poetics*, and (as coeditor) *Essays on Aristotle's De Anima*.

LEROY S. ROUNER is Professor of Philosophy, Religion, and Philosophical Theology; and Director of the Institute for Philosophy and Religion at Boston University. He is General Editor of Boston University Studies in Philosophy and Religion and has also edited *Philosophy, Religion, and the Coming World Civilization*, and *The Wisdom of Ernest Hocking* (with John Howie) and *Corporations and the Common Good* (with Robert Dickie). He is the author of *Within Human Experience, The Long Way Home* (a memoir), and, most recently, *To Be At Home: Christianity, Civil Religion and World Community*.

GEORGE RUPP is the author of numerous articles and several books, including *Commitment and Community*. Currently President of Rice University, he has been named to the presidency of Columbia University, to take office in July 1993. Prior to going to Rice, he was John Lord O'Brian Professor of Divinity and Dean of the Divinity School at Harvard University. He has degrees from Princeton (A.B.), Yale (B.D.), and Harvard (Ph.D.) and has studied and done research at the Universities of Munich and Tübingen in Germany and Peradeniya in Sri Lanka.

NINIAN SMART has written both technical and popular books in the history of religions, Indian philosophy, philosophy of religion, methodology, religious dialogue, religious education, and politics. Educated at Oxford, he founded the first major department of religious studies in England, at Lancaster University. He is currently J. F. Rowny Professor of Comparative Religions at the University of California, Santa Barbara. His books include *The Long Search, Religion and the Western Mind, Beyond Ideology*, and *Worldviews*, and he was editorial consultant for the thirteen-part television series *The Long Search*.

HUSTON SMITH is Thomas J. Watson Professor of Religion and Distinguished Adjunct Professor of Philosophy Emeritus at Syracuse University. The author of many articles and books, including *The Religions of Man* (newly revised and renamed *The World's Religions*), *The Search For America, Forgotten Truth: The Primordial Tradition*, and *Beyond the Post-Modern Mind*, he has also produced television programs for the Public Broadcasting System; films on Hinduism, Tibetan Buddhism, and Sufism; and a phonograph record, "The Music of Tibet."

FREDERICK J. STRENG is Professor of the History of Religions at Southern Methodist University, and is a founding member and Vice President of the Society for Buddhist-Christian Studies. His study for the Ph.D. degree at the University of Chicago took him to Benares Hindu University in India where he lived for a year as a Fulbright Scholar. He has also studied in Sri Lanka, Thailand, Japan, and China. Among the six books he has authored and edited is *Understanding Religious Life*, now in its third English edition, and also available in Japanese and Korean.

Introduction

BARBARA DARLING-SMITH

Human beings have asked questions about what it is to be virtuous, and how to teach goodness to the next generation, for a very long time. Today, in our interconnected and interdependent global community, these questions arise with a greater urgency. Is there a human capacity for learning virtue? Which virtues should be taught — those that benefit the individual or those that benefit the community? What are the most important virtues anyway — and who will decide? Can people from widely divergent cultures learn virtue from one another? Is it possible to instruct college and university students in goodness — and even business school students? What is the relationship between religion and virtue? How does the teaching of virtue relate to the "political correctness" debate? All of these questions are addressed in the essays in *Can Virtue Be Taught?*

The essays in our first section explore the questions of what virtue is and what our aims are for education. We begin with Huston Smith's essay, "Educating the Intellect: On Opening the Eye of the Heart." Smith lays the groundwork for all of the explorations in the book by defending the thesis that humans possess a faculty of knowing which transcends our senses and which unifies our fragmented experiences. He provides an excellent starting point for our discussion of whether this transcendent seat of the human self can be educated in morality and virtue, because, as he points out, "there's little point in talking about educating the Intellect if we don't believe that it exists. The first order of business is to challenge the assumption that it doesn't exist."

Smith finds the awareness of this ability — which he alternately calls the "Eye of the Heart," in spiritual terms, or the "Intellect," in philosophical terms — in a plethora of religious traditions, pre-

1

senting examples from religious practitioners as diverse as Taoists, Sufis, and Hindus. The Eye of the Heart empowers us to know, argues Smith, because it is directly joined to "the Center of Reality itself."

And the evidence of this mental capacity is found in the philosophical traditions as well. Smith's *Intellect* is very similar to the *nous* in Plato, Aristotle, and Plotinus. Our Intellect, operating in a way we cannot explain, lies deeper in us than our cognitive abilities and enables them to function. Smith sees himself as "retrieving . . . the view of the human mind that preceded the rise of modern science and its pivotal spokesperson, Descartes." Our Intellect connects us to this world and thereby overcomes modern philosophy's gap between the *noumena* and the phenomena. The human *nous* derives its power from its relation to the cosmic *Nous*.

Smith spends most of his essay describing and defending the existence of the Intellect, and leaves the question of whether the Eye of the Heart can be educated to his co-contributors to this volume. Amelie Oksenberg Rorty's essay "Moral Imperialism vs. Moral Conflict: Conflicting Aims of Education" picks up where Huston Smith leaves off, going straight to the question of the aims of education. She surveys two schools of thought on this question: perfectionist aims and liberal aims of autonomous self-determination.

The goals of the perfectionist educator, expressed most clearly in Aristotle, are themselves varied: education "to promote the noblest and best life, that of the contemplator and scientist," education of the free citizen, and training for occupations, such as merchant. Aristotle's perfectionist educator, the *phronimos*, must decide whether to structure education so as to enable individuals to develop their potentialities for excellence, or so as to serve the good of the *polis*. Though Aristotle is clear about these tensions in his perfectionist position, argues Rorty, he does not give a final direction to the *phronimos* as to how to weight these different priorities.

Liberal, egalitarian educational policy also has its internal tensions. It is committed to equality of education for all citizens. But because it is limited to educational aims "which all citizens can be presumed to accept," it requires a neutral stance toward competing understandings of the good. Thus it must make questionable distinctions, such as between intellectual and moral education, and leave moral education to private institutions. Thus neither position — the perfectionist nor the liberal egalitarian — is able to delineate unambiguous policies for the structuring of education. Rorty notes that there have been many attempts to construct hybrid theories which reconcile all these diverse aims. But these are either too general to be helpful or their choice of priorities could be challenged by competing theories which weight the priorities differently. Rorty's proposal for defining and structuring the aims of education is the method of "reflective equilibrium," which requires the recognition that consensus on unambiguous educational priorities will remain elusive. Revisable rules of thumb are preferable to binding principles in deciding educational aims, because educational priorities will appropriately vary contextually. Rorty uses the image of a mobile to picture this method: "any shift or movement in one part effects a corresponding shift in the others."

Having tackled the question of whether we have a capacity for virtue to be educated, and the question of how to decide on the appropriate aims for education, we move to Bhikhu Parekh's essay, "Bentham's Theory of Virtue," which reflects on a possible resource for our understanding of what virtue is. Parekh delineates and challenges Jeremy Bentham's description of the nature of virtue and his classification of virtues and vices. In the end, however, Parekh finds Bentham inadequate for several reasons.

Parekh reminds us that Bentham's ethical hedonism distinguishes right from wrong — virtue from vice — solely on the basis of how much pleasure and pain is produced by the action in question. Moral action is action which maximizes one's own and others' happiness, that is, maximizes present and future pleasure and minimizes present and future pain. Therefore one is virtuous when one exercises the requisite self-denial to act in a way which will bring about the greatest overall amount of human well-being.

Further, for Bentham virtues are socially acquired, consciously cultivated, and action-oriented. The two primary virtues are for Bentham prudence, a self-regarding virtue; and benevolence, which governs one's relations with others.

After clarifying Bentham's treatment of virtues, Parekh provides a devastating critique. First he criticizes Bentham's analysis of the concept of virtue. By restricting virtue to moral qualities leading to consequences which further human happiness, argues

Parekh, Bentham leaves no room for virtues such as integrity and conscientiousness. Yet consequences are not the only criteria for judging moral qualities. Morality should clarify not only the right but also the good, not only what we should *do* but what we should *be*. Virtues are not simply motives for action but are also evidence of an agent's character, "a moral compass for mapping, ordering, and finding one's bearings in life."

Next Parekh challenges Bentham's description of specific virtues, which reduces all virtues to various ways of maximizing happiness and minimizing pain. Chastity or fidelity in marriage, Parekh points out, is for Bentham a virtue identical to abstaining from playing loud music to avoid annoying one's neighbor; both demonstrate negative benevolence by avoiding causing pain. To equate these two virtues, says Parekh, shows an "analysis of chastity [which] has gone seriously wrong." Parekh presents an additional example: humanity. Humanity does not mean, as in Bentham's view, simply to eschew giving pain to other human beings. Instead, argues Parekh, humanity "involves recognizing [others] as fellow human beings entitled to certain kinds of treatment and to whom certain things may never be done."

Parekh's critique of Bentham is salutary as a reminder of the continuous need to challenge the questions and answers of the foundational classical philosophers. A more radical challenge is presented by Elizabeth Kamarck Minnich, and we conclude our first section with her essay, "Can Virtue Be Taught?: A Feminist Reconsiders." Hers is an appropriate approach to keep in mind from the start as we ask the question of teaching virtue. Her feminist perspective on the question is informed by a mode of resistance, of ongoing critique of dominant thought patterns. If we do not approach questions such as virtue and the goals of education "with all our feminist-critical senses awake, we are liable to be led down well-trodden paths, which . . . remain within the maze of a world of meanings defined in male terms claiming to be universal." Because of the continuing effects of male dominance, we need to be aware of old mistakes, perpetuated in the present. Mistakes to be recognized and exorcised include faulty generalization, from a few men to all of humankind; mystified concepts, "such as that of virtue that . . . [makes] women subject to a separate and distinctly unequal notion of womanly virtue that is not human virtue"; and definitions which dissociate Man from women, from nature, and from "lesser men"— indeed, from elements within himself which he has in common with all those "others."

Minnich calls for a reconfiguring which will respect and bring to the center those whose experiences and values have been ignored and marginalized. She speaks particularly of women — women of different races and classes — but she notes the convergence of feminist critiques with those from Third World people and proponents of environmentalism, pacifism, and multiculturalism. Recovering the virtues of those who have been dissociated from Man will lead to a *transformation* of Man's virtues. Reminiscent of Rorty's image of educational priorities as a mobile, Minnich cites the image used by Larry and Sande Churchill of ethical theory as a collage, embracing diverse perspectives.

Minnich's inclusive view of a company with which to ask the questions about pedagogy and virtue — a company including "persons from all countries, cultures, genders, sexual orientations, ages, and regions"— leads naturally to our second section. Since our struggle to teach virtue cannot make assumptions about "universal humanity" without attending to the stimulating diversity of many groups of people, our undeniable context for teaching virtue is the cross-cultural global community. Frederick J. Streng's essay "Cultivating Virtue in a Religiously Plural World: Possibilities and Problems" begins our section on teaching virtues in different cultures. Streng reminds us that we are "in a world network of relationships which, for good or ill, helps to shape our sense of virtuous living." Like Minnich, Streng assiduously avoids the particular model of a world order based on imperialism and on "extending one's ethnic or normative ideology and rules for virtuous living to all others." He notes that different cultures understand virtues on the basis of their vision of the transcendent and the human relationship to it. Some religious communities emphasize the selfhood of the believer her- or himself and others focus on other important selves; some groups define the self individually and others identify the self communally. Virtues are thus evaluated differently in these different communities. Streng celebrates this variety, but recognizes the danger of a relativist reduction to virtue as a matter of personal or cultural preference. To avoid relativism, Streng offers two suggestions.

The first echoes Rorty's call for dialogue about educational aims. Listening to citizens from other cultures about what such virtues as authenticity and justice mean for them, and honestly expressing what they mean for us, is crucial. This dialogue should include tolerance for anger, and an atmosphere of trust. Second, Streng calls for a recognition that virtues are learned by practicing them, and that our skills in evaluating virtues can develop as we exercise them. In a process of dialogue we can teach each other "the way in which different expressions of virtue may increase human excellence and enhance the lived experience among the members of the global community."

A key ingredient in cross-cultural dialogue about virtue, as Streng insists, is to listen respectfully to understandings of virtue in other cultures. Thus we present an essay by Katherine Platt about the acquisition of virtue in the Kerkennah Islands, "Vicarious Virtue: Gender and Moral Education in Muslim North Africa." Platt, an anthropologist, understands virtue to be a "cultural ideal, which is to say a cultural product." Just as Rorty insisted that educational goals must vary contextually, Platt argues that understandings of virtue differ according to the changing pressures and influences on the culture in which they are learned.

Platt's essay explores what it means to be virtuous in the Kerkennah Islands of Tunisia. She finds striking contrasts between the perceptions of male virtue and female virtue, and she demonstrates these contrasts by describing the rites of passage which mark the life cycles of both genders. She notes that the character of males and females is believed to be different even prenatally: "male fetuses are thought to be very rambunctious, whereas females are thought to lie still." This low profile for the female is an important element in her virtue throughout her life.

Forty-Day Ceremonies mark the birth of a male baby with elaborate rituals such as his first haircut, a ritual bath, and greetings of "God willing, may you be circumcised." Female babies' Forty-Day Ceremonies are much less formal, and if the girl is not a firstborn, there is usually no Forty-Day Ceremony.

The next ritual for the male child is circumcision (at approximately age two), which ritually affirms his sexuality *and* demonstrates his separation from his mother. There is no parallel ceremony to ritualize the female's separation from her mother; her identity is not perceived in as autonomous a manner as is her brother's.

The female's sexuality is not ritually acknowledged until her marriage ceremony, when it is quickly subsumed under the protection of her husband and is linked integrally to the symbolism of childbearing. Platt notes that "the bride is at the height of her beauty, purity, and innocence, . . . at the zenith of her moral accomplishment. With carnal knowledge, she is permanently compromised and potentially dangerous." The wedding ceremony for the man symbolizes his reincorporation into the domestic world of women, and he becomes the head of his own family.

From the womb to the grave, observes Platt, male and female virtues are understood differently. Men are buried with only a headstone, whereas women's graves need both a head- and a footstone "to hold them down," to keep them from escaping to cause trouble.

Like Platt, Ninian Smart describes the virtues prized by a different culture in his essay "Clarity and Imagination as Buddhist Means to Virtue." Smart points out that Buddhists — particularly Theravāda Buddhists — name three obstacles to human fulfillment: greed, hatred, and delusion. The first two are recognized among the Christian list of seven deadly sins, but Smart notes that Westerners have been less concerned to combat the third. Buddhism, on the other hand, views ignorance or lack of insight as a crucial human problem.

Clarity and imagination are both central to Buddhist ethics because they are strategies by which to overcome delusion. The knowledge which supplants ignorance is existential and not merely intellectual. But intellectual arguments are important to convince us of the practical implications of Buddhist philosophy. For example, the reasoning process that the world must be impermanent and changing, because otherwise there would be no way to account for change, "helps to dispel egoism, since there is no permanent soul to safeguard and pamper." Similarly, the intellectual realization that all human beings belong to the same species can aid in the practical necessity of treating all humans equally. In this way conceptual clarity promotes virtuous living. The clarity of self-awareness is another guide to virtue. Reflecting carefully on one's motives, Smart suggests, can lead one to discover the hidden egoism or envy which may lurk behind our reactions.

Imagination is a virtue which Buddhist meditation utilizes to achieve equanimity, where one envisions oneself as a stream of causation linked to everyone else's stream of causation, and one is thus enabled to "take other streams as seriously as her own." Imagination is also valuable in learning to perceive an enemy in a positive way. By imagining that some evil person was one's mother or father or son or daughter in a previous life, and in that life showered us with acts of love and kindness, we may be able to extend our empathy to them in this life.

Nurturing these Buddhist virtues related to the dispelling of ignorance and delusion, argues Smart, would have wonderfully salutary results in academic life. Learning how to enter the thought world of others through empathetic imagination and equanimity of emotion toward them can aid us in understanding them—a condition necessary for the human and social sciences. And culti- vating the imagination to improve our attitudes toward others, to remind ourselves of our commonalities, could help us in abolish- ing the evils of racism, nationalism, and sexism in our academic institutions. Smart also suggests that viewing the pursuit of truth as a communal enterprise, open to criticism, "would discourage the tendency to pursue knowledge egoistically, where my theories become my intellectual property. . . . There is much to borrow," Smart concludes, "from the Buddhist tradition."

The academic setting Smart identifies as a pivotal place in which to practice these typically Buddhist virtues brings us to our final section of essays, on contemporary contexts for teaching vir- tue. Each of these essays analyzes academic institutions and the opportunities — as well as crises — related to teaching virtue there. We begin this section with Leroy S. Rouner's essay "Can Virtue Be Taught in a School?: Ivan Illich and Mohandas Gandhi on De- schooling Society."

Rouner's central question for today's students about their teachers is Socrates' question: "What will they make of you?" Can teachers in college and university settings aid their students in finding out who they are, and how they might live a good life? The question is not whether the intellectual discipline of ethics can be taught, because ethics "is only the tuneless prescription of social oughts," whereas "virtue is a song. One has to get the tune right." Virtue, like courage, needs to be learned with the heart as well as the head. "The purpose of teaching someone about courage is to make them courageous."

Rouner analyzes three models of how to teach virtue: Ivan Illich, Socrates, and Mohandas Gandhi. Rouner notes that Illich views schools and teachers as unnecessary—even as obstacles to learning—because teachers wrongly fall into or are forced into the authoritarian roles of custodian, preacher, and therapist. Illich theorizes that schools should be done away with, and people will then automatically learn from life outside of school—from families, the work place, the larger community. But Rouner finds Illich unsatisfactory, because knowledge must be worked at to be achieved, and school is the place where we work at attaining knowledge.

Socrates and Gandhi, unlike Illich, both approve of people especially identified as teachers. Both of them, however, also realize that a true, life-changing understanding of virtue "is finally discovered by individuals in their own souls, rather than imposed by someone else from outside. So one can't 'teach' virtue, but one can help people get to the place where they can learn it for themselves." Socrates' method of trying to get people to that place relied almost entirely on rational argumentation, and Rouner recognizes that the powers of rationality are no longer trusted as they were in Socrates' time.

Gandhi's way of teaching virtue was to personify it. As Rouner points out, Gandhi understood the educator's role as that of guru, and he lived that role in relation to the whole of India. His goal was that the teacher's (his own) insight into virtue would be transferred to the student (the nation of India).

Rouner is drawn to Gandhi's personalizing of teaching, but he finds Gandhi's model, in the end, too authoritarian, and he reminds us that not only is virtue a song; "it is a song sung in one's own voice." Thus the goal of teachers in higher education should be to help students find their own voice—as artists, as scientists, and as human beings attempting to live virtuously. The route to this personal transformation, suggests Rouner, is to personalize education, by focusing on the "inwardness" of both students and teachers, by recognizing the dimension of *spirit* in learning and teaching virtue.

Rouner's call for "spirit-informed" learning strikes a harmonious chord with Robert Cummings Neville's essay about "Religious Learning beyond Secularism." Neville argues that in our cultural context of pervasive secularism, institutions of higher education have a responsibility to teach religious learning. And just as Rouner refuses to allow virtue to be reduced to ethics, Neville insists that religious learning cannot be reduced to simply learning about religion. The religious learning which Neville calls for in educational institutions includes study of mythologies and theologies by which religions make sense of the ultimate; legitimation of spiritual practices; and public rituals to celebrate and recognize the religious dimension of life.

Secular culture, observes Neville, seeks to obscure this religious dimension. It denies the "worldward grace" and "divine creative force of the universe" which religion celebrates. But secularism cannot account for the contingency of the world. Even more disastrously, secularism trivializes the religious virtues: righteousness, piety, faith, hope, and love. Neville maintains that these virtues, though articulated in Christian terminology, have parallels in nearly every other religious community.

The religious virtue of righteousness seeks justice out of respect for the created order of the universe. Secularized righteousness reduces justice to a matter of preference, and falls into relativism.

Piety as a religious virtue perceives each element in the world as the valued creature of a divine creator, and therefore deserving of respect. "Without piety, we act as if the human sphere were the ontological center of the universe, whereas in fact it is only the center of our neighborhood." Secularism distorts piety into aestheticism, which enjoys other creatures only for their utilitarian and/or aesthetic value to humans.

The religious virtues of faith and hope inspire us to struggle on courageously despite difficulties and disappointments and discouraging odds. The secularized distortions of faith and hope allow engaging the world only when we are assured of success, and often end up in escapism or despair.

The religious virtue of love combines and harmonizes all of the other virtues, which, without love, would often be in conflict. It acknowledges the intrinsic worth of human beings *and* non-human beings *and* God. The secularized form of love encourages possessiveness and "sticking with those who love you first." The bankruptcy of secular culture and its virtues, maintains Neville, is powerful evidence of the necessity for colleges and universities to foster religious learning.

Sharon Daloz Parks has studied the teaching of virtue within a slightly different context in the university — business schools. Her essay "Professional Ethics, Moral Courage, and the Limits of Personal Virtue" reports on her studies of business school students and their perceptions of their own public accountability. According to Parks, business schools do recognize their responsibility to teach virtue. But they are asking which virtues should be taught in this continually changing world.

Rouner's essay uses courage as a metaphor for virtue, and Parks too emphasizes the centrality of the virtue of courage. She believes with Winston Churchill that "courage is the most important of all virtues, for it guarantees the rest." And she sees courage as based on imagination — and here she finds common ground with Ninian Smart's praise for imagination as a moral virtue. Parks' study explores "the imagination by which entering MBA students make meaning, because this is our best clue as to how they will ground their day-to-day decision making." The results are revealing. Parks finds a recurring lack in her investigation of students' moral imagination: their values are limited to individualistically oriented virtues. Many of these students have a strong sense of personal integrity and individual virtue. For example, they may participate in volunteer activities, and many of them express a strong desire not to hurt anybody. But when asked in the survey who they thought they might hurt in their careers, these future leaders of society's important business institutions responded only with the possibility that they might hurt their family by working too long hours, or that they might hurt an employee if they ever had to fire anyone. They showed no awareness that their decisions might hurt the ecosystem, or the interdependent economy. Further, they articulate a concern with achieving balance in their lives between work and leisure, job and personal life, etc., and this fear of lack of balance reflects no recognition that they themselves "are on their way to becoming architects of the economic and social structures to which they feel they will be so uncomfortably vulnerable." Again, the restriction of virtue to privatized morality handicaps their ability to imagine virtue as *public* accountability.

Yet Parks is hopeful. She finds business school an auspicious learning opportunity for students, as they are forming their identity as professionals, and she calls for educators and students to imagine beyond an individualized view of virtue to "the now vital virtues of a more interdependent conviction . . . an imagination that embraces the common good of the whole earth community."

Our study of education for virtue concludes with George Rupp's provocative exploration of the currently hotly debated topic of "political correctness": "Teaching Virtue Turns Vicious: 'Political Correctness' and Its Critics." Like Rouner and Neville, Rupp, a university president, sets his discussion in the context of liberal arts colleges and universities. The controversy over "political correctness" has arisen in the pluralistic context earlier described by Streng. Rupp notes that colleges and universities have responded to the undeniably multicultural character of U.S. society by broadening academic study to include previously slighted perspectives — perspectives from a plethora of cultures and ethnic groups, from women as well as men, from gays and lesbians as well as heterosexuals. The critics of political correctness find this variety of perspectives discomforting, but Rupp argues that multicultural education can lead to a strengthened, shared national identity which is enriched rather than strained by its diversity.

Yet those who oppose what they call "political correctness" decry multicultural study as an all-out attack on Western culture. They perceive the addition of other perspectives, some of which are highly critical of Euro-American dominance, as too threatening. Rupp agrees that to teach about Western history "with the intention of systematically defaming it as exclusively a tradition of oppression is irresponsible pedagogy that rests on indefensible scholarship." Yet he contends that not only is the inclusion of multiple perspectives central to free inquiry, but comparison with other traditions can sharpen awareness of the distinctiveness of Western culture itself.

Rupp finds the underlying concern of the critics of "political correctness" to be the question of truth. They fear that colleges and universities are encouraging a relativist approach which will make all truth claims meaningless. Rupp acknowledges that many academic disciplines — literary theory and sociology of knowledge, among others — emphasize the historical and cultural limitations of truth claims, but he also insists that these same disciplines are committed to the pursuit of truth (to use Smart's phrase). While they reject absolutist understandings of truth, they also reject relativism by developing a variety of tests for the adequacy of competing truth claims.

Promoting the free exchange of ideas, encouraging the discussion of conflicting truth claims — Rupp insists that these are the proper purposes of academic institutions. Like Minnich and Streng, Rupp celebrates this lively interaction among different perspectives. This interaction is, he argues, "precisely what a community committed to ongoing critical and comparative inquiry should welcome."

What conclusions can be drawn from our exploration of teaching virtue? Some common themes have emerged in these essays: celebration of the virtues of tolerance and appreciation of different perspectives; insistence on inclusion of previously underrepresented voices in dialogue; pedagogical attention to the student's "own voice"; an awareness of the power of imagination to shape our perception of virtues, and the power of courage to enable us to live virtuously. But I resist the temptation to attempt a final definitive answer to the questions about which virtues should be taught, and how we should teach them. To do so would be false to the data, and insufficiently respectful of the diversity of perspectives these authors express. So I conclude by borrowing Rorty's image of a mobile, where each moving part in a pedagogical scheme influences the others, and Minnich's image of a collage, where varying understandings of virtue complement each other without blending and blurring the distinctions. In this way I hope to express the tolerance for diversity which so many of these authors judge to be vital in any discussion of virtues and education in our interdependent global community.

PART I

Foundational Questions about Teaching Virtue

Educating the Intellect:
On Opening the Eye of the Heart

HUSTON SMITH

THE TOPIC I WISH to reflect on in this essay takes the form of a question. Is there a faculty of knowing that has not evolved from our sensory equipment but instead precedes and empowers the senses while doing much more? My *conclusion* is that there is such an organ. I shall begin by calling it the Eye of the Heart; but then, building on the metaphors I rely on in Section One, I shall shift in Section Two to the abstractions of philosophy where I will call the organ the Intellect. There are many reasons why it is important to recognize the Intellect, but I will concentrate on one. The Intellect, or the Eye of the Heart, accomplishes what Mark Taylor tells us no modern epistemology has been able to do. It enables us to get from the knowing subject to its object, from the epistemic subject that *knows,* to the object *that* it knows. Modern epistemology's inability to effect this splice accounts for a great deal of the confusion of our time, so the stakes are high; whether we rise to them is another matter. Procedurally, each of the three key terms in my title — education, Intellect, and the Eye of the Heart — will be allotted a section in my paper, in reverse order.

I. THE EYE OF THE HEART[1]

References to an Invisible Eye that complements our corporeal eyes are widespread in "the wisdom traditions"— my phrase for the major religions in their traditional, sapiential strands; the phrase distinguishes those strands from their institutional, scientific, and sociological involvements. Plato speaks of the Eye of the Soul, which

"outshines ten thousand [corporeal] eyes," and the Tibetans of opening the Third Eye. In Indian philosophy, Nyaya recognizes *pra-
tyakṣa* as a *pramāṇa* (instrument of knowing) which enables seers
to see transcendental realities. Last year a Taoist master from Tai-
wan sought me out to open my Eye of the Tao, my *shin meng*,
or *tsung yang fa mung*. Both Matthew and Luke speak of a Single
Eye which lights the whole body like a lamp and without which
"how great is the darkness!" (Matt. 6:22–23).

What is this Eye in question, for which I shall use the Sufis'
designation, Eye of the Heart? What Heart is referred to? Why
does it have an Eye, and why do we need to open it?

It goes without saying that this Heart is not the physical organ
that pumps blood; nor is it the seat of our sentiments, the faculty
that experiences anguish and joy. Rather, it is the seat of knowledge. There is such a thing as heart knowledge. In the Upanishads,
as in the Islamic tradition and elsewhere, the seat of knowledge
is located in the heart, not the mind. In Chinese, the character
for heart (*hsin*) doubles for both mind and heart but is literally
heart. In contrast with modernity, which situates knowing in the
mind and brain, sacred traditions identify knowing, particularly
essential knowing, with the heart. They consider the Heart — the
incorporeal heart of which the physical heart is a material pro-
longation or extension — to be a distinct instrument of knowing
that exists as a part of the inclusive anatomy of the human self:
physical, psychological, and spiritual. The reason that all wisdom
traditions speak of the Heart is that there *is*, I am arguing, such
a faculty or organ which constitutes the seat and center of the
human state. It is central because it is directly joined to the Center of Reality itself. It is because of the centrality of the heart for
the human organism — it sends forth lifegiving blood and receives
it back to clean it — that tradition speaks of the Eye of *Heart*, and
not, say, of the liver or the lungs. The corporeal heart animates
our physical body in the way the Heart whose Eye we are addressing animates our knowing and our metaphysical selves generally.

Having noted the symbolic appropriateness of the heart, why
the eye? Why do traditions speak of the Eye of the Heart and not
some other organ? Why not the ear of the heart, or the tongue
of the heart? That is because of the scope that vision commands.
We can taste and touch only what contacts our bodies. Smell reaches

beyond our bodies, and hearing reaches farther still, but we can only see the stars, not smell or hear them. Vision sweeps out the vastest world our senses disclose, and this is why Hindus speak of the Eye of Shiva and the Third Eye, not the ear of Shiva or the third ear.

Having noted the metaphorical appropriateness of "eye" and "heart," I must now say what these are metaphors *for*. What is the traditions' view of the human self that receives these references?

In that view the self is not a simple dualism — a body here and a mind that floats somehow above it. Rather, there are "layers" of body, of which the physical (or gross) body is the cover. (The Hindu scheme is the most explicit about this, with its doctrine of the Five Sheaths and Three Bodies.) All of these bodies have their own centers. We oversimplify disastrously when we think that we are inwardly minds, and outwardly the bodies that physicians deal with. Descartes's simplistic mind/body dualism went a long way toward removing God and spirit from our immediate awareness,[2] and it did so by removing the intermediate spaces in the human self. These intermediate spaces have no meaning to moderns. Ironically, at the very moment that Descartes was erasing intermediate psychic spaces with his dualism, Paracelsus and others in his camp were speaking of astral bodies and the like; Descartes's disjunction couldn't dispel the human intuition that there *are* things besides mind and matter. In our own century, this intuition has spawned research on parapsychology and all kinds of New Age interest in shamanism, channelling, and the paranormal generally. The interest is commendable, but it is lost in the confusion of trying to traverse the labyrinthine soul without a roadmap. The current interest in subtle and astral bodies, along with energies like *ch'i* and *kundalini*, is really an attempt to rediscover in this century regions of the self that the wisdom traditions took note of.

If we pick up with the Hindu formulation because of its explicitness, the rough account is this: animating the gross body, which we can see and touch and weigh, is the subtle body which has its own senses, the *indriyas*, which hear and see and touch and taste metaphysical, invisible realities. All scriptures allude to these occult senses; a nineteenth-century Persian Sufi writes: "Open the Eye of thine Heart so as to see the world of the Spirit" (Hatif Isfahani). In the semitic traditions, God speaks. If we think of

physical speech as involving airwaves and vocal cords, this is metaphorical; but in its own domain, on its own ontological plane, it
is literal. If there were nothing in us which on the inner and esoteric level corresponds to physical speech and hearing, there
would be no possibility of the divine communicating to us. The
references to these corresponding senses in the various scriptures
imply the existence of inner organs to which our physical sense
organs correspond by emanational extension. There is metaphysical seeing — intuitive discernment is my favorite phrase for it —
and the Eye of the Heart is the invisible, and presumably immate-
rial, faculty that effects that seeing.

Why, though, is that Eye depicted as single? Our bodies have
two eyes; why shouldn't there be two Eyes of the Heart? In the
center of Shiva's forehead, why is there only a single jewel?

The answer is: Our physical eyes are multiple because the
physical world they open onto is multiple; in Chinese idiom it is
the realm of the ten thousand things. To comprehend the world's
plurality, our eyes too must be plural. But that plurality is kept
to a minimum — two — because existentially that's the way the world
comes to us or "at us." It splits on every hand into yin/yang dis-
junctions: subject and object, good and evil, self and other. When
Adam and Eve ate the forbidden apple, "the [significantly plural]
eyes of both were opened" (Gen. 3:7) and the world split, con-
comitantly, in two — into the knowledge of good and evil. Spirit
must heal that rift, and with it all other dualities, not by erasing
them but by pulling them together in the way the hand gathers
its multiple fingers into the singularity of hand. Because spirit's
vocation is, precisely, to transcend dualities, its eye *must* be one.
It looks toward the shining point where things transgress their sepa-
rateness and all lines intersect.

Implied, here, is the answer to why the Eye of the Heart must
be opened and not left shut. In the long run we are impelled to
open it because the world we ultimately belong to is the world
of oneness, and our final felicity, our *ānanda*, the peace that we
seek and cannot be happy without, cannot be had unless duality
is transcended. Our entire life is the attempt to overcome separation, and the whole tragedy of life springs from our failure to
accomplish that task. All human love is a partial overcoming of
duality, and all pain of separation is duality seen at close range.

Internally, there is no happiness unless we overcome the barrier that separates us from our own selves. Even when I say "I," I am not fully myself, for I am not attuned to the deepest part of myself that is more *than* myself. This may sound abstract, but sooner or later, in one way or another, we must all be brought to this truth because of who we are. That some of us are materialists and atheists makes no difference. Because we are all human, consciously or unconsciously we all seek to overcome the separation between us and the God who is the true object of our desire, whether we envision that God as within us or without. Happy or unhappy as the case may be, the ultimate object of our desire is to be joined to the Reality for which we were created.

The wisdom traditions tell us *how* to open the Eye of the Heart, but I will not go into their instructions which are mainly versions of Hinduism's four yogas. Instead, I shall conclude this section by considering a final question. Why must the Eye of the Heart be opened instead of being open to begin with? Our physical eyes are open from birth. Why isn't the Eye of the Heart?

However we interpret their mythologies, the mainstream answer of the traditions runs something like this:

The fact that we talk about sight suggests that we have not always been blind. The fact that we seek peace though we live in a world full of war means that the experience of peace could not have been totally alien to us. This suggests that the fact that the Eye of the Heart is cited, independently, in so many traditions means that it is a human possibility that it be open. Most, if not all, of the traditions have an explanation for why the eye has closed. It has to do with the flow of time — what the Hindus would call the circling of the cosmic cycles. We are not, today, fully ourselves. We are not what we should be because we live at a particular cosmic moment that doesn't happen to be the Golden Age. The mark of the Golden Age — the time of Eden, the *krita yuga*, or the Age of the Grand Harmony that Confucius looked back to — was that the Eye of the Heart was then open. People then didn't need revelations or religion. Adam walked directly with God. In an Islamic gloss on that story, the Ninety-nine Beautiful Names, now reserved for Allah, applied originally to Adam as well. He had direct knowledge of things, and was his own prophet. Comparably in the Hindu tradition: in the Vedic Age no special *rishis* were needed, for everyone's Eye was open. But time occasions distancing from the divine source, so gradually the Eye of the Heart closes.

This, roughly, is how the doctrine of the Eye of the Heart shapes up — most directly in Sufism, but with strong analogies in the wisdom traditions generally. I turn now to relate that concept to the second substantive term in my title, the Intellect. Whereas this section has employed the language of religion, fixing on sensible objects — eyes and hearts — to point them toward deeper intangible realities, my next section will ride the momentum thus gained, but will wax philosophical. The intent will be to use abstract language to describe the Eye of the Heart more precisely.

II. THE INTELLECT

In using "Intellect" as the philosophical name for our object, I think of myself as retrieving (on balance) the view of the human mind that preceded the rise of modern science and its pivotal representative, Descartes. In that earlier view, the mind's central faculty was called *nous* in Greek, and *intellectus* in Latin. (Vedanta's *buddhi* and the Buddhist *prajñā* could easily be included.) As I am using broad strokes, I shall not go into the differences between Plato's, Aristotle's, and Plotinus's concepts of *nous,* or how those differences shook down into the *intellectus* of Saint Thomas and the scholastics. When modernity started to think of the mind differently, it lost interest in the Intellect to the point where now it doesn't even warrant an entry in the five-volume *Dictionary of the History of Ideas*[3] (the *history* of ideas!) or its index either. So I shall begin from scratch. Working my way back from the way we now think of the mind, I shall argue that we overlook things that our predecessors had better in view. The ones that concern me coalesce, as I have said, in their notion of Intellect.

We can begin with a mental capacity that baffles current epistemologists completely, one that differs markedly from reason. Reason performs logical operations on information that is in full view and can be described or defined. Through and through, though, we find that our understanding is floated and furthered by operations that are mysterious because all that we seem able to know about them is that we have no idea as to how they work. We have hunches that pay off. Or we find that we know what to do in complicated situations without being able to explain exactly *how* we know. This ability is unconscious, yet it enables us to perform enormously complicated tasks, from reading and writing to farming and composing music. Expertise is coming to be recognized as more intuitive than cognitive psychologists had supposed. These students of behavior and learning are finding that when faced with exceptionally subtle tasks, people who "feel" or intuit their ways through them are more creative than those who consciously try to think their way through the situations. This explains why computer programmers no less than psychologists have had trouble getting the experts to articulate the rules they follow. The experts do not follow rules. Workers in artificial intelligence are coming to see that "human intelligence can never be replaced with machine intelligence because we are not ourselves 'thinking machines.' Each of us has, and uses every day, a power of intuitive intelligence that enables us to understand, to speak, and to cope skillfully with our everyday environment."[4] Somehow it summarizes everything we have ever experienced and done, and enables that summary to shape our present decisions. Programmers cannot instruct their machines to do this because no one has the slightest idea how we ourselves do it.

An example that I have cited before bears repeating because it is so remarkable.[5] Japanese chicken sexers are able to decide with 99 per cent accuracy the sex of a chick, even though the female and male genitalia of young chicks are ostensibly indistinguishable. No analytic approach to learning the art could ever approach such accuracy. Aspiring chicken sexers learn only by looking over the shoulders of experienced workers, who cannot explain how they themselves do it.

We find this example startling, but the talent it shocks us into noticing is one that we all possess. Thus far I have stayed with its importance for thinking, but it orders our practical life as well via a virtue we can call prudence. Prudence is a subliminally mobile but focused concentration which again (as in cognition) works for us instinctively, without our knowing how it works or even thinking of it as a distinct operation. Functioning in something of the manner of a hidden gyroscope it monitors our inclinations, directing our "yeses" and our "nos," those two magical words of the will. To do this, it spins no system of ideas. Instead, it synthesizes all we have learned and brings this synthesis to every decision we make. In doing so it provides dozens of answers to dozens of questions, and — because it gives no evidence of caring about their mutual agreement — conveys the impression that each particular answer is absolutely *ad hoc*. This gives it an air of practical poetry, for each particular answer arises spontaneously and ingenuously, while being for the most part appropriate and, for the moment in question, conclusive. Its spontaneity is only seeming, however, for if we reflect on the matter we find that all its *ad hoc* answers arise from a whole that directs them and makes them appropriate; its activities are prodigiously married. The integral truth of our being from which it springs envelops and inspires everything we consciously and even unconsciously do, giving our lives their form and style and seeing to it that each action and decision reflect that style.

I propose that we use the practical and cognitive power I have been pointing to as our entree to the intellect. In this first formulation, we can characterize it as an invisible and mysterious X — invisible because it attaches to no anatomical organ; mysterious because we don't know how it works — that powers and directs our conscious thoughts and actions.

In a way, nothing that I have thus far said is news. For some time Michael Polanyi, evolutionary biologists, and developmental psychologists have been talking about cognitive underpinnings that are indispensable to our knowing but which operate unconsciously. The Intellect, though, differs from "tacit knowing" of this sort in a decisive respect. All the above-mentioned investigators assume that mental operations that we can't explain ride the wave of simpler operations that are rationally explicable. In short, they assume that the more derives from the less. I, for my part, am positing the opposite: that the Intellect is prior to, and the driving power of, all other modes of knowing. To make the difference plain, I shall summarize the evolutionary hypothesis that cognitive psychology works with.

From a "population" of stimulus-response pairs, born of random responses to a given stimulus, the nervous system reinforces pairs that are adaptive. This "selects" them by increasing the probability that they will recur while their maladaptive or merely neutral brethren suffer "extinction" by failing to reproduce. The analogy with Darwinism is very strong, very satisfying, and very familiar. It is equally strong in the so-called dry, as opposed to biological or wet, approach to the study of learning and intelligence, the science of artificial intelligence which works with "thinking machines." Problem-solving computer programs are designed to generate and test. At a given point or points, the program sets up generating and testing units. The generating unit invents candidates for the problem's solution and transmits them to the testing unit, which accepts or rejects them on the basis of stored criteria. This again is like natural selection, as Herbert Simon points out. Artificial intelligence and cognitive psychology work from opposite ends of the scale. Artificial intelligence begins with mechanisms that obviously lack intelligence — magnetic tapes whose segments do or do not conduct electrical currents — and tries to construct intelligence from these, whereas cognitive psychology begins with creatures that obviously have intelligence and tries to work back to neuron firings, nerve reflexes, and selector mechanisms that are as mechanical as computer operations. Forward or backward, though, the object is the same: to derive intelligence from things that do not possess it — or at the very least, things that possess it in lesser degree. For, as Daniel Dennett has written,

> psychology must not of course be question-begging. It must not explain intelligence in terms of intelligence, for instance by assigning responsibility for the existence of intelligence in creatures to the munificence of an intelligent Creator, or by putting clever homunculi at the control panels of the nervous system. If that were the best psychology could do, then psychology could not do the job assigned to it.[6]

What I am seriously suggesting is that, given the way it has set things up, psychology *can't* do the job that it has assigned itself. One phenomenon that won't fit its model — Aldous Huxley called my attention to it during the semester that he was visiting professor at the Massachusetts Institute of Technology — is the talking parrot.

What goes on when a parrot imitates the voice of its owner, or the bark of a dog, or human laughter? Presumably, it has some sort of conscious life. It hears the voice, it hears the bark or the laughter, and presumably, in a way that rudimentarily corresponds to our wish to do something, it wishes to imitate this. But then what happens? When you come to think of it, it is one of the most extraordinary things you can imagine. Something incomparably more intelligent than the parrot itself sets to work and proceeds to activate a series of sound organs that are totally different from those of human beings. People have teeth, a soft palate, and a flat tongue, and the parrot has no teeth, a rough tongue, and a beak. From these, however, it proceeds to organize its absolutely different apparatus to reproduce words and laughter — so exactly that we are very often deceived by it into thinking that what is in fact the parrot talking is the person himself or herself making an utterance. The more we reflect on this, the stranger it is, because obviously in the course of evolutionary history parrots have not been imitating human beings from time immemorial; people arrived after the parrots' adaptive mechanisms were in place. We have here an *ad hoc* piece of intelligent action, carried on by some form of intelligence within the parrot, that cannot be explained by its evolutionary conditioning.[7] This doesn't prove that the Intellect precedes the learning that the developmental model works with, but it leaves the door open to that possibility.

We now have two propositions about the Intellect: (a) it operates subliminally and mysteriously, and (b) it precedes and empowers simpler cognitive components rather than deriving from them. From this base we shall now posit a third feature, (c). It connects us to the world. Working through our sense organs it brings the world to us sensuously, while through the cerebral cortex it enables us to think about the world and reason generally.

This third property is my strongest reason for introducing the Intellect, for anything that holds the hope of removing the wedge that modernity has driven between us and our world deserves attention. I quoted Mark Taylor as saying that no modern epistemology has been able to get from subject to object, and I suspect that this is the root cause of the alienation that so characterizes our age. The failure Taylor points to should not surprise us, for if we begin with Descartes's mind/matter disjunction — which translates into the self/world divide — there's nothing more basic that can unite them. Garbage in, garbage out, as computer programmers say; to hope to arrive at the known after distancing it from the knower categorically is Kafka's cage going in search of a bird. So why accept Descartes's premise to begin with? He had *his* reasons for doing so, but as they were historical ones, having to do with the need to create an epistemology that would give free rein to science, and we live in different times that have their own needs, there is no reason why Descartes's needs should shackle us.

Logically, the epistemological issue reduces to this. Aristotle distinguished between reason (which grasps universals), and sensation (which locks into the world's particulars), both of which faculties are in direct touch with the world. Because the universals in the knowing soul are the same as those in the object known, "actual knowledge is identical with its object" (*De Anima* 430.20). Descartes replaced Aristotle's reason/sensation distinction with the distinction between consciousness, which resides within us, and the material world, which lacks consciousness and is outside our consciousness. This distinction has led to an epistemic impasse (inability to get from the knower to the known), and human alienation (our sense of being adrift in an alien universe). Why, then, should we continue to let it replace the notion of mind that preceded it? My answer, of course, is that we should *not* let it do so, but as my argument turns as much on Cartesian failures as on Aristotelian successes, I will cite those failures and not just assert their existence.

Epistemic Impasse

If we try to connect an animal in the wilds to its environment via what textbooks say about the physiology of perception, we encounter so many inexplicable gaps that rationally we would have to conclude that the animal does not perceive its world at all. This is the psychological outworking of philosophy's inability to bridge Descartes's mind/matter divide. Yet all the while the animal behaves as if it perceives the world; it proceeds toward food and shelter almost unerringly. With J. J. Gibson's *The Ecological Approach to Visual Perception* pointing the way, animal psychologists are coming to see that they have lost sight of this incontrovertible fact.[8] Trying to account for knowledge as inference from noetic bits does not work. We must begin the other way around, Gibson insists: with the recognition that there is a world out there (realism), and that animals are oriented to it.

Human Alienation

I will let Richard Rorty tell the story.

> The Cartesian change from mind-as-reason to mind-as-inner-arena [marked] the triumph of the quest for certainty over the quest for wisdom. [It opened] the way for philosophers either to attain the rigor of the mathematician or the mathematical physicist, or to explain the appearance of rigor in these fields, rather than to help people attain peace of mind. Science, rather than living, became philosophy's subject, and epistemology its center.[9]

It is dissatisfaction with this denouement that drives me back to pre-Cartesian views of the mind which, in their most impressive instances, always centered in the Intellect. None of the different ways that *nous* was nuanced doubt that it locks into world; no Kantian unknowable *noumena* trouble their worlds. Hilary Armstrong characterizes Plotinus's Intellect as "the level of intuitive thought that is identical with its object and does not see it as in some sense external."[10] This is virtually identical with Aristotle's position as earlier quoted.

I ask one final question here: Is the Intellect divine?

Authorities differ somewhat on this question. For Alexander the Aphrodisian and Ibn Sina, Aristotle's Agent Intellect is the Deity communicating itself to individuals through the Affectable Intellect which belongs to individual souls only. For Ibn Rushd, both Agent and Affectable Intellects are separate from individual souls and are alike in all souls, but are less than God. For Thomas Aquinas, the Intellect in both its active and passive aspects belongs to individual souls.

We can leave them to these differences. All of the philosophers mentioned would accept Eckhart's minimal formulation that "there is something in the soul (*aliquid est in anima*) which is uncreated and uncreatable";[11] which something, of course, is God, God being the only reality that is not created. That God is omniscient and we are not does not refute Eckhart, who does not say our souls are pure Intellect, or Intellect only. Eckhart's wording leaves room for other components of the soul to obscure the Intellect, or crowd it into a corner in the way the Vedantic *kosas* —sheaths that overlay the Ātman—explicitly assert.

I have for the most part steered away from technicalities concerning the Intellect, but a letter from a philosopher at the University of Iowa, James Duerlinger, contains a conclusion reached about Aristotle's view that is interesting enough to quote, even though I cannot pursue it.

> Philosophers have reconstructed Aristotle's active mind into a force that abstracts universals from particulars so that the passive mind can have objects. Far from the truth. The active mind is the divine activity of pure self-knowledge present in our souls, producing in them, as out of soul-stuff, likenesses of itself, these likenesses being our own minds, our organs of thought, which are soul-stuff made capable of thinking themselves—gaining self-knowledge, when they become likenesses of the forms of sensible things. Our minds are images of the divine mind, but which, unlike it (which thinks itself per se) think themselves per accidens. In other words, when we think of the forms of things we imitate the divine self-creation—we achieve the divine life as far as our minds are capable. The divine activity produces the form of our minds, whose matter is the soul-stuff Aristotle calls the affectable/passive mind; and it is the very same activity for the sake of which there is eternal motion in the heavens, as laid out in *Metaphysics*.[12]

III. EDUCATION

"If the sun and moon should doubt, / They'd immediately go out," Blake wrote.[13] Doubting the Intellect, we, comparably, have caused *it* to "go out"; which is to say, drop from our attention. This explains why I have left little room for this closing section on education. There's little point in talking about educating the Intellect if we don't believe that it exists. The first order of business is to challenge the assumption that it doesn't exist.

Having done that, I shall enter a single point on its education; it relates to education for virtue. An important component of traditional epistemology was its concept of *adequatio*. Distinct kinds of objects call for distinct faculties to register them, ones that are adequate for their recognition. The skin can fathom the sun's warmth, but not its luminosity. Sense organs can register the solidity of a book and how the words on its pages appear, but minds are needed to comprehend the words' meanings.

It follows that if there are spiritual objects, spiritual faculties of discernment will be required to take note of them. In human beings, this faculty is the Intellect. It came as something of a shock to me to realize as I began this concluding section of my paper that I had completed everything I had intended to say about the Intellect without as much as mentioning its spiritual capacities. That's shocking, but it's explainable. My strategy was to approach the Intellect by way of epistemology, and current epistemology doesn't recognize spirit. And the reason that it doesn't is clear. Faculties for knowing presuppose realities they might know, and there is no general agreement today that spiritual realities exist, much less what they might be. So accounts of knowing proceed without them.

Not long ago things were different. The colleges in this country were founded to train ministers; and from England we have the anecdote of the student at Balliol College who, on confiding to his don (Benjamin Jowett) that he had lost his faith in God, was ordered to find it before breakfast the next morning. Page Smith's book *Killing the Spirit: Higher Education in America*[14] traces the course of events since then; and another Smith — that redoubtable watchdog, Wilfred Cantwell Smith — picked up the fact that in Harvard University's latest book-length statement of aims for undergraduate education the word "truth" doesn't appear.

These, though, are thoughts for another season; songs — or dirges? — for another day.

NOTES

1. This section of my paper was written shortly after hearing a stunning address by Seyyed Hossein Nasr on its subject and is indebted to him for many of its points.

2. See William Barrett, *The Death of the Soul* (New York: Doubleday, 1986).

3. *Dictionary of the History of Ideas*, 5 vols. (New York: Charles Scribner's Sons, 1974).

4. Hubert L. and Stuart E. Dreyfus, *Mind over Machine* (New York: Free Press, 1986), p. xiv.

5. Huston Smith, *Beyond the Post-Modern Mind* (Wheaton, Ill.: Quest Books, 1989), p. 243.

6. Daniel C. Dennett, "Why the Law of Effect Will Not Go Away," *Journal of the Theory of Social Behavior* 5, no. 2 (1976): 172.

7. On the illogic of the biological claim that the fact of microevolution (small adaptations within species) provides grounds for insisting that macroevolution (the theory that natural selection accounts for the origin of species) occurs, see my essay, "Two Evolutions," in *On Nature*, ed. Leroy S. Rouner, vol. 6 in Boston University Studies in Philosophy and Religion (Notre Dame, Ind.: University of Notre Dame Press, 1984). An important book has appeared since that paper that supports its thesis: Phillip E. Johnson, *Darwin on Trial* (Washington, D.C.: Regnery Gateway, 1991).

8. See Marjorie Grene, "Perception, Interpretation, and the Sciences," in David Depaw & Bruce Weber, *Evolution at a Crossroads* (Cambridge, Mass.: Massachusetts Institute of Technology Press, 1985).

9. Richard Rorty, *Philosophy and the Mirror of Nature* (Princeton, N.J.: Princeton University Press, 1979), p. 61.

10. A. H. Armstrong, "Plotinus," in *The Concise Encyclopedia of Western Philosophy* (London: Hutchinson, 1960).

11. *Meister Eckhart*, trans. Edmund Colledge and Bernard McGinn (New York: Paulist Press, 1981), p. 13.

12. Letter to me from James Duerlinger, 1992.

13. William Blake, "Auguries of Innocence."

14. Page Smith, *Killing the Spirit: Higher Education in America* (New York: Viking, 1990).

Moral Imperialism vs. Moral Conflict: Conflicting Aims of Education

AMELIE OKSENBERG RORTY

WHOM SHOULD WE EDUCATE for what? Whose benefit should education serve, and how should that benefit be conceived? What picture of the shape and structure of a human life should guide the way we structure education and the vast range of educational institutions?

I

We were educators even before we described ourselves as rational political animals, or thought of ourselves as free and equal citizens, or projected ourselves as creators of value, a bridge to a super-race. Despite the long history of our educational experiments, we are as uncertain — and as conflicted — as ever we were. There are good reasons for this. This is an area where we are better served by following Socrates' example, by raising intractable problems, than by defending confident answers. Strangely enough, it may also be one of the areas where a certain amount of chaotic anarchy serves us more honestly, and perhaps even better, than principled, regimented order.

Before we turn to what we should do, let's consider what we *think* we should do, the range of aims that we actually project for education. I propose to use indirections to plot our directions. By examining a small sample of the philosophical systems that have, in an indirect way, formed, informed, and reformed our educational aims, we might be able to see how we should go about defining those aims. The cast of our native informants not only includes the long tradition of philosophers from Plato to Dewey, via Loyola and Kant, but also reflective moralists from Homer to the Grateful Dead, by way of Flaubert, Trollope, and Tolstoi. When we engage in what we grandly consider to be rational, critical reflection on our practices, the raw material of our thought is composed of the shreds and shards, the archaeological remains, of the work of all these figures. It should not be surprising that having jumbled all these figures together, we will discover that our native informants disagree, and that we are correspondingly torn.

Consider, then, the range of aims that we actually project for education. Let's provisionally classify a small selection of these as: perfectionist aims, liberal aims of autonomous self-determination, and utilitarian welfare aims. As our investigation proceeds, I hope you'll see why it is so misleading to freeze these positions into "isms."

Obviously each of these positions has its internal divisions, with quite different implications for educational programs. Moreover, these aims can be conjoined in various ways: achieving autonomy can, for instance, be regarded as among the perfectionist excellences or as ingredient in utilitarian projects. I shall return to significant differences in the ways these aims can be conjoined: as setting side-constraints within the primary, dominant direction of a theory, or as mutually tensed in an uncharted and unchartered system of checks and balances. But first, let's examine some of these aims more closely, concentrating on two that seem, on the face of it, to be furthest apart. Perfectionist and liberal aims each direct and structure our system of education. But attempting to combine them in a single hybrid theory only produces the illusion of unity and rationality: it is precisely the continued politically enacted tension among our various aims that provides at least some of the integrity of our education.

II

Aristotle presents the clearest analysis of some of the assumptions and internal tensions of perfectionism. The point and direction of any individual life is that of developing its essential excellences, the potentialities that define and constitute it. Fortunately, biology endorses metaphysics: every individual is intrinsically, naturally motivated to engage in this process. Indeed living just *is* the activity of developing and exercising these basic potentialities.

Even in the best of states, under the best conditions, the ideal Aristotelian educator is pulled in a number of different directions, to fulfill radically different aims whose relative priority is constantly in question.

First, he must determine whether education should be structured to develop the potentialities of each individual, or whether it should be structured to attain and preserve the aims of the *polis*, as they define a way of life as well as a political system.[1] The tension between these two aims arises from a tension within Aristotle's account of substance.

Second, he must determine whether education should be structured to promote the noblest and best life, that of the contemplator and scientist, or whether it should be structured to promote the most comprehensive civic life. The tension between these two aims arises from a tension within Aristotle's ethics.

Third, he must define the boundaries between education and training, between the education of the free citizen, capable of deliberating, and the directions to be given to the shadow class of those who, by constitution or by occupation, are not suited for self-rule. The tension between these two aims arises from a tension within Aristotle's philosophy of mind and his politics.

These tensions do not indicate cracks and flaws in Aristotle's theory; on the contrary, they reveal his proper sensitivity to the complexities and tensions within the phenomena themselves. He can — as many commentators press him to do — reconcile these tensions at a formulaic and abstract level of theory construction; but he recognizes — as many of his commentators do not — that such general principles do not by themselves resolve the dilemmas of the politician and educator.

The first dilemma the perfectionist educator must face derives from Aristotle's two characterizations of the substances that are the ultimate constituents of the world.[2] Early in the *Metaphysics*, Aristotle introduces a rough general characterization of substances: everything else is either predicated of them, or part of them, or a conglomeration of them. They are capable of existing and being understood independently of other things; their aims are not defined to serve a higher aim, and the proper functioning of their "parts" is directed to what serves them as self-sustaining substances. They have essential properties and excellences, endogenous activities whose exercise and fulfillment constitute their existence and their well-being. Some of these activities — those formed by friends and citizens, for example — may involve binding, mutually constitutive associations. What matters for the independence of a substance is that its associations are essential expressions of its nature, acting to fulfill its own ends, rather than reactions or responses to external circumstances beyond its control.

In one sense, individuals are the primary substances, the ultimate constituents of the world. The examples that Aristotle initially gives are those of an individual man or horse. Nature sets norms: though the capacities of individuals vary in degree and quality, every individual should be so educated as to be enabled to fulfill and realize his essential nature, and his domestic and civic associations should be structured and directed to serve his thriving.

But Aristotle introduces a second strand in the theory of substance. On this view, the primary constituents of the world are the species and the genera to which individuals belong. Biologically, human beings form a single unchanging species whose essence defines the potentialities and activities of the individuals who are its members. Presumably, Aristotle's reason for treating species as substances is that the world would remain essentially unchanged, even if any particular individual human or horse had never existed. But there are distinctive psychological and political subspecies, varieties of human beings. A polity has a distinctive form (*eidos*) of life: it is self-sustaining, capable of existing and fulfilling its aims independently of other polities, and of any particular individual citizen. It has a distinctive self-perpetuating constitutional structure; its citizens have distinctive psychologies, with specific aims and virtues. Individuals can only function, can only realize their aims, within a well-constructed polity. Indeed many of an individual's central ends are properly defined by those of his polity, even when it is far from being ideal. When we focus on polities as substances, then what's good for the individual is ultimately fixed by what is good for the *polis:* the education of individuals must be guided by the aims and needs of the polity of which they are members.

"Even if the good is the same for the individual and the state," Aristotle says, "the good of the state is clearly the greater and more perfect thing to attain and to preserve. It is something to obtain the good for one man alone; but to secure it for a nation (*ethnos*) and for a state (*polis*) is nobler (*kallion*) and more divine (*theioteron*)" (I. 2 1094b7ff.). But different kinds of polities appropriately structure the desires, abilities, and virtues of their members in distinctive ways. The citizens of democracies, aristocracies, and oligarchies properly have distinctive *specific* desires and aims that would best be fulfilled by distinctive types of education. While Aristotle concentrates on the education of the best sorts of citizens for the best sort of state, it is left to the political *phronimos* of each type of polity to define, direct, and balance its diverse aims, including those of education. While the *phronimos* is just, he is not impartial. He places the civic good above general human compassion. His characteristic virtues are practical astuteness, a range of debating and rhetorical skills, measured boldness. Odysseus-like, he has no compunction about lying, and measures justice proportionately to nobility rather than by the rights or dignity of every individual. But precisely for this reason, he must address the formidable problems of aggregation. To what extent should the fulfillment of individuals constrain or direct civic aims? And to what extent should civic aims constrain or direct the fulfillment of individual lives?

The second dilemma that the perfectionist educator faces derives from Aristotle's two characterizations of the best life. The first is the comprehensive practical life, the life that fulfills the widest range of human excellences, organized around the virtues of civic activity. The second is the life structured around the contemplative and scientific activity that expresses our highest and best potentialities. To what extent can the education of the best legitimately override the education of the good? What constraints should the assurance of the best civic life impose on the development of the best intellectual life?

The third dilemma that the perfectionist educator must face derives from the tensions in Aristotle's views about the psychological and intellectual capacities of "the many." On the one hand, Aristotle holds that "the many" have the raw materials of virtue. They are, by nature, directed to desire what is good. In the best of circumstances, their perceptions and thoughts need not mislead their actions; they are capable of rudimentary and regional forms of deliberation. It is an open question whether they might become capable of engaging in the kind of "all-things-considered deliberation" that would qualify them for citizenship.[3] On the other hand, Aristotle thinks that the occupational activities of "the many"— activities required for any soundly functioning state — form intellectual and psychological habits that undermine the capacities for genuine systematic deliberation. Charitably setting aside Aristotle's views on the constitutional incapacities of natural slaves and women, the perfectionist educator faces the enormously difficult problem of designing a system of education for the ordinary working populace. On the one hand, the occupations and services of craftsmen and simple merchant-traders are essential to a complex polity; on the other, it is precisely their occupations that unfit this class for citizenship and for the education that it requires.[4] "In every domain," Aristotle says, "actions of a certain type produce a corresponding type of character" (*Nicomachean Ethics* 1114a7–8). A person *is* what he thinks. The direction and content of his thought — as it fills his activities, the occupations that form his preoccupations and his priorities — marks what he is. We can use the merchant to represent the educational problems set by the whole class of those who are not constitutionally unfit for citizenship, but whose occupations require the kind of specialization that, according to Aristotle, in fact unfits them for it.[5] Mercantile activities are specialized; even if they are not directed to the unacceptable aim of accumulating wealth for its own sake, they are focused around cost-benefit calculations directed to unexamined low-level aims. To be sure, the citizen is, as the head of a household, also engaged in cost-benefit financial transactions. But his domestic economy is regulated by a further range of familial and political concerns that do not guide the merchant.[6] In any case, the merchant does not himself deliberate about what place trade should have in the larger scheme of civic aims; and indeed his contributions to the polity might be less useful if he were to introduce considerations of high honor in his calculations (*Politics* I. 3–4).

It might seem that the educational problems set by mercantile activity need not affect the education of craftsmen. In principle, technology might liberate at least some craftsmen to engage in deliberation.[7] But the contrast between leisure and occupation is not marked by the availability of free time. It rather concerns the freedom to engage in self-regulated and defined activities, whose aims are not directed by others. Sound civic deliberation requires the kind of education that detaches the citizen from the limited aims of the specialized occupations, and proposes to determine what is, on balance, genuinely noble (*kalon*) and good (*Politics* 1333a40–b5).

Aristotle is confident that the educative aims and policies designed to fulfill these two forms of life are compatible, even though they may not coincide. In the best of states, in the best of times, the education and activities of a merchant, a poet, and a philosopher like Socrates should not — even if fully developed in their own terms — threaten common political life. The assumption that supports Aristotle's confidence is that a sound polity can construct its institutions in such a way as to assure the compatible, harmonious fulfillment of the basic varieties of human lives: it can channel a significant sector of the population towards socially useful occupations. *Given such structuring, given the institutions of the society*, a mercantile life might, for instance, be the best *available* alternative, all things considered, even for someone who might be constitutionally suited to citizenship. In deciding to become a merchant or craftsman, a man acts voluntarily, even if he acts under the pressure of family and the influence of public rhetoric. He is typically not coerced, and he knows what he is doing. But since occupational choices are made in youth, they are rarely made in the light of full deliberation, which requires the education of a free, leisured man. While the educator-statesman has presumably deliberated on behalf of everyman, he has done so from a point of view that can override individual interests.

It emerges that there are really three modes of perfectionist education. Setting aside the special conditions for the education of the contemplative scientist, there is first and foremost the *paideia* directed to the education of the citizen; there is the training required for the specialized occupations; and there are the civic institutions, including the social and economic rewards, that draw

the members of the *polis* to the occupations that effectively constitute the form of their lives. Despite his distance from Plato, Aristotle clearly envisions a strong alliance of the educator and the
statesman, an alliance that must also enlist the active cooperation
of the rhetorician who sways the population towards — or away
from — becoming full-fledged deliberators.

Just how should the *phronimos*, the perfectionist educator,
structure social institutions to channel individuals to those sorts
of lives that, while not realizing their best potentialities, nevertheless are as satisfactory as possible, considering their long-range
interests? What *is* the proper balance of specialized and civic education? Aristotle's formula is "Get it right: hit the mean." The metaphor of "hitting the mean" suggests that there is a ratio, a measure,
and a rationale for "getting it right." But our various ends are not
weighted in a definite order of priority; and attempting to place
them in a clear lexical order reintroduces the very uncertainty and
conflicts it is meant to resolve. It is for this reason that Aristotle
leaves all these matters in the hands of the *phronimos*. He gets it
right, but not even Aristotle can tell him just how to measure what
would be right in various circumstances, let alone what to do to
realize it.

III

It is much more difficult to summarize the liberal, egalitarian
aims focused around self-determination. For one thing, their sources
and directions are extremely diverse and complex, even though they
were originally formulated as basic metaphysical principles. Some
derive from a secularized version of the Christian postulate of the
will, as the unconditioned capacity for autonomous choice. It is
through the exercise and direction of this freedom that individuals
define their lives; it is in the exercise of their freedom of choice
that their thriving consists; and it is what makes them responsible
for their actions, capable of citizenship. On this view, every individual is equally and innately endowed with a free will whose
exercise is independent of constitutionally based abilities and
socio-political conditions. Rousseau and Kant added some Stoic
strands to this position: rationality defines the directions of genu-

ine autonomy. For Kant, the argument is transcendental: rationality provides the preconditions for the possibility of a causally unconditioned, free exercise of the will; freedom provides the preconditions for the possibility of rationality. Freedom is the exercise of rationality, in its practical employment; and rationality is the free exercise of the will, in its theoretical employment. Rousseau's argument is psychological and political: the individual only becomes genuinely *active* when he is capable of acting in accordance with his conceptions of general principles, rather than from impulse and instinct. But Rousseau and Kant differ from most classical Stoics in connecting rational autonomy with active political self-determination in a community of mutually respecting equals, each willing that his own motives be directed by universalizable principles.

The three strands in liberalism — the libertarian strand, the egalitarian strand, and the rationalist strand — are, of course, independent of one another. Each, taken alone, would dictate a distinctive educational policy. Much of liberal political theory is directed to attempting to reconcile these views, sometimes by the use of additional principles inherited from natural rights theories. Post-Kantian liberals who attempt to detach themselves from the transcendental postulate of an unconditioned will face an unwelcome dilemma. They must choose between retreating to undemonstrable intuitions or forging an uneasy alliance with some version of utilitarianism. Some liberals attempt to block the retreat to intuition with a contractarian theory meant to provide a rational justification for a set of specific principles of justice.

The principles that define the domains and the lexical ordering of equality and liberty would, it is argued, receive universal consent under conditions of purely rational choice, where decisions were unaffected by the natural and social lottery.[8] But as Rawls and many contractarians acknowledge, their "foundational arguments" presuppose and express rather than ground or justify their liberal commitments.[9] They articulate the structure of democratic liberalism as a normative position whose appeal admittedly relies on historically conditioned intuitions. Onora O'Neill puts the point nicely: "Far from deriving a justification of democratic citizenship from a metaphysical foundation, Rawls invites us to read *A Theory of Justice* as providing a recursive vindication of those principles of justice we would acknowledge if we drew deeply on our underlying conceptions of free and equal citizenship. The vindication of [this conception of] justice is not to be seen as addressing others . . . who do not start out with such ideals of citizenship; it has nothing to say to those others."[10] But since liberals remain committed to justifying their fundamental principles as well as their actions, this acknowledgement places them in a delicately embarrassing position.

Other liberal theorists attempt to support their position by arguing that it brings the benefits of utilitarianism, without incurring some of its difficulties or costs.[11] Welfare, construed as the aggregate satisfaction of individual preferences, is argued to be typically best served by liberal politics.[12] The argument is that far from being a threat to human happiness, freedom is one of its constituents. When metaphysical freedom is demystified, it emerges as political liberty. Its exercise requires — and presumptively assures — the promotion of an appropriate level of material welfare. The hope is that the kind of egalitarian education that develops every citizen's capacities for self-determination also provides the best and most effective assurance of material welfare.

Amy Gutmann puts it this way: education in a liberal democracy should be directed to "what will maximally expand each child's future civil and political freedom to choose a way of life, compatible with the equal freedom of others."[13] The aim of education is, on this view, "to equip every child with the intellectual means to choose . . . or at least to evaluate . . . a way of life compatible with the equal freedom of others."[14] The criterion of freedom is practical and political. It is "what leaves open the most reasonable options."[15] One might have thought that education should not only equip a child to make rational choices, but also equip her to lead the life she chooses. But since liberal policy is committed to remaining neutral between competing conceptions of the good, it cannot undertake to develop the intellectual skills and virtues necessary to realize distinctively *different* conceptions of the good.

The recognition that individuals or groups might reasonably and rightfully be committed to radically different educational aims forces liberals like Gutmann to accept several questionable distinctions. There is, first, the distinction between the private and the public domains which allocates morally distinctive education to the private domain. (But many associations that have a strong educational import — unions and private hospitals, for example — bridge the private and the public sectors. While they are under public regulation and sometimes receive public benefits, still their memberships, funding, and primary activities are self-defined and determined.) Secondly, they introduce a distinction between specific substantive conceptions of moral goods and the good of justice, which would, ideally, be defined by principles to which any rational person, whatever her conception of the good, would consent. (But both equality and liberty represent specific substantive conceptions of human goods. It may be foolish or mistaken, but it is not irrational or immoral for a society to question their primary value.) Thirdly, they require a distinction between intellectual and moral education, on the assumption that intellectual education is, along with civic education, neutral between competing conceptions of the good. (But moral systems typically disagree about the moral worth of various intellectual abilities. Consider, for example, the checkered history of the imagination as a morally significant capacity.)

Since liberal democratic education confines itself to aims which all citizens can be presumed to accept, it leaves the education of the specific abilities required to realize diverse conceptions of the good to the private sector, to individuals and their associations. The regulation and funding of such differential education is assigned to public agencies and institutions, on the presumption that their decisions would be reached by fair and equal rational deliberation, unaffected by power politics. The comforting but questionable assumption is that the education that serves all citizens equally also serves the diversity of distinctive substantive ends fairly, even if it only does so indirectly. Liberal theories of education suppose that the diverse aims of education are mutually compatible, if not actually harmonious; and that the education required for self-determination would not conflict with any of the diverse substantive educative aims that citizens might set for themselves.

Despite the profound chasm that separates Aristotelian metaphysics from political liberalism, the educational consequences of their views face similar dilemmas, and their attempts to resolve these dilemmas involve similar assumptions. Both are convinced that the competing aims of education are in principle compatible, that in the best political circumstances, the structure of education that best serves one aim also typically serves the others. Nevertheless, despite that optimism — or perhaps because of it — both Aristotelian perfectionism and liberalism leave the articulation and specification of particular policies and decisions open. Because practical decisions cannot be derived from a set of rules or principles, Aristotle places decisions about the priorities of potentially conflicting educational aims in the hands of the *phronimos*. And because contemporary liberals recognize that participants in civic debate may never form a consensus about their substantive aims, they concentrate on defining just procedural principles, the guiding criteria for fair debate on the formulation of policy. Both perfectionism and liberalism are left with similar bootstrap problems: both presuppose a set of virtues that only a sound education in a sound polity can provide.

IV

I want now to return to the questions with which we began. Who should be educated for what? Whose benefit should education serve, and how should that benefit be understood? It doesn't take much reflection to recognize that Aristotelian perfectionist and liberal aims are, along with many others, alive and well within our practices. Despite the fact that few of us can accept Aristotle's metaphysics, the consequences of that metaphysics continue to form many of our motives and directions. Much of our educational system is directed to the twin aims of developing individual potentialities and achieving political excellence, construed as political supremacy. We share Aristotle's confidence that fulfilling individual aims and fulfilling those of the polity can be brought to coincide; that an educational system directed to advancing the pure sciences is directly compatible with one directed to developing comprehensive, civic virtues. As liberals, we also believe that political and economic institutions can appropriately define and channel the specialized professions without jeopardizing the free and equal right of self-determination; and that the aims of high-level specialized education and those of general civic education are not only compatible but mutually supportive.

There are, of course, many attempts to construct hybrid theories that attempt to conjoin and order the various aims that should guide our educational practices. Some philosophers attempt to combine the primary directions of perfectionism with liberal side constraints;[16] others devise a two-level utilitarian theory constrained by a set of primary virtues and rights;[17] still others develop deontological liberal theories that either incorporate utilitarian commitments or designate a set of primary virtues.[18]

Our question is not "Which of these is true?" Nor is it "How can we reconcile these views to form one grand hybrid, synthetic theory?" As Dewey—who is clearly the hero of our story—well knew, our problems are, initially and finally, practical and political. Ours is the problem of constructing educational practices that express and serve the tropisms that rightly pull us in different directions. The problems of formulating our educational aims are *practical* problems, best addressed by arbitration, negotiation, compensation, and accommodation.[19] Theory construction is appropriately set within a frame of practical arbitration and accommodation. Separated from these, it presents an illusory, misleading hope of finding a purely rational solution to the problems of defining and structuring the proper aims of education.

There is nothing wrong with constructing hybrid theories. Indeed, as the Aristotelian and the liberal cases show, it is typically the desire, if not the actual need, for hybrid combinations that typically impels theory construction in the first place. It is through the construction of hybrid theories that we gradually specify our initial general — indeed our vague — aims and principles. But interpreted as if they were primarily *theories* about the good, hybrid systems have two major drawbacks: first, we can construct too many sound, reasonable, appealing theories. Attempting to demonstrate one and refute the others typically enmeshes us in arguments and evaluations that our friends call "recursive vindications" and our opponents deride as circular and question-begging. Second, hybrid theories that attempt to combine incommensurable ends disguise the fact that the process of specifying and applying them reintroduces the very tensions that the theory was designed to avoid. All the competition for specifying the dominance and priority among the various directions for education typically re-appear as practical problems about the application of the most general aims.

Hybrid systems should not be interpreted as if they were competing hypotheses, to be demonstrated or falsified. They should rather be understood as shared practical deliberations and investigations in which the participants do not initially know precisely what they think.[20] The conversations embedded in hybrid systems are not exchanges of monologues among the dead, each presenting and justifying their views. They are closer to what Bakhtin called the dramatic interanimation of voices.[21] The minutiae of continuous practice-oriented, contingency-sensitive interactive deliberation presses toward gradual closure. It moves from general to more determinate programs, sometimes by opposition, sometimes by elaboration or improvisation. Interpreted as *theories*, hybrid systems are the reconstructed minutes of such conversations. They codify the mutual influences and accommodations of the voices. When deliberation goes well, what emerges is a further specification and determination of our several aims and intentions. When things go well, we emerge with a program that suits us all — temporarily. A slightly less happy resolution produces a set of grudgingly accepted compromises. The worst outcome declares a winner, with the loser retreating to gather forces for another attack, often a sneak surprise.

The method of reflective equilibrium presents one of the most estimable models for constructing a hybrid system.[22] Instead of selecting a single primary normative stance and attempting to do justice to competing principles by setting them as side constraints, the method of reflective equilibrium involves a mutual adjustment of the most abstract principles or aims with the range of considered convictions concerning just and fair outcomes.[23] This method has the advantage of attempting to balance competing claims in a way that allows for their mutual criticism and correction. It acknowledges the provisional and relatively arbitrary character of the initial commitments, and provides an account of the way that we can refine, revise, and specify them.

But the method of reflective equilibrium can itself be interpreted in several ways. Construed one way, it is a method to guide the construction of a demonstrable *theory*, one which is Janus-faced with the rejection of alternative theories. Construed this way, reflective equilibrium attempts to conjoin a range of aims and principles with a set of specific convictions to form a consistent, well-ordered, determinate, and justified system of beliefs. Ideally, the principles of a theory are unambiguous; and ideally, there are well-defined procedures for determining what they entail. The desire to articulate and to *demonstrate* a rational reconstruction of our fundamental beliefs is a powerful and admirable desire. It is powerful because relinquishing it seems to threaten rationality itself, and because we think that rational principles are our only defense against the ravages of power politics. And the desire is admirable because it presses us to explain and to *justify* ourselves to our fellows. But even the most powerful legitimate desires cannot always be satisfied. A unified hybrid theory will either be too general to provide practical guidance, or it will have a host of competitors with equally serious claims to our allegiance.

Construed as a method for producing a *system of practice*, the method of reflective equilibrium presents a workable interpretation of Bakhtin's dialogic interanimation. So construed, reflective equilibrium attempts to construct a dynamic system of checks and balances among the diverse and incommensurable aims and interests of different systems. It leaves major issues open for continuing arbitration, compensation, and accommodation. Despite the misleading metaphors of "balance" and "equilibrium," it does not assume that we should attempt to reach a consensus about unambiguous principles for distributive norms or educational priorities. Recognizing that the priorities accorded to our various ends might properly vary contextually, it substitutes revisable rules of thumb for principles. It acknowledges the utility of ambiguity in enabling people with different aims to have different reasons for cooperating. It recognizes that the mutual adjustment of general principles and considered convictions has a suspiciously circular movement. Today's considered convictions were formed by yesterday's general principles, and tomorrow's general principles bear a marked resemblance to today's considered convictions. Construed as a *system of practice* rather than as a *theory*, the method of reflective equilibrium does not assume that political theory can replace or rationalize politics, or that politics primarily involves applying the aims and principles that have been demonstrated and articulated by political theory. Sometimes the mutual adjustment of principles and considered convictions only emerges accidentally, as a result of politicized negotiation; and sometimes it does not emerge at all. But this recognition need not belittle or deny the arbitrating role of reflective deliberation.

Whom should we educate for what? Whose benefit should education serve, and how should that benefit be construed? One of the significant dangers of attempting to answer these questions by constructing general theories rather than by adjusting systems of practice is that doing so is likely to distort and mislead the directions of education. Educators may focus on developing the abilities for debating-team justification rather than on developing the kind of imagination, empathy, and cooperation that promote mutual accommodation. The practical aims and principles of education pull us in different directions; they can only be worked through by a political process whose procedures are themselves under constant critical examination.

In attempting to define and structure the ends of education, we are — at best — like well-constructed mobiles, so adjusted that any shift or movement in one part effects a corresponding shift in the others, in such a way as to rotate toward an indefinite number of well-formed configurations. The point of equilibrium does not control the patterns that the mobile can legitimately be permitted to form. It is rather the point at which the resolution of balancing dynamically equilibrated forces occurs.

Stuart Hampshire captures the direction of this image in an address appropriately entitled "Justice is Strife." "What emerges from a fair political contest will often be described," he says, "by those who are intent on a specific form of substantial justice, as a 'shabby compromise'. . . . For the individual . . . as for society, compromise . . . is both the normal and the most desirable condition of the soul for a creature whose desires . . . are often ambivalent and always in conflict with each other. . . . Political prudence . . . must expect a perpetual contest between hostile conceptions of justice. . . . The contests are unending; . . . the rock-bottom justice is in the contests themselves, in the tension of open opposition, always renewed."[24]

NOTES

1. In speaking of Aristotle's perfectionism as it affects his theory of education, we must perforce use the masculine pronoun throughout. Women are for Aristotle constitutionally incapable of genuine *autarkeia*, of the kind of rationality that marks contemplative or civic excellence. They can at best be trained to perform the tasks of administration, following the orders of a higher command, as applied to the domestic sphere.

2. Cf. *Categories* 5 and *Metaphysics* V. 8 for Aristotle's survey and summary of accepted definitions of substance, the entities that are the basic components of reality, the fundamental entries in the table of contents of the cosmos.

3. Aristotle EE 8. 3 1248b16–25; 1248b26–1249a16. Cf. Stephen A. White, "Doing Fine in Seeking the Good: Aristotle on Virtuous Motives," *Proceedings of the Boston Colloquium in Ancient Philosophy*, 1991–92.

4. It is just this consideration that leads Rousseau to argue that women should not be citizens. The abilities and traits required for motherhood are highly specialized; they necessarily involve a kind of particularity and partiality that undermines the commitment to the common good fixed by General Will. Like Aristotle, Rousseau supports this view with the further claim that women are, by constitution and nature, best suited to domesticity: that is — happily — where their potentialities are most fully realized.

5. Cf. *Politics* I. 8–10; III. 5; VII. 8–9. Aristotle distinguishes sharply between the kind of businessman engaged in (what Aristotle considers to be the despicable aim of) accumulating wealth for its own sake, and the householder who engages in a certain amount of economic activity, selling his produce and buying household goods. He allocates the detailed discussion of political economy to a specialist, who would presumably analyze the proper functions of the merchant class — the class of small shopkeepers (who may have many other aims than the sheer accumulation of wealth) and import-export traders. In the *polis* that Aristotle envisions, such traders might be resident aliens who present no special educative problems; and perhaps the former might be assimilated to the class of craftsmen who sold their own products. But even if the mercantile and artisan classes can be divided in this way, the educator still faces the problem of designing a system of education for those who might, in principle, be capable of civic deliberation but who are engaged in civically useful occupations that undermine their capacities for genuine deliberation.

6. Cf. Michael Oakeshott, "Rationalism in Politics," "Political Education," and "Reflection on Modern Politics," in his *Rationalism in Politics and Other Essays* (Indianapolis: Liberty Fund, 1991).

7. Cf. Aristotle, *Politics* I. 4 1253b33ff.

8. John Rawls, *A Theory of Justice* (Cambridge, Mass.: Belknap Press of Harvard University Press, 1971), chap. 3.

9. Cf. John Rawls, "Kantian Constructivism in Moral Theory," *Journal of Philosophy* (1980), and "Justice as Fairness: Political not Metaphysical," *Philosophy and Public Affairs* (1985); see also Onora O'Neill, "Ethical Reasoning and Ideological Pluralism, *Ethics* (1988): 707.

10. O'Neill, "Ethical Reasoning," p. 707.

11. Amy Gutmann, "What's the Use of Going to School?" in *Utilitarianism and Beyond,* ed. Amartya Sen and Bernard Williams (Cambridge: At the University Press, 1982).

12. But this claim is strongly denied by Tim Scanlon ("Contractarianism and Utilitarianism," in Sen and Williams, *Utilitarianism and Beyond* [pp. 119ff.]). It would take us far afield to see whether Scanlon's argument affects all liberal positions, or only those which, like his, rest on a modified contractarian base.

13. Gutmann, "What's the Use?" pp. 268–71.

14. Ibid., p. 269.

15. Ibid.

16. Cf. Martha Nussbaum, "Nature, Function and Capability," in *Oxford Studies in Ancient Philosophy* (Supplement Volume 1988).

17. Cf. H. Sidgwick, "The Establishment of Ethical First Principles," *Mind* (1879); S. Scheffler, "Moral Demands and their Limits," *Journal of Philosophy* (1986); P. Railton, "Alienation, Consequentialism and the Demands of Morality," *Philosophy and Public Affairs* (1984).

18. Onora O'Neill, *Constructions of Reason* (Cambridge: At the University Press, 1989); Barbara Herman, "Mutual Aid and Respect for Persons," *Ethics* (1984).

19. Cf. David B. Wong, "Coping with Moral Conflict and Ambiguity," *Ethics* (1992–93); and my "The Advantages of Moral Diversity," *Social Philosophy and Policy* (1992).

20. Cf. Henry Richardson, "Specifying Norms as a Way to Resolve Concrete Ethical Problems," *Philosophy and Public Affairs* (1989–90), esp. pp. 293 ff., and fn. 30.

21. Cf. M. M. Bakhtin, *The Dialogic Imagination* (Austin: University of Texas Press, 1981), pp. 51, 275–85; and my *Mind in Action* (Boston: Beacon Press, 1988), pp. 15–21, 324–29; and "Varieties of Pluralism," *The Review of Metaphysics* 44 (1990).

22. As Rawls remarks, this is the method which "goes back in its essentials to Aristotle's method in the *Nicomachean Ethics*" (*A Theory of Justice*, p. 51, fn. 26).

23. Ibid., pp. 19–21.

24. Stuart Hampshire, "Justice Is Strife," *Proceedings of the American Philosophical Association* (November 1991): 26–27. I am grateful to William Ruddick for many fruitful, illuminating conversations. Steven Gerrard's patience and generosity — and his acute questions — helped shape this paper.

Bentham's Theory of Virtue

BHIKHU PAREKH

ALTHOUGH JEREMY BENTHAM'S MORAL THEORY has been a subject of considerable discussion, his analysis of the nature and classification of virtues has received little attention. This paper is a small step toward filling that gap. In the first section I shall outline his concept of virtue, and in the second his classification of virtues and vices. Since the utilitarians are generally thought to have considerable difficulty giving a coherent account of justice, I devote the third section to it. In the last section I briefly indicate why Bentham's theory of virtue is unsatisfactory.

I

For Bentham the "principle of utility" is the only correct or valid standard of right and wrong. Although his formulation of it varied over time and seemed to point in different directions, basically he intends to say that an action is right or wrong depending on whether it promotes or diminishes the greatest happiness overall.[1] Since pleasure and pain alone are respectively good and evil, the moral agent has a duty to consider the claims of all human beings impartially and to act in a manner that maximizes human happiness overall, irrespective of who its bearers are. We are, however, also socially situated beings related to different people with different kinds of bonds, and these give rise to different levels and degrees of expectations. Rather than ask abstractly what we can do to increase the overall quantity of human happiness, we should generally concentrate on those to whom we are bound by ties of expectations, whom we know and whose happiness it is within our power to influence, without ignoring the consequences of our actions for others.

53

For Bentham human actions fall into two categories, depending on whether they "primarily" or "in the first instance" affect the agent alone or others. In the former case, he maximizes human happiness by pursuing his own greatest happiness. If he overate, or ate food that did not agree with him, or slept awkwardly, he would have to pay the price the next day. At a different level if she organized her personal life badly, developed the habit of worrying over trivial matters, lacked self-discipline, or tended to brood over unpleasant incidents, she would make her life miserable. Because others have only a limited interest in and knowledge of our personal lives, if we do not properly organize our lives and pursue our happiness, no one will; and the sum of human happiness will diminish. The pursuit of one's own happiness in the self-regarding area of life thus is the requirement of the principle of utility itself, and the right thing to do. Far from being immoral or "selfish," such a pursuit of self-interest is deeply moral, and indeed a matter of what Bentham calls a "duty to oneself."

If the agent's action affects others, the principle of utility requires that she should act in a manner that maximizes their happiness. But she should take care that in so doing she does not cause greater unhappiness to herself or to those not directly involved, as that would diminish the overall quantity of happiness and violate the principle of utility. It is irrational "sentimentalism" to make great sacrifices of one's own happiness for others' relatively trivial gains, Bentham argues. Similarly the pursuit of others' happiness might cause harm to those not directly involved, and if the latter is greater in quantity, the action in question is to be avoided. In short when his action affects or is capable of affecting others, the moral agent should act in a manner that promotes their happiness without doing any or much damage to himself or to those not directly involved. Such an action promotes the greatest possible human happiness in a given context.

For Bentham, then, to live and to act morally is always to act in a manner that maximizes the overall sum of happiness in the universe. So far as the self-regarding area of life is concerned, it involves so conducting oneself that one maximizes one's happiness over the entire course of one's life. This often involves sacrificing short-term pleasures or incurring short-term pains in order to enjoy greater pleasure later. So far as the other-regarding area of life is concerned, morality involves maximizing others' happiness, and this sometimes involves sacrificing one's own lesser happiness. In either case moral life necessarily involves sacrifice, a measure of self-denial, giving up some pleasure. This is against "natural" human inclination. We tend to pursue immediate pleasures even if they produce considerable pain later. And we like to pursue our own happiness even if it results in greater unhappiness to others.

It is in this context that Bentham introduces the concept of virtue.[2] To resist this natural inclination and to practice the required self-denial in the interest of one's own or others' maximum happiness, argues Bentham, is to display virtue. No action is virtuous unless it promotes human well-being. But the reverse is not true. Eating, sleeping, and making love promote human well-being, but we do not call them virtues. Bentham thinks that this is so because we do them as a matter of natural necessity. They do not go against our natural inclination, and hence they do not involve sacrifice, reluctance, struggle, and self-denial. Although eating is not a virtue, it becomes one when one eats what one detests for medical reasons, or when one abstains from eating to avoid indigestion or in order that a famished friend may eat more. As Bentham puts it, "under the system of utility, virtuous is a common epithet attributed to such [actions] only as are meant to be of a tendency beneficial to the community upon the whole, considered in the light of their being apt to be repugnant to the inclination of the agent," and "to a certain degree and in a certain respect painful to him."[3]

For Bentham, virtue has four features. First, it is concerned with action rather than with understanding, and is an "appetitive" rather than a "perceptive" faculty. The ability to solve mathematical problems or to speak a foreign language is an intellectual, not a moral, quality and is neither a virtue nor a vice. Second, virtue relates not to all kinds of actions but only to those that affect happiness. Whether to wear a blue or a red tie, to visit rather than write to a sick friend, or to eat an apple rather than a pear when hungry are largely a matter of taste, convenience, or social convention, and do not raise questions of virtue and vice. Actions without materially or hedonistically significant consequences are amoral, and do not involve exercise of virtue.

Third, virtue implies choice between two actions, one producing a greater amount of happiness than the other. If two actions give equal quantities of happiness, for example visiting a bereaved friend and going for a swim, the choice between them is a matter of moral indifference and no question of virtue or vice arises. The exercise of virtue is involved only when the moral agent needs to sacrifice her own pleasure in the interest of her own or others' greater pleasure, and suffers self-denial and pain. If it has become habitual to her, she might not find the self-denial painful. But that does not alter the fact that she practices self-denial and that this is *generally* painful. For Bentham a sacrifice of even "the least particle of pleasure" is a loss, and is to be avoided, unless it is likely to produce a greater quantity of pleasure. A sacrifice lacking such a justification is "not virtue but folly," and to cause others to make it is "not virtue but vice," an act of "malevolence."[4]

Fourth, since human beings "naturally" seek pleasure and avoid pain, they find self-denial painful. Virtue involves "fighting" this tendency, an element of "struggle" and "exertion," and is not a "gift of nature" but a product of social training. This does not mean that every exercise of virtue should involve struggle, only that it should do so when it is being acquired. Nor does it mean that all human beings should acquire it after struggle, only that most should. Those born impotent or undersexed have little difficulty restraining their sexual impulses and practicing chastity or self-restraint, but this is not the case with most human beings. Bentham argues that once an individual acquires a virtue, he not only gets rid of the initial "uneasiness and regret" and the "original repugnance" associated with self-denial, but also finds a new source of pleasure in exercising his newly acquired skill. When a virtue becomes "habitual" to him, a part of his "second" nature and a "source of delight" and "pure pleasure," it can be said to exist in the "highest degree of perfection," in "its most consummate state." Such a person has a "virtuous mind habitually inured to the exercise of virtue."[5]

For Bentham, then, virtue is a socially acquired, consciously cultivated, and action-oriented moral "quality" or "disposition," which is conducive to human well-being and whose acquisition and exercise generally involves an element of self-denial and pain. Given this view he argues that several virtues traditionally so called are not virtues, and many not so called are in fact virtues. Thus good nature or cheerfulness is not a virtue because it is "natural," not socially acquired, and "is no more a virtue than beauty or strength is a virtue." Discretion is socially acquired but, since it is not action-oriented, it too is not a virtue. Presence of mind, quick wit, and so forth are not virtues, as they neither lead to action nor involve self-denial. Cleanliness, generally not called a virtue, in fact possesses all the features of one. For similar reasons politeness too is a virtue.

II

Following his division of human actions into self- and other-regarding, Bentham divides virtues and vices too into self- and other-regarding, while recognizing that some may be both. Such virtues as temperance, self-control, and fortitude are self-regarding, whereas generosity, charity, compassion, benevolence, and so forth are other-regarding. All self-regarding virtues enable the individual to forego her immediate pleasures in order to obtain greater pleasure in the long run. Since this is how Bentham defines prudence, he contends that all self-regarding virtues are forms of or means to prudence. So far as other-regarding virtues are concerned, they consist in sacrificing one's happiness in the interest of others' greater happiness. Since this is how Bentham defines benevolence, he thinks that all other-regarding virtues are forms of or means to it. He is not entirely consistent on this point. For him other-regarding actions affect others negatively or positively. He therefore divides other-regarding virtues into two: probity, or refraining from harming others; and benevolence, or positively promoting their happiness. Sometimes he calls probity negative benevolence; on other occasions he treats it as an independent virtue.

Bentham is not entirely sure if self-regarding virtues should be called virtues. Those able to sacrifice their immediate pleasures in their own long-term interest have "firm" or "sound" minds, whereas those unable to do so are "infirm" or "frail." Bentham wonders if anything is gained by calling the former a virtue and the latter a vice. He thinks that *virtues* and *vices* are powerful terms which evoke strong feelings of approval and disapproval, and should be reserved for those moral qualities that produce "great" quantities of pleasure and pain. To extend them to such ordinary qualities as firmness and strong will or infirmity and weak will is not only to give them an "ill-proportioned measure" of importance, but also to "diminish the abhorrence which ought to be reserved" for those affecting the happiness of society at large.[6] Bentham, however, is not entirely happy with this view. Individual happiness is just as important as the happiness of others, and the moral qualities required for its maximization have all the properties associated with virtues and vices. Bentham therefore opts for the wider usage of the terms *virtue* and *vice*.

For Bentham prudence and benevolence are "basic," "primary," or "cardinal" virtues, "virtues of the first rank," or "intrinsically useful virtues." Prudence relates to the self-regarding area of life and ensures maximization of the agent's happiness over the entire course of her life. Benevolence deals with her relations with others and ensures maximization of their happiness. Between them they exhaust all virtues, and hence Bentham calls them "all-comprehensive." He calls prudence and benevolence cardinal or primary virtues, first, because they are irreducible to other virtues; and second, because they are "intrinsically useful," that is, they promote happiness always and under all conditions. All other virtues are "secondary," "subservient," "ancillary," or of the "second order"; that is, they are virtues because they lead to or are reducible to the two primary virtues, and because they do not promote happiness under all circumstances.

Having concluded on utilitarian grounds that prudence and benevolence alone are cardinal virtues, Bentham goes on to give a utilitarian account of other virtues and to show why they are secondary or of the second order. A few examples will illustrate his method of analysis.[7] Mercy is often called a virtue. Bentham agrees for his own reasons, and with important qualifications. For him mercy, which consists in forgiving the harm done by others, is a virtue because it terminates the cycle of revenge and establishes a spirit of good will, and is a form of benevolence. But it is not always a virtue because sometimes the agents of harm must be punished in order to prevent them and others from causing future harm. Since mercy is reducible to benevolence and is not always desirable, it is a secondary virtue of limited moral value.

Gratitude too is an instrumental virtue. It is a virtue because by reassuring people that their good deeds will not go unrewarded, it encourages a constant flow of benevolence and creates a climate conducive to mutual help and maximization of human happiness. Bentham seems to think that unlike mercy, it is thus not a form of but a means to benevolence. Gratitude is not always a virtue, as when the benefactor is an evil person or when an act of gratitude is misconceived and likely to be socially harmful. Loyalty to friends too is an instrumental virtue. It leads the moral agent to promote his friends' greater happiness at the cost of his own, and is "benevolence on a small scale." But it becomes a vice when it is blind and leads the agent to ignore the interests of others. Generosity, which is "friendliness on a larger scale and extended beyond the narrow circle of acquaintance," is a virtue because it promotes others' happiness. It is a secondary virtue because it is a "form of benevolence," and becomes a "vice and folly" if it involves an excessive cost to the agent or to those who are not its direct beneficiaries.

Patriotism is a virtue because it leads the agent to promote the greater happiness of the community at the expense of her own, and is a form or species of benevolence. But it becomes a "very pernicious" vice if the government is run by sinister interests and is not committed to the pursuit of the greatest happiness of the community. Humanity, which consists in alleviating the suffering of a fellow human being, is a species of benevolence. But it ceases to be a virtue when released from the restraints of either prudence, as when one risks one's life for a relatively trivial gain to others, or of benevolence, as when one gives alms to the able-bodied poor and encourages idleness. Truthfulness is a virtue both because it raises the speaker in others' esteem and gives him pleasure, and because by giving others correct information it helps them avoid harm. It is, therefore, a form of both prudence and benevolence. It is not, however, always a virtue, and Bentham thinks that its importance is often exaggerated. In his view "falsehoods of humanity" (as when a doctor gives the dying patient a false hope), "falsehoods of necessity" (as when one tells a lie to save one's own or another life), "falsehoods of urbanity" (as when one admires the hospitality of an incompetent host), and falsehoods uttered to those who have no right to ask personal questions, or seek certain information, are all fully justified by the greatest happiness principle.[8]

We have so far sketched Bentham's analysis of some traditional virtues. Although his discussion of vices is along similar lines, it is even more sketchy and lacking in rigor. Since prudence and benevolence are cardinal virtues, their opposites are basic vices. Imprudence is the opposite of prudence, and consists in pursuing one's immediate happiness at the expense of one's greater happiness in the long run. Bentham is not sure what to call the opposite of benevolence, and reluctantly settles on ill will or antipathy, defined widely to include causing pain to others or pursuing one's own happiness at the expense of their greater happiness. All other vices are reducible to these two and instrumental in nature.

III

Traditionally moral and political philosophers have called justice a cardinal virtue, and some have considered it the most important social virtue. In his own peculiar way Bentham arrives at a similar view.[9] For him human life is based on and would be rendered impossible without settled expectations. Human beings do not and cannot live in the present alone. They hope to continue living for as long as they can foresee, and they need to plan their future. They cannot plan their future without having firm expectations about it. They must know what they can call their own, which will not be arbitrarily taken away from them. And they must also know what form of behavior they can legitimately expect of each other. When their expectations are frustrated, their plans get disturbed, their lives lack order and predictability, there is a great deal of social chaos and confusion, and they all suffer acute pain. Indeed Bentham thinks that the frustration of expectations is the greatest source of pain in human life. Every society must therefore both develop a consensus on the expectations its members are legitimately entitled to entertain, and provide institutions to prevent and punish interference with them.

For Bentham expectations are of three kinds. First are natural expectations, or those inherent in certain types of human relationships and common to all societies. For example, children expect to be looked after by their parents, even as the latter in turn expect to be looked after by their children in their old age; and husband and wife entertain appropriate expectations of each other. Second are habitual or moral expectations, that is, those based on long-established and largely unwritten practices, usages, and conventions. Thus in most societies those who have long possessed land or enjoyed certain benefits and privileges expect to continue to do so in the foreseeable future. Bentham's distinction between moral and natural expectations is confused; but he seems to think that unlike the former, the latter are not contingent but inherent in certain relationships which cannot be sustained unless the relevant expectations are met. Third are legal expectations, or those derived from positive laws enacted by a sovereign authority.

Expectations give rise to claims. When people are agreed on what they may legitimately expect of each other, they demand these things not as a matter of good will or charity but as a socially sanctioned claim whose disregard entails a strong social disapproval. Since the claim is socially recognized and enforced, Bentham thinks that we can call it a right in the wider sense of the term. Justice consists in satisfying these claims or rights or, what comes to the same thing, in giving each individual his or her socially acknowledged due. The three bases of expectations give rise to three kinds of claims and three kinds of justice, namely, the natural, the moral, and the legal.

As societies increase in size and become more complex, natural expectations and unwritten usages can no longer provide a stable basis of social relationships and expectations, and come to be replaced by the positive law. In the modern society, argues Bentham, justice is for all practical purposes legal justice. It is therefore both accurate and proper to confine the term *justice* to legal justice, and to say that justice consists in respecting others' legal rights. Unlike moral rules and social conventions which lay down "imperfect duties," the law imposes a "perfect duty," which Bentham calls an obligation. Bentham therefore argues that justice consists in discharging perfect duties or obligations. As he puts it, when conduct "is a matter of obligation, it becomes justice."[10]

Unlike Hobbes and other positivist philosophers, Bentham argues that a law too can be just or unjust. Although the law is the source of all claims in the modern society, it does not exist in a vacuum and cannot prescribe whatever form of behavior catches the fancy of the sovereign. The law is embedded in and preceded by a long-established body of practices and customs, on which members of the society concerned have traditionally relied in planning their activities and lives. If a law were to disregard these practices, it would disturb their habitual expectations and cause enormous frustration and unhappiness. Since justice consists in nondisappointment of expectations, in satisfying well-grounded claims, Bentham thinks that such a law is unjust. As he puts it, the legislator "ought to maintain the distribution which is actually established. This, *under the name of justice,* is with reason regarded as his first duty."[11] Since the settled expectations are sometimes called "vested interests" in the technical sense in which the term is used by lawyers, Bentham says that "a just law . . . is one that protects vested interests."[12]

Bentham acknowledges that some of the established practices such as slavery and primogeniture might discriminate against or ill-treat and thus cause considerable unhappiness to a section of society, and need to be changed. For him this is a case of conflict between justice and utility. In a slaveholding society slaveholders have well-founded claims to their slaves, and justice requires that the claims be respected. At the same time the slaves suffer considerable unhappiness, which has to be relieved. The law needs to find a way of arbitrating between the justice-based claims of the slaveholders and the happiness-based claims of the slaves. Bentham argues that since the traditional moral philosophy viewed justice and utility as independent moral principles, it had no common ground in terms of which to resolve their conflict. He thinks that since he has reduced justice to nondisappointment of expectations, and thus to the principle of utility, he has available to him a more general principle by which to translate and compare the two claims. In his view the conflict is resolved by ascertaining whether the sum of human happiness will be increased by retaining or changing the practice of slavery.

For obvious reasons Bentham argues that the law should change it, but slowly and with minimal damage to the slaveholders' expectations. Since such a law violates established expectations, it is unjust. But since it violates them minimally, it is not grossly unjust. Besides, such injustice as it causes is outweighed by the increase in the overall quantity of human happiness, and hence fully justified. The new law establishes a new set of claims which, being in greater harmony with the principle of utility, represents a higher level of justice.

For Bentham, then, justice or observing rules and respecting socially established claims is a virtue because nondisappointment of expectations is a vital component of human happiness. That is, justice is a virtue because it produces a balance of pleasure. When it produces a great quantity of pain, as in the cases of legally enforced slavery, primogeniture, and polygamy, it ceases to be a virtue and needs to be corrected and redefined in the light of the principle of utility. Furthermore justice is essentially a negative virtue: it maximizes happiness not by increasing pleasure, but by not causing pain. As Bentham puts it, it is at bottom negative benevolence or probity, with which it is "pretty completely synonymous."[13] Since justice is a virtue because it minimizes pain, and since it may be overridden under certain circumstances, it is not a cardinal but an instrumental or second-order virtue. If it were a cardinal virtue as the moral philosophers have traditionally maintained, argues Bentham, we would not be able to explain *why* we should give each his or her due, nor provide the *grounds* on which to criticize the prevailing principles of justice.

IV

In the previous sections I outlined Bentham's theory of virtue. Since I cannot undertake here a detailed critique of it, a few general remarks should suffice.

Bentham's theory of virtue aims to do two things: to analyze the concept of virtue, and to show what moral qualities constitute virtues and vices and why. His discussion of neither is persuasive.

As Bentham understands it, a theory of virtue presupposes and is derived from a theory of right conduct. For him morality is exclusively concerned with actions and their consequences, and virtues are those moral qualities or dispositions that promote human happiness and entail a measure of self-denial. In his view no moral quality is a virtue unless it leads to desirable consequences. The limitations of this view would become evident if we took a couple of examples.

It is generally agreed that integrity is a virtue. Broadly speaking it implies being true or honest to oneself, speaking, choosing, and acting in a manner that is congruent with and expresses the kind of person one thinks one is. Integrity is a form of self-integration, a search for inner wholeness. It refers *both* to what one does and especially to *how* one does it, and is tied up with self-reflection and self-interpretation. It does not indicate what the agent will do, but rather that whatever he does will be done honestly, sincerely, and in harmony with his self-conception. As such it does not *cause* actions, but regulates them. It may or may not promote the agent's own or others' happiness, yet it is a desirable moral quality and a virtue.

Like integrity, conscientiousness, which is closely connected with it, is generally regarded as a virtue. Broadly speaking it implies acting with due deliberation, moral seriousness, and a sense of responsibility, taking great care over what one does and ensuring that one gives it one's best. It refers to how an agent approaches her choices and actions and the spirit in which she chooses and acts. It may or may not promote her or others' happiness, but that does not detract from the fact that it is a desirable moral quality. Two individuals may undertake identical actions producing equal amounts of happiness. One does it out of habit, love of reputation, or a fear of the charge of inconsistency; the other because it is the right thing to do, which she must undertake conscientiously. We would generally commend the latter. This is not because she offers a more reliable guarantee of similar future conduct as Bentham suggests, for conscientiousness offers no such guarantee.[14] Rather she displays such qualities as seriousness of purpose, a sense of responsibility, thoroughness, and a desire to put the whole of herself into her actions. We value these qualities not only because of their likely consequences, but also because they conform to our notion of how a good person should approach life.

If what I have said is correct, morality cannot be reduced to actions and their consequences. It is also about the kind of person a moral agent should aim to be and the kinds of qualities she should seek to cultivate. Morality is about *both* conduct and character, about rules and principles to regulate conduct *and* ideals to inspire and mold character, about *both* rightness and goodness. The two *are* related, but they are not mutually reducible. Since Bentham looks at morality solely from the standpoint of consequences and sees the inner moral life as only an extension of the outer world of conduct, he commits four interrelated mistakes. First, he confuses virtues with motives and sees them merely as causes of actions rather than as expressions of the agent's character and moral identity. Virtues are not moral qualities or even skills which a moral agent may or may not "possess"; they are relational in nature and refer to the way he relates to himself and to others. A just man does not merely desire to act justly and know how to do so; he also perceives and relates to others in a certain way, brings a high degree of moral seriousness to matters involving justice, is provoked by acts of injustice, and seeks a world in which justice flourishes. Virtues are a moral compass for mapping, ordering, and finding one's bearings in life, and have not only practical but also epistemological and ontological dimensions.[15]

Second, Bentham's consequentialism leads him to give a reductionist account of virtues. Consequences do enter into our assessment of moral qualities, but not in the crude causal manner suggested by Bentham, and they are not the only factor. Virtues span both rightness and goodness, both what human beings should be like and what they should do, and cannot be adequately accounted for in terms of either alone. Third, Bentham's moral theory leads him to concentrate on what might be called active virtues. It blinds him to, and prevents him from giving a coherent account of, such virtues as integrity, conscientiousness, sincerity, and critical self-reflection, which either are not directly and causally related to action or are primarily concerned with *how* it is done rather than its outcome.

Finally, since Bentham analyzes virtues solely in terms of actions and consequences, he thinks that like the latter, virtues too can be divided into self- and other-regarding. As we saw, virtues do not merely lead to action but also enjoy a measure of autonomy. They cannot therefore be classified on the same basis as actions. Even if we agreed that actions can be satisfactorily divided into self- and other-regarding, virtues cannot be so divided. Virtues refer to the agent's character and moral identity and have a unitary character. As such they inform and are expressed in *all* her actions, be they self- or other-regarding. Temperance is not only about what and how much to eat and drink, but also about how to organize one's relations with others, what emotions to express in public and in what form, and so forth. Conversely justice is not only about giving others their due but also about one's relation to oneself, including forming a just estimate of one's abilities and achievements, establishing a just relationship between one's emotions or impulses, and creating order in one's life.

I have so far questioned Bentham's analysis of the concept of virtue. His discussion of specific virtues is no more convincing. As we saw he reduces all virtues to so many different ways of maximizing happiness, and subsumes them under the highly abstract, largely empty, and arbitrarily separated virtues of prudence and benevolence. In so doing he highlights their abstract similarity, but ignores their specificity and the distinct pattern of qualities and relationships that makes them the kinds of virtues they are. As a result he is unable to grasp their unique nature and place in moral life as well as their differences from each other. A couple of examples will illustrate the point.

For Bentham chastity or matrimonial fidelity is a virtue because it avoids hurt and pain to the spouse. It is a form of benevolence, and no different from its other forms except in the agent's relationship to the person involved. I may play music quietly and avoid annoying my neighbor; I may eschew an extramarital liaison and avoid causing pain to my wife. For Bentham both are forms of negative benevolence, and there is no qualitative difference between the two. Similarly I may resist the idea of throwing a party in a colleague's honor, and thereby avoid causing pain to my asocial wife. For Bentham this form of negative benevolence too is qualitatively no different from not striking up an extramarital liaison. It is obvious that Bentham's analysis of chastity has gone seriously wrong.

Bentham cannot explain how chastity differs from other forms of negative benevolence, and why infidelity causes pain and of what kind. Chastity is a distinct kind of virtue because it is embedded in a certain kind of relationship based on specific obligations, commitments, and mutual loyalties, and sustained by a climate of trust. When detached from this context and reduced to an abstract form of negative benevolence, it loses its meaning and specificity. Infidelity hurts because it violates the very basis of the relationship and involves elements of exploitation, dishonesty, and selfishness. As such the hurt and pain it causes is distinct in nature, and has depth, poignancy, and intensity missing in the annoyance my loud music causes to my neighbor.

What is true of chastity is also true of other virtues. Humanity is not just about refraining from causing pain to other human beings. It involves recognizing them as fellow human beings entitled to certain kinds of treatment and to whom certain things may never be done. Truthfulness is not just about giving correct information to others, but involves mutual respect, trust, honesty, and a concern to establish a pattern of relationship based on these. Contrary to what Bentham says, virtues are not phenomenal manifestations of an identical essence. They are differently constituted, signify different kinds of interpersonal relationship, involve different kinds of emotions, and generate different types of pleasure and pain. A theory such as Bentham's, which treats pleasures, pains, and emotions as homogeneous entities and ignores their ineliminable diversity, is inherently incapable of appreciating the specificity of virtues and giving even a remotely satisfactory account of virtues. It is striking that J. S. Mill introduced the concept of qualitative distinctions between pleasures and pains precisely when he found it impossible to give a coherent account of virtues and vices on Benthamite grounds.

NOTES

1. Many of Bentham's critics, including David Lyons, interpret the principle of utility differently. For my reasons for disagreeing with them, see the "Introduction" in Bhikhu Parekh, *Jeremy Bentham: Critical Assessments*, 4 vols. (London: Routledge, 1993), vol. 1.

2. For Bentham's discussion of virtue, see Amnon Goldworth, ed., *Deontology* (Oxford: Clarendon Press, 1984), pp. 154ff., 178ff., and 208ff.; and Bhikhu Parekh, ed., *Bentham's Political Thought* (London: Croom Helm, 1973), chap. 6.

3. Parekh, *Bentham's Political Thought*, p. 91; Goldworth, *Deontology*, pp. 154–55, 178–79.

4. Parekh, *Bentham's Political Thought*, p. 91.

5. Goldworth, *Deontology*, pp. 156, 179.

6. J. H. Burns and H. L. A. Hart, eds., *An Introduction to the Principles of Morals and Legislation* (London: Methuen, 1970), p. 125.

7. Goldworth, *Deontology*, pp. 208ff., 350ff.

8. Jeremy Bentham, *Works of Jeremy Bentham*, ed. John Bowring (Edinburgh, 1859), vol. 6, p. 267.

9. Parekh, *Bentham's Political Thought*, pp. 97–98; Goldworth, *Deontology*, pp. 219ff., 308–9. There is also important unpublished material on this subject in Bentham Manuscripts, University College London, boxes 14 & 15.

10. Goldworth, *Deontology*, p. 127.

11. Bentham Manuscripts, box 14, pp. 155–56.

12. Ibid.

13. Goldworth, *Deontology*, p. 220.

14. Bentham Manuscripts, box 14, pp. 181–82.

15. Alasdair MacIntyre's otherwise excellent *After Virtue* (Notre Dame, Ind.: University of Notre Dame Press, 1981) suffers from his failure to take a consistently coherent view of the nature of virtue. Sometimes he sees it as a kind of moral skill, sometimes as a disposition, and on other occasions as a form of excellence. Only rarely does he see it as a form of relationship and a mode of being in the world.

Can Virtue Be Taught?
A Feminist Reconsiders

ELIZABETH KAMARCK MINNICH

Surely it is time for the true grace of women
Emerging, in their lives' colors, from the rooms, from the harvests,
From the delicate prisons, to speak their promises.
The spirit's dreaming delight and the fluid senses'
Involvement in the world. . . .

Coming close to the source of belief, these have created
Resistance, the flowering fire of memory. . . .
Muriel Rukeyser, from "Letter to the Front," Part X[1]

FRAMING THE QUESTION

I WOULD KNOW, or think I did, whether virtue can be taught had I a philosophical position specifying what sort of thing it is that we wish to teach. I could respond had I a theory of pedagogy framing for me what teaching is, what it can and cannot do. Had I such grounding, I not only could but confidently would proceed directly to an answer: my work, then, would be to convince others that I am right, that I have achieved that desired philosophical creation, an Impregnable Argument. However, not only do I not have a theory of virtue that suffices, nor a completed theory of pedagogy, but I am not convinced that it is safe for me to respond directly to the question precisely because it is one of the oldest and most fundamental within the dominant Western tradition. The vast amount of thought given to it affords me the opposite of aid or comfort: it is precisely in such areas that we most need to be careful. If we do not approach such culturally central topics with all our feminist-critical senses awake, we are liable to be led down well-trodden paths, which, however clear and distinct and elegant

69

and proper, remain within the maze of a world of meanings defined in male terms claiming to be universal. Some may indeed be universal, but we will not know that until/unless we submit them to critique. Our tools of thought—to change the metaphor to recognize also method—having been developed through the centuries in which "man" was imperially proclaimed actively to "embrace" women, to subsume us by right, by logic, by "nature," need to be carefully examined lest they betray us once again.

A feminist stance is informed, then, by a spirit of *resistance*. "Feminist ethics is born in women's refusals to endure with grace the arrogance, indifference, hostility, and damage of oppressively sexist environments. It is fueled by bonds among women, forged in experiments to create better environments now and for the future, and tried by commitments to overcome damage already done."[2] It is also informed by *respect* for the lives and experiences of those whose wisdom has not been consulted: "Ethics benefits from reflection upon our own experience, upon choices we have actually faced,"[3] where "our" is remembered to include the extraordinarily diverse people who have for so long been forced into the singularity of the Woman who is Man's Other.

We are, then, required to face the basic problems posed by an effort to comprehend that which and those who have been predefined in ways we do not accept. "Comprehension," as Hannah Arendt knew, "does not mean denying the outrageous, deducing the unprecedented from precedents, or explaining phenomena by such analogies and generalities that the impact of reality and the shock of experience are no longer felt. . . . Comprehension means the unpremeditated, attentive facing up to, and resisting of, reality —whatever it may be."[4]

Thus, feminist critique of dominant modes of thought and their related systems and forms of life moves and helps us to learn to think ourselves free, to think more freely, recognizing but also resisting reality. Such work is also now, as it always has been, carried forward for the sake of loving creative vision, a radical stance: "The feminist religious revolution thus promises to be more radical and far reaching than liberation theologies. It goes behind the symbolic universe that has been constructed by patriarchal civilization, both in its religious and in its modern secular forms. It reaches forward to an alternative that can heal the splits between 'masculine' and 'feminine', between mind and body, between males and females as gender groups, between society and nature, and between races and classes."[5]

Feminist critique, as I invoke it here, is, then, an expression of a commitment to a resistant, respectful, reflexive, critical, creative approach that asks us to look behind, or below, received knowledge and dominant traditions in an effort to locate whether, when, where, how modes and methods of thought, deriving from old exclusions and devaluations, may continue to skew our ability to think on all levels.

Such critique is required of us today because of the historical creation and enduring effects of the system of male dominance called patriarchy. It is possible as well as required because we are embodied creatures of place and time who are capable of thinking about and beyond any given construction of meaning and truth. I believe, then, that we move toward some understanding of what we will choose *virtue* to mean as we think about how we need to think about it in the first place. That is, we enact some notions of what *virtue* means and how we might teach it by how and with whom we approach the question itself.

CONTEXTUALIZING

We are creatures as well as creators of history, of language, of culture; we are meaning-making creatures, born as such into a world that we take into ourselves from the moment we are born. To resist reality in the name of comprehension involves preparing to confront the meanings and systems that are most deeply entrenched.

At the beginning of the master narrative of the dominant Western tradition, as Nicholas Lobkowicz reminds us, "When the Greeks opposed to each other *theoria* and *praxis* . . . what they had in mind was a distinction between various kinds or walks of life — a distinction which permitted them to tackle the kind of question of yore it was customary to ask at the Delphic oracles: Who is the most pious, the most happy, the wisest, the best man?"[6] "The Greeks"— meaning, of course, the few males who had the leisure to consider such questions — then prescribed the sorts of virtues, understood as excellences of kind, characterizing lives to be led only by some "kinds" of people: "the 'citizen's virtue'— that is, his being capable of participating in government — would not belong to every citizen; only those released from necessary and menial occupations, have the leisure required for governing."[7]

We must notice now that the citizen's virtue, like the virtues of any life then considered worthy of "a free man," is premised on the exclusion and devaluation of those forced to serve him, to "free" him from all that sustains us in being. We cannot simply say, "That was then; this is now. There is no point in dwelling on the prejudices of a past age, or imposing on them our values." To rush past the context is to ignore that what was actually said about "man" is fundamentally implicated with a gender hierarchy that hides as it marginalizes and devalues one half of humankind, along with male slaves and those who worked with their hands — and with them, the virtues of labor, both productive and reproductive. Functioning here are the historical injustices we are still struggling to set right, and those remain with us as both practices and modes of thought.

UNTANGLING OLD KNOTS

We see in Lobkowicz's study of "the Greeks" their and his *faulty generalization*, from a few men to humankind and from a few Greeks to "the Greeks"; *circular reasoning*, defining virtue by reference to those few men's lives, and then justifying their being the only ones allowed to live those lives by referring to the virtues ascribed to them; and *mystified concepts*, such as that of virtue that obscures its exclusion of women from the possibility of achieving it, leaving women subject to a separate and distinctly unequal notion of womanly virtue that is not human virtue. Thus, we end up with *partial systems of knowledge*[8] as of belief and morality that perpetuate as they derive from, and return to justify, entangled gender and class hierarchies of "kinds" of humans.

We need, then, to watch for where and how *invidiously hierarchical definitions* of "man" and "his" virtues are worked into the ways we think about humans and our virtues at all levels, and all the time, lest we perpetuate them. The past, as has been said, is not only not dead; it isn't even past.

Still with us are also *oppositional definitions* which not only distinguish male from female but oppose them in a way that divides us at the same time it holds us together as mutually defining through our opposition: "the opposite sex." "Virtue" derives from the Latin *virtus*, "manliness, valor, worth, etc., from *vir*, man," and means "the possession or display of manly qualities; manly excellence, courage, valor."[9] By such definitions there cannot be a "virtuous" woman, except as that "unnatural" creature, a "manly woman." She does not thereby become human, as Man is, but aberrant, neither a proper woman nor a natural human. As Mary Wollstonecraft put it, "If there be but one criterion of morals, but one archetype for man, women appear to be suspended by destiny . . . ; they . . . must not aim at respect, lest they should be hunted out of society as masculine."[10]

For women, virtue has been defined quite differently, as we all know. A "good woman" is one who successfully enacts her gender role, which is distinguished sharply from that of man, and is fundamentally based, as a man's virtue is not, on sexuality. A good woman is not sexually "loose," out of the control of a man to whom she belongs. For the meaning of virtue for woman, see "chastity, sexual purity, esp. on the part of women. Of easy virtue: see Easy. . . ."[11] This is, of course, both a gendered oppositional definition, by which females cannot have/display human virtue because we cannot properly be "manly," and a sexualized definition that supports the hierarchy by requiring "sexual purity" of women as it is not required of men.

This is, *mutatis mutandis*, a theme of the relations between women and men we see around the world. Any definition of Woman that defines her/us primarily as a sexual/reproductive being leads to the reduction of our humanity. It locks us all into that terrible dance of repulsion and yearning, of unequal mutual dependency, that is so familiar between men and women and that poisons the highly sexualized relations of white and black, colonist and native, civilized and primitive—"us" and "them."

Such entangled, mutually constitutive, naturalized oppositions play against the *Man/Nature division* in any of its forms. They all place males—to varying degrees, depending on how "civilized" and "rational" their "kind" is held to be—against, rather than mutually within, a Mother Nature that both sustains and is felt to threaten to engulf him. Thus Man/civilization/rationality is not only distinguished from but radically separated from Woman/the primitive/the sexual/emotive.

This is dualistic and divisive; it is also dangerously because faultily abstract. Man, taken to be the defining kind of human, is alienated, dissociated, not only from women and from Nature and from "lesser" men, but from those aspects of himself that he in fact shares with them. That is, since all the qualities and activities and modes of life of the lesser people are also always human, Man, in distinguishing himself from them/us, splits himself from himself as well. The privilege explained and justified by the old division between thought and action, mind and body, has many costs. As Stanley Cavell observed, "The requirement for purity imposed by philosophy now looks like a wish to leave me out, I mean each of us, the self, with its arbitrary needs and unruly desires."[12]

Thinking about our thinking as a result of his searing experiences in war, the philosopher J. Glenn Gray noted:

> The dissociation of man as individual and as species from the limitless backgrounds of his being is another quality which constitutes the monstrous character of contemporary civilization. . . . Thoughtlessly we conceive nature as external environment. Thinking, and presumably remembering, too, is supposed to be "non-natural." But that which sustains us in being is surely as much these nonmaterial activities of thinking, remembering, creating as digesting, breathing and locomotion, and the like."[13]

Even Glenn Gray, trapped by the faultily universalized and purified "man," oddly does not note, as we must in a spirit true to his work, that "the dissociation of man . . . from the limitless backgrounds of his being," from all "that which sustains us in being," is profoundly related to the early and persistent dissociation of a few privileged males from the lives of all those who took care of the necessities of life from which virtuous men were freed by the labor of defined-as-lesser Others. We have all paid the price of such dissociation. It does indeed run through the "monstrous character of contemporary civilization." It defines a virtuous human as manly, masterful, in control, and in opposition to others. Those others have been identified with Nature, while Man has been supposed to rise above nature through dominance, in order to be free.

ACTION

The question of freedom reminds us that successful critique of concepts and systems of thought does not of itself change social, cultural, economic, political systems that have realized those concepts and systems. Revealing the errors and curiosities on which constructions of gender as of class and race have been based does not change the fact that such tragic nonsense is implicated in almost all present systems of thought as in daily life. Thus, moral inquiry must be critical, resistant, respectful, reflexive, and responsible to action.

Here it is critical to note the complementarity of philosophical-political strands of critique from feminist scholars, Third World people, environmentalists, pacifists, proponents of multiculturalism. No matter where we begin critique of the dominant tradition we arrive at similar observations. When a few define themselves as the inclusive term — the norm and the ideal — there is nowhere for the rest of us to go except out of the central category, and down the scale of worth. Thus is injustice, and the violence that attends it, established and justified. Thus do we become divided against each other and ourselves, trapped in sterile combat. It is difficult, then, to conceive of *human* virtue.

TRANSFORMATIONS

Let me, then, explore a few of the ways we are attempting to think ourselves free of the old and still present invidious hierarchies of thought, of method, of action.

Recentering

Those who have been most marginalized and oppressed have turned to their own lives of struggle and resistance, fury and love. They have put at the center that which was marginalized, divided, repressed.

Seeing knowledge as grounded in experience, theorists such as Nancy Hartsock, Sara Ruddick, and Hilary Rose argue that the activities assigned to women, understood through the categories of feminist theory, provide a starting point for developing claims to knowledge that are potentially more comprehensive and less distorted than those of privileged men. They believe that women's sensuous, relational, and contextual perspective allows them to understand aspects of nature and social life not available to those men who are cut off from such activities. Thus women's experiences provide a basis for developing an alternative epistemology that unifies manual, mental, and emotional activity.[14]

Such recentering is not singular. We do not move from Man to an equally mystified, abstract, dissociated Woman. We struggle to remain in conversation with many women as well as to speak of our own experiences so that we do not once again suffer the loss of multiple realities. As Patricia Hill Collins notes in her effort to explore an epistemology developed from Black women's experiences: "First, Black women's political and economic status provides them with a distinctive set of experiences that offers a different view of material reality than that available to other groups. The unpaid and paid work that Black women perform, the types of communities in which they live, and the kinds of relationships they have with others suggest that African-American women, as a group, experience a different world than those who are not Black and not female. Second, these experiences stimulate a distinctive Black female consciousness concerning that material reality."[15]

Pushing us not only through the barriers between kinds of women, but through those between the conscious and the repressed, Ruth Ginzberg, learning and thinking with Audre Lorde, notes that Lorde "identifies the erotic as 'a considered source of power and information within (women's) lives' that 'rises from our deepest and nonrational knowledge'. The erotic, she claims, provides 'the power which comes from sharing deeply any pursuit with another person,' as well as 'the open and fearless understanding of . . . [the] capacity for joy'. . . . This," says Ginzberg, "is a political claim, not a claim about hedonism or 'rights' to pleasure. . . . [Lorde] sees the erotic as an epistemic force that tempers the individualistic sense of self; it is the source of both power and information, which encourages resistance to atomism and unchecked individualism and which leads to understanding. . . ." And she concludes, "I suggest that there is a conception of moral philosophy emerging from the writings of Audre Lorde and other lesbian feminist theorists that is based in the very acts of surviving. . . ."[16]

Reconfiguring

Such efforts to bring that which was denied and hidden fully into consciousness, culture, and thought undo the dangerous dissociations we have been noting. They erupt them from within, not by turning old hierarchies upside down, or collapsing ego into id, but by reconfiguring what was always there. With *more* now relating us, we must learn to make distinctions that are not divisions; to think far less crudely about *sameness* and *difference* in order to escape the old pattern of mutually created oppositions. As Agnes Heller puts it, thinking about the relations of sameness and difference reconceived in relation to "the good life" as public life: "Although the good life of each and every person is unique, it is simultaneously shared by the members of a community, a group, a society; however . . . all these shared ways of life are again unique: they cannot be ranked and compared."[17] We need to be able to think not of difference and sameness across the old hierarchical lines, but of uniqueness that is discernible and has meaning precisely because of our human commonality.

But because we persist in respecting the experiences of those we have now put at the center, we do not fall back into understanding uniqueness or commonality in ways that erase either actual individuals or particular communities. We are precisely not trying to locate the good life in abstraction from real and possible lives led by those whose existence is constantly at risk. "Survival . . . is central to any conceptualization in which the summum bonum (if there is such a thing) is not taken to be something that transcends physically, psychologically, and socially embedded life but rather that is taken to be just exactly that. The sketch that emerges is that of an immanent rather than a transcendent philosophical theory, in which survival is not transcended but embraced."[18] We are seeking to reconfigure, not to reinscribe in and for different bodies, the good life of the "free man," and thus we no longer flee but attempt to comprehend the wisdom of human life in its intimate relations to necessity.

Revaluing

We are thus revaluing the lives prescribed for women in different groups, at different times, in different cultures. This, of course, is a research project as well as a conceptual task. The qualities of women as of Woman are evidently prescribed in all sorts of ways in philosophies, religions, political theories, economic systems, in codes of mores, manners, and morals. If we would locate a fuller array of the virtues discerned and prescribed for humans of all sorts, we can do so by remembering and revaluing what it has meant to be a woman. This is the sort of work Mary Daly, Katie Cannon, Patricia Hill Collins, Carol Gilligan, Sara Ruddick, and Nell Noddings, among others, have been doing. What was both prescribed for women and scorned in relation to the falsely generalized or even universalized Man is reevaluated.

Thus, among other coexisting and complementary efforts, we begin work on an "ethics of care," in which the "maternal" (Ruddick), the "caring" (Gilligan), the "feminine" (Noddings) are recast from the qualities "naturally" to be expected from females, to become suggestive of virtues to be attained by humans. We undo the dissociation of Man from all that sustains us, all of us, in being. We reconsider notions of justice that exclude care, and struggle to rethink care as it interrelates with justice, drawing, as Ruddick does, on experiences within the family, and as Hill Collins does, on the paid and unpaid work Black women perform.

Redefining

Once having begun such philosophical and empirical work, we find that revaluing is much more than an effort at addition. It requires more basic transformation of our theorizing, as of our action. While "manly" strength is considered central to a citizen or a leader's virtue, gentleness and compassion remain problems, signs of weakness, marks of the devalued effeminate. While power is defined as the ability to make people do as one wills, we continue to conflate power with domination. The military remains the epitome of masculinity, and pacifism can only be scorned as effeminate. It is no accident that the effort to revalue "feminine" virtue has led to rethinking pacifism, nor that it has led other feminist thinkers to create "ecofeminism."

We redefine culturally central terms, concepts, frames of meaning and hence of action. As Sara Ruddick writes,

> A feminist maternal politics of peace: peacemakers create a communal suspicion of violence, a climate in which peace is desired, a way of living in which it is possible to learn and to practice nonviolent resistance and strategies of reconciliation. This description of peacemaking is a description of mothering. Mothers take their work seriously and create a women's politics of resistance. Feminists sustain that politics, devising strategies, celebrating strength, resisting violence and contempt. Together mothers, feminists, and women in resistance are members of an "imaginative collective" . . . (which) subverts the mythical division between men and women, private care and public defense, that hobbles both maternal and peacemaking endeavors. As men become mothers and mothers invent public resistance to violence, mothering and peacemaking become a single, womanly-manly work — a feminist, maternal politics of peace.[19]

With the redefinition of "maternal" to become a human term, our move to recenter with the marginal within the material reconfigures the old transcendent/immanent division as well. We need not choose between the life of the mind, the spirit, and the body. "Man is mortal" must yield to the recollection that humankind is also always *natal*.[20]

J. Glenn Gray understood the violence of forgetting such foundational human connections. He related "dissociation" to "living godlessly," a product of that "remoteness from reality" that Hegel diagnoses as the "fury of abstraction." Notions of virtue that are built on and require splitting off aspects of humanness that are then projected onto Others over whom some few men are justified in exercising dominion reveal that "fury." The passions of the masculine mind, uncontrolled by the realities of human embodiedness within real human natural and historical contexts, are more dangerous than those of the body uncontrolled by reason because reason is, unlike body, limitless.

REASON

We ask how any thought relates to body. As Maxine Sheets-Johnstone notes, "The consequence of leaving the body behind is unexplained concepts, that is, concepts that are simply taken for granted with no thought as to how they might have originated . . . (which) not only perpetuates the errors of a partial and in consequence biased metaphysics (but) also creates conceptual problems in the very real sense of assuming concepts to arise *sui generis*."[21] We are attempting to undo such bizarre dissociations of thoughts from thinking, and of thinking from the embodied natal/mortal, reproductive/productive, meaning-created and creating particular person who thinks as, of, and beyond what and who she or he is.

Thus, having undertaken to begin revaluing the virtues of dissociated/alienated Man's Others, we uncover again the need to transform, and not merely add to, Man's virtues. As Alison Jaggar notes, "Typically, although again not invariably, the rational has been contrasted with the emotional, and this contrasted pair then has often been linked with other dichotomies. Not only has reason been contrasted with emotion, but it has also been associated with the mental, the cultural, the universal, the public, and the male, whereas emotion has been associated with the irrational, the physical, the natural, the particular, the private, and, of course, the female."[22] There are now many studies of reason, often focused especially on science and the Enlightenment dream, that discern hidden but potent biases on many levels. Such critiques come also from nonfeminist scientists. As Abraham Pais wrote, in a study of the great physicist Niels Bohr, "the best we can say" about nature, according to Bohr, "is always partial and incomplete; only by entertaining multiple and mutually limiting points of view, building up a composite picture, can we approach the real richness of the world. (Bohr) called this important idea 'complementarity' and applied it not only to explain why matter sometimes acts like a particle and sometimes like a wave, *but also to rebuke Nazi claims of cultural superiority. . . .*"[23] (emphasis added)

These critiques underline the fact that the claims we make for reason *have effects* in, even as they also reflect, the world. If we would rethink reason, the defining virtue of Man from Aristotle on, we must do with it what we have done elsewhere. We must critique it to uncover its biases, its definitional and operational implications with foundational invidious divisions and dissociations. We do this in order also more creatively to explore its functioning in all the modes written out of its "proper" sphere as characterizing lesser humans. We then find that what John Dewey called "the quest for certainty" is, as he argued, closely related to Man's quest for dominion over others, and over the earth. Bohr's idea of "complementarity" provides an intriguing alternative model that is consonant with Dewey's move to transactional analysis, Gilligan's ethics of care, Ruddick's drawing on and drawing together of maternal and pacifist thinking, Noddings' revaluation of the virtues of femininity, and J. Glenn Gray's plea for the undoing of abstract thinking that perpetuates dissociation from all that sustains humans in being.

NEW WAYS

A picture, a collage, a weave of many strands old and new begins to emerge, suggesting a way of thinking that is resistant, respectful, reflexive, and critical. It refuses dualistic and/or invidiously hierarchical divisions that cannot be breached in favor of distinctions within wholeness. It emphasizes transactional mutuality over oppositional relations. It explores connection, complementarity, relationality within the matrix of experience where we are called to practice both care and justice. And it struggles to retrieve and revalue all aspects of the meaning of being human, from the bodily to the rational to the transcendent, in the name of our fullest unique and common potential. Such a vision has always threaded its way through the dominant tradition, never disappearing entirely, often emerging into full view. Nevertheless it needs to be rediscovered and reconfigured so that it can be freed of the startling lapses from its own intellectual and moral coherence it has suffered because of the depth and range of always divisive gender constructs that have entangled with the other primary divisions of humans into "kinds."

There are models. Working herself free of old ways by immersing herself in them to find the Ariadne's thread, listening for guidance to "the orphic voice," the philosopher, poet, and novelist Elizabeth Sewell discerns in poetry a method, a logic, that does not suffer from the "fury of abstraction":

> It is not a matter for specialists, but for people. . . . The method, the postlogic, is a way of using mind and body to build up dynamic structures (never fixed or abstract patterns) by which the human organism sets itself in relation to the universe and allows each side to interpret the other. The mind's relation to its structure or myth is inclusive and reflexive. It is not detached; the working mind is part of the dynamic of the system, and is united, by its forms, with whatever in the universe it is inquiring into. The process of making the interpretive myth is carried out in language, and the structure of its language in its dynamic with the mind both conditions and is conditioned by the mutual interpretation. The body is an essential part of the method. The method bears a close relation to sex and fertility. Love is a necessary part of its working. . . . It lies to everyone's hand and we have to return to it, not as a vague ornament of life but as one of the great living disciplines of the mind, friendly to all other disciplines, and offering them and accepting from them new resources of power.[24]

We can see some fruits of Sewell's teaching in the collaborative work of Sande and Larry Churchill, philosophers who are her students as well as being involved with both the dominant tradition and feminist critique. Here, they prepare to think about ethics brought into creative tension with the realities of clinical practices:

> Human ethical activity is complex and multi-faceted. It includes deciding and acting, reflection and contemplation, sustaining habits over time, nurturing character, and many other kinds of activity. It is part logic, part acts of will, part turning of emotional sensibilities, part feats of imagination. Because ethics embraces such diverse kinds of activity, ethical theories need to be diverse and multifaceted as well. Yet this is frequently not the case. . . . We invite you to think of the approach to ethical theory we will undertake in this essay not

as a linear and progressive rational argument which makes additive and cumulative points for the purpose of unifying or totalizing a theory. Rather we think of our approach as a collage. . . . The emphasis is on showing how images are interdependent and gain their meanings from the whole, rather than being serially or chronologically anchored.[25]

The Churchill critique, like that of Elizabeth Sewell and others, has also led them to accept the challenge to create which that critique carries with it. They know the intellectual, political, and ethical importance of changing methods of thought, and recognize that such a method often entails shifting our shaping metaphors. Just how imaginatively stimulating such shifts can be is vividly displayed by Cornel West, who envisions "new world bricoleurs with improvisational and flexible sensibilities that side-step mere opportunism and mindless eclecticism; persons from all countries, cultures, genders, sexual orientations, ages and regions with protean identities who avoid ethnic chauvinism and faceless universalism; intellectual and political freedom fighters with partisan passion, international perspectives, and, thank God, a sense of humor . . . with intellectual rigor, existential dignity, moral vision, political courage, and soulful style.[26]

Inspired by this evocation of a virtuoso of humanity, we return to an old question: How is one to realize well all that one might be? How is one to help others do so as well? There are no prescriptions, although there are methods of thought and practice as there are inspiring models to be found everywhere, among us all. For the moment, it is no small thing to recognize that how and where and with whom we *begin* will make the difference in our own undertaking of the old quest. We begin again with the inspiration of the great African-American educator Anna Julia Cooper, who wrote in 1892:

It is not the intelligent woman vs. the ignorant woman, nor the white woman vs. the black, the brown, and the red,— it is not even the cause of woman vs. man. Nay, 'tis woman's strongest vindication for speaking that *the world needs to hear her voice.* . . . The world has had to limp along with the wobbling gait and the one-sided hesitancy of a man with one eye. Suddenly the bandage is removed from the other eye and

the whole body is filled with light. It sees a circle where before it saw a segment. The darkened eye restored, every member rejoices with it.[27]

NOTES

1. Muriel Rukeyser, "Letter to the Front," from *Out of Silence* (Evanston, Ill.: TriQuarterly Books, 1992). © William L. Rukeyser.

2. Claudia Card, ed., *Feminist Ethics* (Lawrence: University Press of Kansas, 1991), p. 4.

3. Ibid.

4. Hannah Arendt, *The Origins of Totalitarianism* (Cleveland: World Publishing Co./Meridian Book, 1966), p. viii.

5. Rosemary Radford Ruether, *Women-Church: Theology and Practice* (San Francisco: Harper & Row, 1985), p. 3.

6. Nicholas Lobkowicz, *Theory and Practice: History of a Concept from Aristotle to Marx* (Notre Dame, Ind.: University of Notre Dame Press, 1967), p. 3.

7. Ibid., p. 20.

8. For discussion of these conceptual errors throughout the dominant tradition, see my *Transforming Knowledge* (Philadelphia: Temple University Press, 1990).

9. *The Oxford English Dictionary* (Oxford: Oxford University Press, 1978), p. 239.

10. Mary Wollstonecraft, *A Vindication of the Rights of Woman* (New York: W. W. Norton & Co., 1967), p. 69.

11. *The Oxford English Dictionary* (Oxford: Oxford University Press, 1978), p. 238.

12. Stanley Cavell, *Conditions Handsome and Unhandsome* (Chicago: University of Chicago Press, 1990), p. 77.

13. J. Glenn Gray, *The Warriors: Reflections on Men in Battle* (New York: Harper & Row/Harper Colophon Books, 1970), p. xix.

14. Nancy Tuana, *Woman and the History of Philosophy* (New York: Paragon House/Paragon Issues in Philosophy, 1992), p. 116.

15. Quoted in ibid., p. 117.

16. Ruth Ginzberg, "Philosophy Is Not a Luxury," in *Feminist Ethics*, ed. Card, pp. 131–32.

17. Agnes Heller, *Beyond Justice* (Oxford: Basil Blackwell, 1991), p. 324.

18. Ginzberg, "Philosophy is Not a Luxury," p. 132.

19. Sara Ruddick, *Maternal Thinking Toward a Politics of Peace* (Boston: Beacon Press, 1989), p. 244.

20. Cf. Hannah Arendt, *The Human Condition* (Chicago: University of Chicago Press, 1970).

21. Maxine Sheets-Johnstone, *The Roots of Thinking* (Philadelphia: Temple University Press, 1990), p. 289.

22. Alison M. Jaggar, "Love and Knowledge: Emotion in Feminist Epistemology," in *Gender/Body/Knowledge: Feminist Reconstructions of Being and Knowing*, ed. Alison M. Jaggar and Susan R. Bordo (New Brunswick: Rutgers University Press, 1989), p. 145.

23. Richard Rhodes, review of *Niel Bohr's Times: In Physics, Philosophy and Polity* by Abraham Pais, *New York Times Book Review*, 26 January 1992.

24. Elizabeth Sewell, *The Orphic Voice: Poetry and Natural History* (New Haven, Conn.: Yale University Press, 1960), pp. 404–5.

25. Sande and Larry Churchill, "Reason, Narrative and Rhetoric: A Theoretical Collage for the Clinical Encounter," in *Theological Analyses of the Clinical Encounter*, ed. Gerald McKenny and Jonathan Sande (Kluwer Academic Pubs., forthcoming).

26. Cornel West, in *Out There: Marginalization and Contemporary Culture*, ed. Ferguson, Gever, Minh-ha, West (Boston: Massachusetts Institute of Technology Press, 1990), p. 36.

27. Anna Julia Cooper, *A Voice From the South* (New York: Oxford University Press, 1988), pp. 121–23.

PART II

Teaching Virtue
in
Different Cultures

Cultivating Virtue in a Religiously Plural World: Possibilities and Problems

FREDERICK J. STRENG

When the Tao is lost, only then does the doctrine of virtue [*te*]
arise.
When virtue is lost, only then does the doctrine of benevolence
[*jen*] arise.
When benevolence is lost, only then does the doctrine of propriety
[*li*] arise.
Now propriety is only the husk of loyalty and faithfulness [*chung
hsin*];
It is the beginning of all confusion and disorder [*luan*].
Tao te Ching, chapter 38[1]

The [Aristotelian] tradition of virtues is at variance with central features of the modern economic order and more especially its individualism, its acquisitiveness and its elevation of the values of the market to
a central social place.
Alasdair MacIntyre, *After Virtue*[2]

FOR OVER TWO MILLENNIA down to the present, morally reflective
people have criticized their contemporaries for allowing true living to degenerate into a semblance of best living, from virtuous
living to mere virtuosity. The pursuit of the authentic good life,
however, continues an effort documented in many cultures during
at least the past six millennia. Religious seers, philosophers, and
honored leaders have called on their people to awaken to what
superior human beings recognize as excellent, effective, and true.
They encourage their compatriots to celebrate the sources of goodness and well-being, and to choose profound joy over ephemeral

pleasure. They have defined and promoted authentic living, however, primarily for a given community centered in its own ancestors, language, and tradition. When the rulers of a community extended their political and economic power over other communities, they sought to incorporate the strangers into their own (normative) traditions. The formulations of true virtue and the assumptions about the relation of virtue to the comprehensive purpose for living arise from their own cultural context, ancestral memories, and military-economic power base.

While we stand in this long human heritage of wrestling with the form and content of true virtue, we also recognize that we stand in a historical pivotal point for an emerging global consciousness. The technological and socio-economic revolutions in western Europe during the nineteenth century brought an important shift in the sources of knowledge. This was a shift away from traditional cultural values and ecclesiastical institutional authority to a dependence on scientific discovery and constitutional political power. By the middle of the twentieth century the imperial dominance of European political authority was defunct. The freedom that many nations gained in Asia, the Middle East, and Africa during the mid-twentieth century has resulted in a resurgence of traditional values in these nations, combined with technological advances. We are now in a world situation in which there are many centers of personal and cultural value, and diverse political-economic bases. We stand today in a global horizon of history without, as yet, a global consensus of values or common understanding of virtue.

In this context of religious and ideological pluralism that itself rests on a long heritage of the human effort in virtuous living I want to place the theme question of this volume: Can virtue be taught? To place this question in such a context is to forego the issue of the teachability of virtue as defined in fifth-century BCE Athens: Can *arete*, effective power and social (including moral) excellence, be taught by a teacher for a fee to someone who might or might not be concerned to perform in such a manner? Nevertheless, this question set in today's context does relate to the larger issue found also in Plato's *Meno* of the relation between the development of social-moral aptitudes, sensitivities, and behavior and the fundamental nature or capacity of human beings.

PRESENT SOCIAL CONDITIONS
FOR CULTIVATING VIRTUE

Our physical and social environment, our "experienced world," is one which we often take for granted. It is often quite local — that which we experience daily in a direct sensory way: where we eat, sleep, work, and play. At the same time our extended communication systems of TV, radio, and printed material, our economic trading network, and our military capacity — including the continuing ICBM posture between nations — force us into a global consciousness of living in a worldwide community. People from different parts of the globe are aware that we live in mutual cultural, economic, political, and military relationships, sometimes in harmony and sometimes in conflict or tension. High stone walls, mountain ranges, deserts, or oceans can no longer isolate and protect us from each other, nor save any of us from nuclear fallout or environmental disaster. Today technology makes information available momentarily to people whose ancestors only four or five generations ago had little knowledge. Ignorance of alternate lifestyles, moral systems, and ideologies cannot insure the validity of long-held tribal or cultural value systems. Thus, today we already are in a world network of relationships which, for good or ill, helps to shape our sense of virtuous living.

If the present situation in which we cultivate virtue requires recognition of a worldwide community for which virtuous living is relevant, we need to consider briefly a definition of "virtue" as a general term, and the significance of the diversity of the content and roles of virtue in different religions, and *within* religious and cultural traditions. As a general working definition of virtue I find that used by Lee Yearley, in his *Mencius and Aquinas*, to cover most of the concerns that we will take up here. He writes:

A virtue, then, is a disposition to act, desire, and feel that involves the exercise of judgment and leads to a recognizable human excellence or instance of human flourishing. Moreover, virtuous activity involves virtue for itself and in light of some justifiable life plan.[3]

This definition focuses appropriately on the capacities and skills of character whereby a person can pursue an "internal good," such as justice, benevolence, or sympathetic joy (in someone else's success); at the same time, it does not sufficiently emphasize — as will the following discussion — the concrete social expression of virtue in practice. This is to say that the capacity of "human flourishing" in its moral dimension will unite the disposition and practice when the virtue is well expressed.

This general, formal definition of virtue can help us identify the kind of human experience and behavior that can be classified within a concept of virtue. It does not have any normative content by which to judge whether any given behavior exhibits true virtue or only a semblance of it. By contrast, when we examine concrete cultural forms that fit this classification we must note the divergent, sometimes conflicting and sometimes similar claims about the social forms, psychological dispositions, and roles that virtue has in a larger "life plan." These differences and similarities have been noted and analyzed by a number of scholars; I call attention to a few examples of comparative studies of virtue (as broadly defined above). I wish to avoid any suggestion that when we affirm the *goal* of a world community, as well as the *fact* of an economic, political and communication network on a worldwide scale, we assume it is an easy process to cultivate those virtuous dispositions necessary for such a world community. We can begin by looking at some examples of traditional theories of virtue. In his comparison of the theories of virtue in the Christian Saint Thomas Aquinas and the Confucian literati Meng-tzu (or Mencius), Lee Yearley notes:

> Mencius's benevolence (*jen*) . . . seems to resemble Aquinas's benevolence (*benevolentia*), but the virtue is central to Mencius and peripheral to Aquinas. In fact, charity (*caritas*) often functions for Aquinas in the way that benevolence (*jen*) functions for Mencius, and charity differs substantially from benevolence.[4]

Similarly, after making a survey analysis of the contents and role of virtue in the social behavior advocated by Homer, Aristotle, New Testament authors, Jane Austen, and Benjamin Franklin, Alasdair MacIntyre asserts: "There is no single, central, core conception of the virtues which make a claim for universal allegiance."[5] In an earlier study of "personal transformation" in the Christian

Protestant reformer Martin Luther's *Lectures on Romans* and the spiritual transformation found in the Indian Buddhist Mahāyāna text *Eight Thousand Line Perfection of Wisdom* I found that their expression of virtues and moral behavior both diverged and overlapped; while virtues such as patience, charity, serenity, and joy are advocated in both traditions, they are understood differently in relation to alternate understandings of reality and the relative importance of faith and wisdom.[6] In another study of three twentieth-century religious philosophers—a Christian, Paul Tillich; a Confucian, Chun-i T'ang; and a Buddhist, Keiji Nishitani—and their approaches to "authentic existence," I suggested that because of their different ontologies and anthropologies they had quite different understandings of what constituted true religion and its expression, including moral obligations.[7]

The recognition that honorable people in other cultures and different institutional bodies within a society have different values, approaches to authentic existence, and understandings of the role of virtue within a comprehensive purpose of life is, indeed, disturbing. One way to overcome the discomfort experienced in the differences is to disregard them. Such disregard is often found among those people who assume that variations or differences represent external expression of an essential, common reality that transcends particular cultural expression. Thus, different interpretations of such virtues as patience, friendliness, or conscientiousness —including the rules for practicing these virtues—are seen to be less important than the generalized notion of each. By contrast to that orientation, my assumption here is that differences are significant; and the necessity to consider the differences informs the manner in which a world community can be developed. Only by taking the present conflicts and differences seriously can we develop the character dispositions, the "virtues," including the intellectual and emotional skills, to handle the "otherness" of other people.

The urgency of the need to understand the way in which other people are different from oneself and still necessarily interrelated comes from the fact that all human beings are either nourished or poisoned by each other. All of us have become physical and cultural neighbors in a shrinking world. We must deal with the differences and conflicts through a strategy and sensitivity other than a dichotomizing flight-or-fight mentality. Flight is no longer possible, and to fight results in mutual destruction. The aspiration of a world community, as presented here, then, recognizes a strong continuity among human beings, with overlapping general goals such as security, justice, freedom, some control over one's life, and a sense of well-being, but does not entail the hope or expectation that one orthodoxy or orthopraxis will reign supreme. Given divergent immediate needs and particular perceptions of concrete goals for enhanced living, it is likely that human beings will remain ideologically and religiously pluralistic. The critical issue, then, is whether human beings can aspire toward the goal of a world community within a recognition that there are divergent visions and strategies for attaining such a world community. As indicated before, one model for a world order is the imperial model of extending one's ethnic or normative ideology and rules for virtuous living to all others. In the next section we want to examine some of the considerations that must be taken into account if we are to affirm both the likelihood of continuing diversity in practicing true virtue, and the need to identify workable social rules that permit diversity and mutual life enhancement.

VARIATION IN, AND VARIANCE FROM, TRUE VIRTUE

The first point is that character dispositions and their expression in social action are seen within a larger ontological and anthropological context. Virtue is grounded in claims about ultimate reality, about the "way things really are," about what is self-transcending, while it is also expressed through particular historical forms. The experience and practice of true virtue manifests one's destiny; it actualizes one's greatest potential. Virtue is the capacity, or power, to express true humanity.[8] Thus, virtue is seen to be based in reality that is beyond the particular personal or socially determined goals, desires, or purposes of the individual. By way of example we note that the grounding of true virtue in a final purpose or superlative expression of life is recognized in the analyses of Alasdair MacIntyre regarding Aristotelian ethics, and of Robert Thurman regarding Mahāyāna Buddhist social activism. MacIntyre states with regard to the basic structure of Aristotle's *Nicomachean Ethics:*

Within that teleological scheme there is a fundamental contrast between man-as-he-happens-to-be and man-as-he-could-be-if-he-realised-his-essential-nature. Ethics is the science which is to enable men to understand how they make the transition from the former state to the latter. Ethics therefore on this view presupposes some account of potentiality and act, some account of the essence of man as a rational animal and above all some account of the human *telos*.[9]

In a different ontological context, Thurman describes the attainment of wisdom and merit for the goal of enlightenment as arising within the three-fold body (*trikaya*) of the Buddha. He writes:

A perfectly enlightened Buddha is defined in the Universal vehicle [Mahāyāna] to be a superhuman who has spent aeons in evolutionary development, acting out of both self-interest (*svartha*) and altruistic interest (*parartha*) to gather the stores of wisdom and merit (*punyajnana-sambhara*). These ultimately come to the fulfillment of self-interest in the Body of Truth (*Dharmakāya*) and to fulfillment of altruistic interest in the Bodies of Beatitude and Emanation (*Sambhoga-nirmana-kāya*).[10]

It is only within a context of some self-transcending reality or ultimate purpose that the seers and sages of different cultures distinguish between true and false virtue. Life is full of ambiguities; different virtues themselves provide the bases for conflicting moral action in specific situations. The self-transcending reality is both the deepest resource for variation in virtuous expressions *and* — perhaps paradoxically — the normative guideline marking off which semblances of virtue are at variance with true virtue. As saints and aspiring righteous ones know, it is all too easy to become a transgressor in the Promised Land! In light of this dilemma, can we have a model of the transcendent which has an internal openness to allow for significant variation while avoiding a pernicious relativism that precludes judgments of true and false virtue? I believe we can if we do not assume that the transcendent is known or realized only by a concept or symbol — even though we must use a concept or "model" to communicate this claim verbally. I do not have the space to elaborate such an internally open model of the transcendent here, but I can make a few suggestions.[11] The key notion is that there are different ways, or modes, of knowing and expressing the ultimate context or purpose of life, and that the role of virtue changes in relation to the understanding of its function within the mode of knowing the ultimate reality. Four different modes of knowing and realizing the ultimate reality are symbolic meaning, feeling, moral social action, and aesthetic sensitivity. In different ways each makes the apprehension of the transcendental reality possible; and this awareness of self-transcendence is a constituent element of the participant's perceived state of being.

Thus, transcendental concepts, such as God, Tao, Brahman, or Buddha-nature, are important indicators of a *context* of awareness, as well as descriptions of ultimate reality, and this context reflects a particular mode of experience which, in turn, also expresses a mode of valuation. It is the value-granting, or valorizing, processes which provide the means to overcome the self-deceptions inherent in life's ambiguities. It is the modes of self-transcendent awareness that indicate the procedures in life practices, including the cultivation of virtues, whereby a person actualizes the transcendent context or purpose of life. When we take seriously the embeddedness of the ultimate context in cultural expressions, and the multiple modes of human awareness/practice, we find no transcendent, Archimedian process of actualizing the ultimate context that is self-evident for all people. The self-transcending ordering of life, including the cultivation of virtue, requires a reaching out to others by way of implementing the interconnection with others as part of a self-transcending awareness. Such a self-conscious reaching out to others as a way to explore the many dimensions of the transcendent ordering of life requires a theological or philosophical shift in thinking. The shift is from an exclusivistic, or essentialist, way of conceiving the normative task to an interactive multidimensional procedure. We are required to live in a tension — which hopefully will not be debilitating — between our own procedures and cultural constructs of self-transcending awareness and a recognition of the "otherness" in which we also, at least partially, participate.

If the cultivation of virtues functions differently in relation to different modes of actualizing the self-transcending reality, it will also take a variety of shapes in one's understanding of the self.

Just as a multidimensional transcendent reality requires the recognition of different modes of experience/expression that have their own valuation procedures, so these same modes will inform one's experienced self-identity. This is to say that once we allow conceptions of selfhood, and procedures for self-consciously identifying authentic selfhood, other than those given in our immediate cultural social context, we can appreciate alternative modes of actualizing an authentic self.[12] Psychologists remind us that people normally recognize self-consciousness by direct intuition; this is the basic sense that one exists as a person with some freedom, personal choice and memory of distinctive experiences, recognition of pain in "my" body and personal emotions. This immediate awareness of self-consciousness is on a continuum with the experience of other "selves" in a family, community, and, by extension, all humanity. A basic religious orientation can focus on the personal mind, "heart," or "soul" or "self-emptying" experience, on the one hand. On the other hand, it can emphasize the other pole of the continuum: a vivid experience of other important "selves" such as divine persons, ancestors, or "Great Beings" (*mahasattva*) and "celestial Buddhas" in Buddhism, for example, a deep feeling of trust in Amida Buddha's vow to aid all beings by rebirth in his Buddha-realm. Another dimension of the self, or personality, is the continuum of self-disclosure or self-image. At one pole of this continuum is the self-narrative in which the experiencing self is symbolically defined as a particular entity; for example, in all monotheisms the self is defined as a creature created by God. At the other pole of this "self-disclosure continuum" is the socially defined self-image as identified by a communal language, rituals, myths of "my people," and socially prescribed law. Any of the four poles of the two dimensions of the self can be identified with the transcendent, which also constitutes comprehensive value (or some combinations of different aspects of self-identity can be placed together in an ultimate context of self-awareness). From the standpoint of self-identity, then, there are not only different images of selfhood found in different religions and cultures; there are diverse *modes of perception* which have different mechanisms for evaluating such virtues as patience, friendliness, or conscientiousness. If we perceive each of the poles of the continua as structurally constituting human self-consciousness, we must allow for any basic

mode of awareness to become the central organizing and evalua-
tive principle whereby a person distinguishes between authentic
or inauthentic virtue.

If we intend to take seriously the plurality of ways that people have cultivated authentic selfhood and the plurality of modes
by which the self-transcending reality is known, we might ask if
there can be a single mode of self-awareness or self-transcendent
awareness that is in all cases normative. To that I must say: no.
We still must make judgments about the authenticity of virtuous
acts, about authentic self-awareness, and about authentic self-
transcendent realization. There can be a coherence, I believe, between the judgments a person uses even as one moves from one
mode of valuation to another. The virtue of patience, for example,
might take the form of a feeling that a loving but incomprehensible God was testing one with suffering in a mode of immediate
self-awareness that responded to an other-self. In a mode of contemplating the Ultimate in a mystical, or profound aesthetic,
awareness, however, a sensitivity of release from any self- or other-
identity as described in the "perfection of patience" in the Mahāyāna "Bodhisattva Path" might be more appropriate.

THE VIRTUOUS LIFE AS CULTIVATING THE GOOD
FOR INDIVIDUALS WITHIN A GLOBAL COMMUNITY

So far I have tried to convey the notion that behind, or within,
the question: Can virtue be taught? is another question: What is
the nature of virtue?—virtue not as an eternal quality of an unchanging good human being, but as a disposition of character that
is able to select and practice the good within the recognition that
authenticity of action is related to multiple dimensions of selfhood
and self-transcending behavior. I have suggested that in the present knowledge of the diverse understandings of virtue, we must
consider multiple transformative— as well as formative— processes
of self-awareness and realization of the self-transcending "other."
These processes are different modes of experiencing and valuing
which cannot be reduced to a single mode, and which place the
development of virtues and their practice in quite different contexts of valuation. This recognition of multiple modes in which

virtues are assessed may lead some students of virtue to despair of any way to distinguish the practice of true virtue from pretend or fake expressions of virtue. I have, however, argued that we can discriminate the true expression of virtue from the false. The danger in the approach which I am taking, that affirms both a variety and a diversity of modes for valuation of authentic virtuous action, is that it may turn into a vicious kind of relativism that reduces all claims to virtue to private "taste" preferences, or momentary "good feelings." To avoid such reduction I propose two qualifications which would help to structure the criteria within which particular valuations of virtues would be made.

The first qualification is that authentic virtuous expression would be assessed within a process of dialogue between sincere people who represent diverse cultures, ideologies, religions, or modes of valuation. For example, in order to assess a particular instance of justice, patience, conscientiousness, or compassion, it needs to be understood within diverse perspectives. This affirms the principle that the virtuous life is not simply a matter of my individual taste, nor of a cultural, class, or gender bias. In the context of a world community, where people have divergent moral and religious sensitivities, the discovery of authentic justice, for example, requires shifting away from simply projecting our own notion of, and strategy for attaining, justice onto everyone else. Rather, we (and they) must develop an openness for listening to people's deepest visions and commitments, and make an all-out effort to perceive the intention of another person's viewpoint. Then the process must continue, beyond simply judging the quality of another person's notions of justice, to making decisions together. This kind of engagement, of course, requires the development of skills in understanding, and psychological strength to risk self-exposure.

The participants in this dialogic process of engaging another person in such a way as to learn and perhaps redefine one's own perception of virtue requires a willingness to expose the depth of one's own convictions while recognizing the depth—if not accepting the formulations—of another person's convictions. Each person must attempt to evoke the best, the deepest, the most enlightening aspects of the dialogue partner's orientation. Instead of looking for ways to discredit one's partner, one must continually ask whether he or she has probed the deepest intention of the partner's view. One must continually ask: Is there a misunderstanding over the use of a term, a symbol, or an ethical alternative that is preventing true communication? The crucial need for dialogue in learning what authenticity means in virtuous action comes from a judgment that a basic aspect of humane living is the spontaneous response of one human being to another. Direct human engagement evokes a response. Of course, communication in such an engagement may or may not occur. It is not assured. It depends on the personal resources, including the virtues of patience, courage, sense of justice, and psychological openness. The courage to risk oneself includes the willingness to arouse anger and hostility in the exchange of strongly held conflicting views. Perhaps an even greater risk is the surprise in receiving new insights that require changing one's own perspective. It is possible that one could discover unexplored horizons of meaning and truth. In real engagement one can not fully foresee what will happen. At the same time, risk must be matched with trust. We must trust the other person as someone who is conscientious and caring in order to provide a context in which we can test our sensitivities and understanding which will arise from a particular cultural, class, gender, age, ideological, and religious perspective.

The second qualification is the recognition that the character dispositions and performance which we label "virtuous" are developed, learned, and cultivated by practice as well as by testing and exploring in dialogue. This is to say that virtue is honed *and* spontaneously manifested by particular decisions, by "subsidiary awareness" and "tacit learning"— to use two phrases from Michael Polanyi[13] — and by appropriating the unarticulated selective processes of a tradition. This can be summed up by saying that judging authentic virtue appropriate for individuals in a global community is a matter of developing skills in learning, cultivating "taste," evaluating, and placing specific events in perspective.

The difference between this kind of cultivation and what we earlier called an "imperial" incorporation of strangers into an essentialist normative tradition is that the skill development, the cultivation of character dispositions, requires multiple experiences within oneself and among people. This cultivation of virtue rejects an imperialist procedure, and substitutes a "family relationship" or a "federal" procedure for solving problems, developing authentic virtue, or fostering well-being of all members of humanity. This procedure assumes no identity, or unity in the sense of total sameness, of all humanity; rather it affirms that there are strong continuities, as well as important differences, between members of *Homo sapiens*. The model of the human family provides an expression of a continuity between members, whose roles in relation to each other continually change, and which finally disbands into other families. It correlates with the recognition that there is no one complete solution to self-understanding, and that one or another process for attaining authentic self-consciousness may be appropriate at one specific time, but not for all times or conditions. The skill development for this understanding of virtue comes through engagement with "the stranger," "the other," and this engagement is a kind of mutual apprenticeship in learning from the other. This is a skill development which might also be called an art and a practical judgment which then become embodied in one's performance. The "master" under whose tutelage the participants learn this skill is "emerging humanity," which is also being created in the process. Here, of course, "skill" is not simply a technique, which can be used merely for performance. Such techniques in the learning of virtue could easily lead to performing a semblance of virtue, a facsimile that is used to deceive another. Rather, it is a skill development that promotes character building, a sensitizing that structures and energizes many facets of human experiencing.

The possibilities, then, of cultivating virtue in a religiously and ideologically plural world are exciting precisely because they must use the diversity which is often seen as the problem because it leads to conflict and to anxiety about the finality of any one perspective. By redefining the context of self-awareness and self-transcending realization as one in which truly virtuous people operate in relation to others in a global community, the plurality becomes a resource rather than a hindrance. The risk of allowing the plurality to become a pernicious relativism in which one can no longer distinguish between authentic and fake virtue is real. It can be overcome to some extent, however, by engaging others from different ethnic and cultural circumstances and by conscientiously learning (and unlearning) the way in which different expressions of virtue may increase human excellence and enhance the lived experience among the members of the global community.

NOTES

1. N. J. Girardot, *Myth and Meaning in Early Taoism* (Berkeley: University of California Press, 1983), p. 119.

2. Alasdair MacIntyre, *After Virtue: A Study in Moral Theory* (Notre Dame, Ind.: University of Notre Dame Press, 1981), p. 237.

3. Lee Yearley, *Mencius and Aquinas: Theories of Virtue and Conceptions of Courage* (Albany: State University of New York Press, 1990), p. 13. Yearley adds (p. 14): "Two abstract considerations . . . inform a virtuous person's deliberations. One is a tendency to see certain acts as duties; the other is a propensity to consider the consequences of actions." These I judge to be less universal than those capacities and skills of character which he depicted on p. 13.

4. Ibid, p. 172.

5. MacIntyre, *After Virtue*, p. 173. See also Jean Porter, *The Recovery of Virtue* (Louisville, Ky.: Westminster/John Knox Press, 1990), pp. 165–71. She analyzes the differences between the natural good found in the "cardinal virtues," which depend heavily on Aristotelian thought, and the supernatural good found in the "theological virtues" which "direct their subject toward a personal union with God" (p. 169).

6. Frederick J. Streng, "Understanding Christian and Buddhist Personal Transformation: Luther's Justification by Faith and the Indian Buddhist Perfection of Wisdom," *Buddhist-Christian Studies* 2 (1982): 15–44. On virtues see pp. 41–42.

7. Frederick. J. Streng, "Three Approaches to Authentic Existence: Christian, Confucian, and Buddhist," *Philosophy East and West* 32, no. 4 (October 1982): 371–91.

8. *Virtue*, etymologically, is derived from *vir*, Latin for "man."

9. MacIntyre, *After Virtue*, p. 50.

10. Robert Thurman, "Guidelines for Buddhist Social Activity Based on Nāgārjuna's *Jewel Garland of Royal Counsels*," *The Eastern Buddhist* 16, no. 1, New Series (Spring 1983): 20.

11. I have made a beginning in stating such a model in Frederick J. Streng, "The Transcendental in a Comparative Context," in *Culture and Modernity*, ed. Eliot Deutsch (Honolulu: University of Hawaii Press, 1991). Several adapted paragraphs from that paper are included here.

12. I have given a diagrammatic model of authentic self-consciousness to indicate how different dimensions of personal awareness and social

experience contribute to quite divergent, though related, expressions of authentic selfhood in Frederick J. Streng, "Meeting of East and West: The Self in Global Consciousness," in *The World and I*, ed. Morton A. Kaplan (August 1989): 543–59. Several adapted paragraphs from that paper are included here.

13. See Michael Polanyi, *Personal Knowledge: Toward a Post-Critical Philosophy* (Chicago: University of Chicago Press, 1962), part 1: "The Art of Knowing," chap. 4, "Skills."

Vicarious Virtue:
Gender and Moral Education
in Muslim North Africa

KATHERINE PLATT

As an anthropologist, I am going to answer the question about learning virtue in both a general and particular way. From a general theoretical perspective, I hold that virtue is and can only be learned. Virtue is a cultural ideal, which is to say a cultural product, and it is in the nature of cultural products that they are learned. It is also in the nature of cultural products that they are somewhat specific to the culture and period which transmits them and responsive to the pressures and challenges that culture is subject to at any given time. What constitutes virtue and even the modes of transmission are culturally and historically specific and mutable. What is universal, I believe, is the presence in every human culture of a model or set of models of ideal behavior. There may be one code for the whole population or a number of variations for different categories within that population. The code may focus on individual character attributes more than social behavior or vice versa. I do not believe that there is a culture without a transmissible model of human goodness which is necessary for its self-perpetuation and continuity. That is my general answer.

My particular answer is in the form of a culturally and historically specific example, the Kerkennah Islands of Tunisia. What does it mean to be virtuous or have virtue on the Kerkennah Islands of Tunisia, a small rural Islamic community of 15,000 linked to the cities of the mainland by the constant flow of labor migrants? How is virtue learned by the inhabitants of these islands? And how is it passed on to the next generation?

Virtue as a cultural ideal in this case is greatly shaped by two systems of meaning: religious meaning and a related set of gender meanings. Male and female virtue are distinct variations expressed within an Islamic idiom. However, while these gender "styles" are distinct, they are also mutually defining and highly interdependent.

One feature of this interdependence might be called "vicarious virtue." This is a culture where to a high degree individual family or community members often function as symbols of each other or as symbols of the whole. In this sense, a male's virtue will have both a masculine and feminine aspect. The male will manifest his own variation of masculine virtue, but this masculine virtue would be incomplete or flawed without its feminine component which is the virtuous attributes and behaviors of the females who are associated with this male. This pertains for females and their male associates, also, but it is not a symmetrical relation because of the structural differences in male and female social and cultural power. In general, females' reputations for virtue are more intertwined and embedded in the group than males'.

In spite of this important feature of interdependence, male and female Kerkennah virtue are essentially incomparable. Males and females are thought to have different capacities for virtue; they are thought to develop morally at different rates and to "peak" at markedly different stages of their life cycles.[1]

Females become physically independent and acquire personal responsibilities earlier than males. They are also thought to reach their full intellectual and moral growth earlier. Males are thought to develop more slowly and to go through more abrupt stages. They are also thought to continue to develop well past adolescence. Ultimately, males achieve a level of rationality and capacity for moral and religious judgment (*baṣira*) that is not possible for females. In many ways, females are thought to reach their highest human potential while still in maidenhood. This pinnacle of virtue includes a combination of spirit (*nafs*), purity of motive or intention (*niya*), intelligence in the form of social propriety (*akhlaq*) and responsibility (*'aqel*), and most important, modesty and shame (*hishma*). With marriage, sexual knowledge, and experience, women are more likely to deteriorate morally than to develop. Perhaps the disciplines of female virtue — modesty, obedience, and restraint — should be seen as palliatives against the inevitable moral decay that comes with the female life experience.

By contrast, the parallel attributes of male virtue — eloquence (*balagha*), influence or power (*qadr*), and judgment (*baṣira*) — are all thought to enhance a male's natural moral inclinations. His moral development is thought to accelerate throughout his life cycle, reaching its zenith only in old age. Affectionately considered little donkeys or devils (stubborn and naughty) when young, males are thought to steadily increase in rationality (*'aqel*), morality (*akhlaq*), and wisdom (*'alm*) until they ascend into the heavenly garden. (It is interesting to note that the only female inhabitants of the heavenly garden described in the Qur'an are all young maidens.)

Unsurprisingly, these beliefs about the inverse relationship of male and female moral development are found elsewhere in North Africa.[2] They are pithily expressed in the following proverb of the Chaouia in the Aurès mountains of Algeria:

> The child of the male sex comes into the world with sixty *jnun* in his body; the child of the female sex is born pure; but every year, the boy gets purified of a *jinn*, whereas the girl acquires one; and this is the reason that old women, sixty years old and with sixty *jnun* are sorcerers more malignant than the devil himself. Blind she sews more material, lame she jumps over rocks and deaf she knows all the news.[3]

Another general characteristic of Kerkennah virtue is that it is seen as a combination of personal attributes and social abilities. However, the focus is often on the external abilities as outward signs of personal qualities. A person's intrinsic quality (or virtue) is thought to be manifested in his or her style of speech, work style, and many other aspects of the social presentation of the self.

How is virtue acquired? There are a number of explicit mechanisms through which virtue is taught. These include self-conscious childrearing practices, religious training, formal education, and different kinds of mentoring and apprenticeships. There are also a number of implicit mechanisms through which virtue is inadvertently learned. These include the built environment and the use of space, and social control mechanisms such as gossip and ostracism. Rites of passage, marking the transition from one social role to another, have both explicit and implicit lessons about male and female virtue.

Perhaps the best way to review these purposeful and unintentional teachings of gendered virtue is to walk through the male and female life cycles, using the ritual punctuation marks of the different stages as a framework for examining many of these related issues. We will start with the perceived behaviors of the fetus.

Long before birth, males and females in this culture are perceived to have different kinds of character: male fetuses are thought to be very rambunctious, whereas females are thought to lie still. The labor pains of a male baby are said to be continuous and unrelenting and those of a female child rhythmic. These beliefs reveal a conviction that behaviorally males and females are profoundly different from the earliest possible moment. There is moral coloring in these beliefs in that males are expected to be very active, somewhat difficult, and to draw attention to themselves, while females *in utero* are already perceived as quiet, cooperative, and able to "roll with the punches" of life.

This, of course, is not to say that females are more desired or welcome than boys just because they are thought to be somewhat "easier." In general, a male birth provokes a loud public response and the announcement, "It's a follower of the Prophet!" Already the little boy has a religious identity linked to gender, the essential framework of male virtue. A female birth is greeted more quietly with the exclamation, "May the mother be well!" with no mention of the baby herself. She will keep a low social and religious profile throughout her childhood and adolescence. This is the seed of her virtue.

The rituals of childhood dramatize, teach, and reinforce these differences. The first ritual of childhood is the Forty-Day Ceremony, a kind of social "coming out" party for the infant. It also marks the mother's emergence from the dangerous and polluted state of childbirth. This ceremony is often very elaborate for a male baby, including his first haircut, first pair of trousers, and first sitting up in a chair (with assistance, of course). There are many references to his being a little man and to the upcoming circumcision ceremony for which there is no female equivalent. Formal greetings to male infants at this stage are "God willing, may you be circumcised." For a female infant they are "God willing, may you be happily married," for this is the first (and in most cases, only) ritual in a female's life of which she is the focus. Forty-Day

Ceremonies for female infants are much abbreviated, more like a tea party, and very often, especially for non-firstborns, not observed at all.

The ceremony takes place at a maraboutic shrine or in the infant's home and is attended exclusively by close female relatives and friends of the mother as well as multitudes of small children. The attending women are those most likely to be actively involved in the child's upbringing and, not incidentally, also those most likely to be envious of the new mother's good fortune. These women are obliged to come to the ceremony to show that they are not envious and the sweets and refreshments are extended partially as an appeasement offering.

The disarming of envy through hospitality is a ritual element employed in all celebrations of good fortune. All members of the society, especially those with good fortune, are vulnerable to the malevolent forces of envy in the community. There are well-known protective measures to be taken against its ill effects, including uses of Qur'anic texts, amulets, charms, and defensive hospitality. Although anyone can be the victim of envy, it is women, especially later in life, who are thought to be the main perpetrators of these forces of ill will which are used to explain various kinds of mishaps and reversals of fortune. This dynamic is consistent with the concept that after their maidenhood, women are on the moral decline.

As far as the infant is concerned, the ceremony achieves three things. First, he is formally introduced to the immediate social world through songs with his name in them and he is acknowledged as an independent social being through the chair-sitting ritual. Second, his maleness is recognized for the first time in the sex-specific clothing, the haircut, and the blessings concerning his upcoming circumcision. Third, as he enters the dangerous real social world, he is given many layers of protection through a ritual bath, the anointment of olive oil, blessings, and the pinning on of an amulet. In essence, the value of his being as an autonomous male is being celebrated.

The new mother is also going through a rite of passage in that she is re-entering the community after the dangerous and polluting experience of childbirth. At forty days she performs a complete ritually prescribed ablution identical to the one she performs after sexual intercourse and menstruation. The purpose of these ablutions is to protect her husband from contamination which would invalidate his prayers. Not only is she re-entering the social world, she is also re-entering relations with her husband by making herself pure, at least temporarily, which is the most that any woman can achieve. The image of the woman as both vulnerable and dangerous is symbolically and ritually underlined throughout her life cycle.

Although the focal point of the ritual is the baby and, peripherally, the new mother, it is the community of women who perform, attend, and ultimately control the whole event. While female babies may be ignored ritually and later in life are infrequently the center of ritual attention, it is largely females who are organizing and paying this attention. And the proper paying of attention is a central female virtue which women begin to practice from their earliest days.

Unlike the Forty-Day Ceremony, the circumcision ceremony (*tahir*) is addressed to the entire immediate community of both sexes. Close relatives from the mainland and other villages as well as the face-to-face community of the village quarter are expected to come, and all others are persistently encouraged and welcomed. Major rites of passage such as the circumcision ceremony are the only recurring, reliable scenario in which the emigré and island subcommunities come together in large numbers. As such they become a public forum for the expression, reinforcement, or adjustment of loyalties and alignments between households.

These rites of passage are also public statements about the collective virtue or honor (*sharaf* or *arḍ*) of the host household (*dar*). A household's virtue is a combination of its material power (*qadr*), its influence (*ktif*, literally "shoulder"), its magnanimity (*kram*), and its openness (*bibanhum mahluhlin*, "their doors are open"). These are all qualities that the host (*dar*) tries to demonstrate in putting on a ritual such as a circumcision ceremony. The community can affirm or reject the *dar*'s claim to a certain level of honor by the numbers they turn out in and the size of their congratulatory offerings. In this sense, virtuous attributes must be backed up by periodic social demonstrations, and to be effective, these demonstrations must be ritually acknowledged by the community of which the household is a part.

In Islamic terms, circumcision is a critical requirement for admission to the Muslim community. To circumcise literally means "to purify," *tahara*. Without being circumcised, a man cannot achieve ritual purity, and without that, none of his religious acts are valid (*sih*). Ritual purity comes in five stages: purity of intention (*niya*), of the body from physical dirt, of the members from offenses, of the heart from evil desires, and of the spirit of all that is not God.[4] The circumcision is the first step in the male's life-long journey toward increasing religious purity and efficacy. Most Kerkennis would articulate this necessary religious purification as the reason for the circumcision.

They also explain it in terms of health and virility, that a man cannot function properly without being circumcised. Many male Kerkennis hold that European women are promiscuous because their uncircumcised men cannot satisfy them. This is not a secular or alternative explanation to the religious one given. It is part of it. God gives men the means to be both clean and virile to protect and hold women, who do not have the same capacity for purity and strength, within the framework of the patriarchal family as it is prescribed in the Qur'an.

The circumcision ritual demonstrates the essential stages of separation, transition, and incorporation as codified by van Gennep in his classic, *Rites of Passage*.[5] The initiand is being separated from his role as an infant dependent on his mother. This is why boys are almost never circumcised before they are weaned. The dangerous transition from one role to another is marked by a journey on donkeyback through the village to the protection of a saint's shrine, a liminal site, where he is actually physically altered from an infant into a "little man." After the circumcision, his social center of gravity shifts away from his mother and her domestic circle and he is incorporated into the world of his male peers. Not until he goes through the next rite of passage, marriage, does the young male really have a social role again in the domestic unit. Until then, he is more or less banished from the domestic domain and he is relegated to the world of young males where he will constantly be called upon to demonstrate his virility, albeit in boyish ways. His presence in the female domain is disturbing because his sexuality has been actively affirmed, unlike his female counterpart whose sexuality has not and must not be acknowledged.

The female sex role and the virtues which define it are *not* ritually celebrated. Upon weaning, which is usually earlier for females than males (approximately one year as opposed to approximately two years), the female child is immediately and easily incorporated into the multigenerational community of women. The transition from being an appendage to the mother to being an appendage to the wider community of girls and women is smooth and takes place without ritual punctuation marks. From the loud recognition of the male's birth and the Forty-Day Ceremony to the circumcision, the steps and changes in a male's infancy are paid a great deal more attention and are treated with more drama. In their early orientation toward the world, males and females have very different experiences based on the way "the world" responds to them. The smooth and undramatic absorption of the female infant into the multigenerational domestic world predisposes her toward a less demanding, less assertive, and less autonomous sense of self than her male counterpart. Her identity is more submerged in the group and the threshold between individuals is lower. Modest cooperation is a female virtue begotten in this childhood context. The more dramatic and longer intimacy of the male infant with his mother and the later more pronounced separation from her predisposes him toward a more independent, distinct, and demanding sense of self.

These differences in orientation and presentation of self are very important for adult work styles and the sexual division of labor on the Kerkennah Islands. One of the most important and striking differences between male and female childhoods is in the attitudes toward work and play. For female children the distinction between work and play or between productive and recreational activities is blurred. For males the distinction is very sharp. The implications of this difference for adult behavior are vast, for even in adulthood, women make little distinction between work and recreation. They are both simply generalized into the single category of "what women do." In the male sphere, however, work and recreation are very distinct categories. One often sees little girls "playing at work," such as making cakes out of sand, and in the same hour actually assisting their mothers in the real making of cakes. This is also true of playing at cleaning, washing, and childcare. Dolls and little brothers are easily and often substituted for each other. As soon as a little girl can walk, she is involved in the productive activity of the household — often only as a nuisance, but she is involved. By the age of four most little girls have some real responsibility in the household.

Little boys are babied longer and are discouraged from imitating their mothers because "that is women's work." After circumcision, they are largely shooed out of the house to play with their peers. They might run errands or assist their fathers in a specific task but in general they do not socialize with their fathers or their fathers' peers. This would be disrespectful. Nor do they have regular responsibilities except for going to school. Boys are encouraged to play without obligations until about the age of twelve and often a good deal longer. Even if a girl is in school, she will still be fully occupied with household jobs and activities during nonschool hours.

This sharp distinction between work and play for males persists throughout adulthood. Grown men continue to have a special category of activity that could be called "play" which is absent from the lives of girls and women. Adolescent and adult male "play" usually consists of sports, public strolling, and card and table games. Both males and females listen to the radio and, when it is available, watch television, but they do so with different styles. Females knit, shell, husk, or braid away at some task at the same time as they listen to the radio or watch television — always blurring the boundary between work and play.

This recreational sphere of activity, like most of male social life, is informally but distinctly age graded. This informal age grading begins shortly after circumcision when boys start to have some social independence and it continues throughout their lives. This informal separation according to age as well as sex has to do with issues of respect, rivalry, and personal power, all aspects of male virtue that do not have the same relevance in the lives of females. For females, the boundaries between generations are blurred as are the boundaries between work and play.

This compartmentalized quality of male activities has important implications for the sexual division of labor on the Kerkennah Islands. A finite number of jobs are considered male work, usually those related to fishing, building, commerce, and bureaucracies. Most of the vast number of other tasks are done by women. This asymmetry in the sexual division of labor reflects the difference between male and female attitudes toward activity which, in turn, reflects the difference in local conceptions of male and female natures, and the virtuous expression of these natures. Male productive and recreational activities are clearly defined, distinguished, and highlighted, as is the individual male ego. Female activities include many things without distinction between the activities and the doers. They are generalized and shared without much ado just as the female self is submerged and shared in the general female community.

A great proportion of female work is characterized by a corporate idea of productivity. This is related to the female child's early sense of responsibility, the early integration into the multi-generational female world, and the lack of emphasis on personal autonomy. This generalized identification and low threshold between individuals often extends even to creative work. It is not at all unusual for girls to pick up each other's knitting and to knit a few rows or to work on each other's tapestries. By contrast, for a man to weave a few palm fronds into someone else's fish trap would be considered an extraordinary invasion of personal territory. Actually it would probably be laughed at as effeminate behavior.

This cooperative aspect of women's work also extends to childrearing. It is perfectly acceptable for women to feed, embrace, clean, and discipline other women's children. Such acts are not considered trespassing on another woman's domain. Men, however, would not discipline each other's children except within the extended family. Young girls pick up this shared quality of work, while young boys continue in their track of developing their sense of individual autonomy and separate personal skills and power.

Although there is no childhood ritual specifically for girls, much of the conversation, dreaming, and planning in a girl's childhood and adolescence focuses on her future wedding. There is no single event in Kerkennah life that provides more excitement, entertainment, and intrigue, or involves so many people and so much expense as the marriage ritual. In the marriage ritual the distinct "natures" of male and female virtues are most elaborately dramatized and taught. It is also at this time that the vicarious quality of Kerkennah virtue is most highly articulated because there is a systemic transfer of virtue when the daughter of one family becomes a wife in another.

In terms of role symbolism, when a man marries, he is ritually reintegrated into the domestic world which he left when he was circumcised. The circumcision ritual is a ritual recognition of his male sexual identity and with this comes the dramatization of a set of rules concerning maleness. During this sexually "liminal" period of childhood and adolescence, the male has no social role in the domestic routine. At marriage, his sexuality is literally domesticated and he is readmitted into the world of women. He now holds the office of the head of his own nuclear unit which is at least potentially autonomous. His presence now represents protection and not a threat.

Upon his marriage, the groom is also admitted for the first time into the fuller social and political forum of adult men. A man is not considered stable, trustworthy, and serious (*balug*), until he has domestic responsibilities. The weight of these responsibilities is fully acted out during the ceremony and the forum of elders is there to witness it. Graced with new authority, the groom no longer observes the custom of publicly avoiding his father and his father's male peers which is incumbent upon adolescent boys and unmarried men. He has taken a first step toward becoming an elder himself. His company in public gathering places is no longer a foolish nuisance to his father. Rather he adds weight to the collective virtue of the local patriarchy.

The role symbolism of a young woman's marriage is analogous to a boy's circumcision. It is the legitimation and public recognition of her sexual identity for the first time. As a virgin she was protected and "covered" by her family. At her marriage, she is "uncovered" by her family and she is ritually instructed through dance and music in the art of lovemaking. Her sexuality now becomes part of her identity and she is given new mobility in which to demonstrate her womanliness. Like the little boy after circumcision, she is now freed from the intense protection of her natal domain. There are many symbols in the marriage ceremony which recognize the power and danger of female sexuality. The bride is at the height of her beauty, purity, and innocence. In her virginal state she can do no vicarious harm to her father or her brothers. She has been chosen as a bride for her softness of speech, her discretion, her modesty, her willingness to work cooperatively. In this promising state she is at the zenith of her moral accomplishment. With carnal knowledge, she is permanently compromised and potentially dangerous. Active female sexuality is a negative kind of power which affects the entire constellation of family roles and their collective virtue.

Once her sexuality is acknowledged, it is quickly submerged in the symbolism of fertility. According to Kerkennah ideology, the sole reason for marriage is the bearing and raising of children. It is this fact which assuages the sexual shame (*hishma*) between a husband and wife. However, it is also the fact of this active sexual bond which injects an intense element of shame and modesty into the relationship of the bride and her father. He must abandon his role as her domestic protector and shareholder in her virtue. The ritual avoidance of the father and daughter required by this new element of shame helps the bride to demonstratively shift her orientation and loyalty to her husband's family.

Another important systemic shift that takes place in the marriage ceremony is the enhanced position of the groom's mother. Acquisition of a bride expands the female cooperative workteam of which the groom's mother is the leader. A more productive and better kept household allows the mother of the groom to be more expansive in her hospitality, an important collective virtue. Through the principle of vicarious virtue, she has a high stake in the virtue of the new member, especially as it is expressed in the bearing of grandsons. Failure or a long delay in this area can reflect badly on the mother of the groom's judgment because she usually has an active hand in choosing or approving of the bride.

Currently in Kerkennah society, there is a wide spectrum of practice concerning bride choice, ranging from parentally arranged marriage planned in childhood to complete free choice. Most marriages are a combination of family consultation and personal choice. In any case, the choice of a partner is another arena where male and female virtues are in high relief.

Excellence of verbal style is a very important personal quality. The presentation of the self is a phenomenon in which verbal style represents inner character. In this case, form is content.

When young Kerkennis are asked about the characteristics of an ideal spouse, the most desired quality for both men and women is *akhlaq.* In literary Arabic this word means both morality and good manners.[6] When defining *akhlaq,* Kerkennis emphasize the external form: "deportment, good manners and above all, a nice way of speaking."

Yet the ideal style and attitude toward the spoken word differs considerably for men and women. For instance, a man who is admired is called "a man who greets people well," and an intelligent man is "a man with strong words." In Arabic male maturity and eloquence come from the same root (*balagha,* "to achieve male maturity," and *balugha,* "to be eloquent").[7]

A parallel concept to *balagha* and *akhlaq* is *bashart,* which has three meanings: religious reason, male maturity, and the ability to speak in public as the group representative.[8] The emphasis is on attaining the age of reason as far as religion is concerned. The term is never applied to a female, for presumably the female moral sense never develops sufficiently to allow her to make religious decisions. The coincidence of the ideal of speech, the ideal of manhood, and the ideal of religion or morality in these three terms — *balagha, akhlaq,* and *bashart* — form something of a conceptual gestalt of male virtue.

The ideal verbal style and the moral connotations of speech for females are quite different. For instance, the ideal wife must have soft words; "she must not beat her husband with her words," as the Kerkennis say. It is more difficult for a woman to use words publicly to good effect. Her words can easily be used against her, so it is incumbent on her to control her speech as much as possible. Just as the Kerkennis say that a woman's ugliness is her protection, the same is true of her silence. No shame can come to an ugly, silent woman.

Even in private, a woman must be cautious in her speech. There are still some older women on Kerkennah who are ashamed to address their husbands directly by name and use the name of the oldest child as a form of address instead. I was told by one woman of her shame in opening her mouth to eat in her husband's presence and of her insistence on the children introducing any medicine to her husband's mouth. It is very shameful behavior for a woman to open her mouth and laugh aloud. The proper form, if a woman insists on being amused, is a quiet titter behind a hand.

However, a woman's silence can be used as a virtuous social

act. She is admired for being verbally receptive, listening quietly to her husband. In the past, silence or quiet weeping was interpreted as her necessary legal consent to a marriage contract.[9] Also, her silence, lack of social weight, and underdeveloped moral sense allow her to be insignificantly present at many conversations from which her male counterpart would be excluded. This, of course, is a source of valuable information and also the reason why little Kerkenni girls are much more socially knowing than their male agemates.

When applied to sex roles, it is clear that the spoken word has many ambiguous qualities. As a social potency it can be said to have a dual character. The spoken word, *klam*, in the sense of an individual's ability to greet people expansively and to exercise available verbal forms fully, is a measure of a man's influence in the community and a feature of his virtue. *Klam* in the sense of gossip is a measure of the community's influence over him. The former sense is much more important for males and the latter sense is much more important for females. It is a man's job to represent his family in public, to be verbally expansive in the streets and cafes, to make sound verbal contracts in legal and business matters, to express himself politically, and to pray aloud in the mosque. It is a woman's job *not* to be talked about.

We find in this dual idea of *klam* complete consonance between reputation and personality. A person is not only his or her own words, but also other people's words. Gossip, or *klam en nass*, either validates or undermines an individual's presentation of him- or herself. This is another extension of the collective aspect of Kerkennah virtue. That is to say, virtue in some respects is held collectively by family members and it is bestowed (or withheld) collectively by the community. All of these concerns and levels of interdependence are symbolized in the marriage ceremony. They are, of course, also continually reworked in the quieter drama of everyday life.

From marriage to the next major rite of passage, decades of everyday life take place. Certainly, after their marriage rituals, males and females are frequently involved in rituals which affect them deeply, but in which they do not play the leading role. While their social roles are changing, these changes are dependent variables in relation to the key role transformations taking place.

Correspondingly, changes in the status of their virtue in these contexts are vicarious or collective rather than primary. Even in the Forty-Day Ceremony, the all-important mother plays a supporting role to the baby. An essential characteristic of a rite of passage is that it is a once-in-a-lifetime event. A mother can have as many Forty-Day Ceremonies as she has babies, and a father as many circumcision ceremonies as he has sons.

The pilgrimage to Mecca (*hajj*) is somewhat anomalous as a rite of passage, but it is the next once-in-a-lifetime irreversible role transformation that people go through after marriage and before death. It is anomalous because it occurs every year on the Islamic calendar and, technically, a Muslim could go every year. In effect, it is a once-in-a-lifetime ritual because no Kerkenni would consider going twice. Aside from the material difficulty, it would be thought absurd (redundant) and sinful (it would rob someone else in the family of the opportunity to go). It is also anomalous because it is not expected that every "normal" Kerkenni would find the means to go on the *hajj*. This makes it different from other rites of passage where only an abnormality would keep someone from going through it. However, in the Kerkenni context, all people at least profess an aspiration to go on the *hajj* and it is part of the shared picture of a complete, correct, and virtuous life even if only a small percentage of the population achieves it.

In terms of the developmental cycle of sex roles and morality, for a man the *hajj* marks the pinnacle of his lifelong journey toward maturity, judgment, wisdom, and authority. The *hajj* is both the goal and the reward for his increasing religious devotion. For the small number of Kerkenni women who go on the *hajj*, it represents a condition of being almost removed from her sex role. While not actually being made an honorary man, she takes on a somber, devout manner that is characteristic of elderly men and decidedly uncharacteristic of elderly women.

In general, as women get older and pass childbearing age, they become freer in their manner and movements, more outspoken and even boisterous. This is in stark contrast to the bridal ideal of silence and passivity as well as the penultimate male ideal of religious sobriety. At this time women normally have adult sons who are devoted and daughters-in-law whom they can boss around. The postmenopausal woman is no longer a threat to the religious purity of those around her because she is free of polluting female blood. Her sexuality is no longer threatening to the integrity of the patrilineage. Now she can afford to laugh and this is what she does. Older women, unburdened by *hishma* and the heavy male mantle of wisdom and morality, often take on the role of joker or jester. They sing naughty songs at weddings and dance absurdly suggestive dances; they make fun of brides and even greater fun of grooms. They bring some antistructure to the highly structured roles which define so much of life in this community.[10]

This is not to say that there are no devout women, but only that the female sex role does not provide a model for the austere devotion associated with male religious practice. While most women fast for Ramadan, most do not know how to perform the five daily prayers and even fewer can read or recite the Qur'an. Much of their religious practice centers around the intercession of saints. This style of devotion, while not opposed, is quite different from the style required of a pilgrim. In this sense, as a female prepares to go on the *hajj*, she departs from what is typically female on Kerkennah and models her behavior after the more austere male religious style. When she returns, she is treated with a kind of respect normally directed toward men.

All returning pilgrims bring home vast quantities of holy souvenirs from Mecca which are rapidly distributed and redistributed throughout the community. The pilgrims themselves are also received as if they were sacred objects imbued with the blessing of the *hajj*, which, in a sense, they are.[11] They become holy symbols of the pan-Islamic tradition. This objectification of the pilgrims is reflected in the fact that they all take on the common title of *hajj* or *hajja* and cease to use their given names. In a sense, they withdraw from their pre-*hajj* identity and take on the joint identity of this titled category. Both male and female pilgrims, because of their new religious weight, are treated as lay preachers who teach their contemporaries how to pray and other techniques of religious practice and who comment unchallenged about religious matters in general. The pilgrimage is one of the means by which this society connects itself to the message of pan-Islamic orthodoxy and provides itself with a renewable cadre of specialists to pass on this message.

As in all rites of passage, in the pilgrimage there are systemic role changes as well as the focal role transformation. In the case of the pilgrimage, the adult children who are financing the journey, as well as the parents who are fulfilling the religious obligation, are achieving new positions in the developmental cycle of the family. I know of no *hajj* that was not financed by the adult children of the pilgrims. Consequently, this event confers great honor on both parties. The grown child is behaving in an exemplary manner and the parents are proving that they have succeeded in raising a good son (for it is usually a son or sons who pay).

Financing a pilgrimage is an emphatic announcement that the dependent relationship of child on parent has been fully reversed. Throughout the son's childhood and adolescence, the parents have the expectation that the care and expense they invest in him will be reciprocated when he is grown. This is a specific and direct expectation. The financing of the *hajj* is the most dramatic means available for a son to acknowledge his obligation to his parents and his willingness to take up the role of provider. It is one more step along the male moral trajectory of increasing authority and responsibility. For their part, the parents are now free to prepare for the next passage, which is death.

Death ritual, second only to marriage ritual, is dense with messages of gendered and Islamic virtue. Along with numerous other ritual elements, the family of the deceased distributes pieces of bread throughout the village. This is called both a *sudqa* ("act of charity") and *samah* ("peace offering"). A *sudqa* is different from a *zakat* ("alms") in that it is a voluntary act of generosity rather than an obligation. This *sudqa* is offered in the name of the deceased as a last earthly good deed to help him or her get out of purgatory and to improve his record on the Day of Judgment. The response to this offering is, "May God have mercy on him (or her)." The giving of the piece of bread is also a peace offering to anyone in the community the deceased may have offended and a plea for forgiveness. Repentance and forgiveness are not the same thing. As a young Kerkenni explained to me, "If I steal someone's money and I return it with an apology and that person does not forgive me, God will not forgive me either. I must have that person's forgiveness also." The forgiveness of the community is necessary for the release of the deceased's soul from purgatory. The fact that it reaches beyond the grave is a good gauge of the power of public opinion in this local culture.

Unforgiven offenses are sometimes attributed to a woman's

difficulty in delivering a baby and if the labor is very prolonged, a *samah* will be sent out on her behalf to release the fetus. Similarly, a groom will ask forgiveness of anyone he fears he might have offended before his wedding night, because it is thought that an unforgiving victim can cause him to be impotent. Clearly, at these dangerous passages, the vulnerable individual is in the hands of the community, even in death.

The community shows its respect for the bereaved by condolence visits, and the bereaved show the depth of their grief through ritual neglect and abuse of their own persons. In addition to wailing for long periods of time, bereaved women tear their cheeks with their fingernails. For forty days, they neglect their hygiene and do nothing to beautify themselves. They wash, but do not shampoo or comb their hair, do not depilate their faces or their bodies and do not wear any kind of perfume or cosmetics.

It is not surprising that the rules of mourning and the ways of showing grief are different for males and females. This is consistent with all the other rites of passage that have been examined. It is striking, though, that sex role differences and expectations about the moral content of these differences follow the individual beyond the grave, just as they precede the individual's birth. The double layer of clothing that protects the female corpse from immodesty or some other sexual danger is echoed in the head and footstones that distinguish female graves from male graves. When asked why male graves have only a headstone yet female graves have a head- *and* a footstone, a middle-aged Kerkenni man answered, "The stone is to hold the women down; we don't want them wandering around causing trouble." Vicarious virtue to the end.

A society needs models of goodness or virtue in order to reproduce itself through interdependent constellations of social roles. These models are taught, activated, deactivated, revised, and replaced in a multitude of ways. For a cultural outsider, dramatic rites of passage are one of the more accessible and "readable" sites for studying these models of goodness and their transmission.

In Kerkennah society, in addition to being grounded in Islam, these models of goodness are intensely gendered. The Kerkennis think of these differences in orientation and presentation of the self as being part of the difference between male and female natures, not something that is socially or culturally induced and ritually underlined. This belief is a very important force in the reproduction of Kerkennah virtue because a culture's construction of "the natural" is its most powerful means of transmitting its values and virtues.

NOTES

1. Katherine Platt, "Cognitive Development and Sex Roles on the Kerkennah Islands of Tunisia," in *Acquiring Culture: Cross Cultural Studies in Child Development*, ed. Gustav Jahoda and I. M. Lewis (London: Croom Helm, 1988).

2. Daisy Hilse Dwyer, *Images and Self-Images: Male and Female in Morocco* (New York: Columbia University Press, 1978).

3. Mathea Gaudry, *La Femme Chaouia de l'Aurès* (Paris: Geuthner, 1929), p. 246, as quoted in Cynthia Nelson, "Public and Private Politics: Women in the Middle Eastern World," *American Ethnologist* 1, no. 3 (August 1974): 551–63.

4. *The Encyclopedia of Islam* (Leiden: Brill, 1934), p. 608.

5. Arnold van Gennep, *The Rites of Passage*, trans. M. Vizedom and G. Caffee (Chicago: University of Chicago Press, 1960).

6. Michael M. J. Fischer, "On the Changing Concept and Position of Persian Women," in *Women in the Muslim World*, ed. Lois Beck and Nikki Keddie (Cambridge, Mass.: Harvard University Press, 1978), p. 196.

7. Hans Wehr, *Arabic-English Dictionary* (Ithaca, N.Y.: Spoken Languages Services, 1976), p. 73; and Raphael Patai, *The Arab Mind* (New York: Scribners, 1973), p. 49.

8. Jean Cuisinier, "Le Cycle Domestique dans l'Organization Familiale Traditionelle en Tunisie," in *Mediterranean Family Structures*, ed. J. G. Peristiany (Cambridge: Cambridge University Press, 1977), p. 145; and Hans Wehr, *Arabic-English Dictionary*, pp. 60–61.

9. Joseph Schacht, *Introduction to Islamic Law* (Oxford: Clarendon Press, 1964), p. 117.

10. Victor Turner, *The Ritual Process* (Chicago: Aldine, 1969).

11. Victor Turner, "The Center Out There: Pilgrim's Goal," *History of Religions* 12, no. 3 (1973): 191–230.

Clarity and Imagination
as Buddhist Means to Virtue

NINIAN SMART

THIS PAPER IS NOT INTENDED as an analytic or descriptive one. In it I wish to commend certain ideas drawn from the Buddhist tradition and freely adapted to a global view of ethics. The comparative study of cultures is important from a number of points of view: one of them is that denizens of differing cultures can learn from one another. I am sure that the Western tradition of ethics can learn much from the Buddhist tradition, partly because its assumptions are so very diverse from those of most of the West. Of course, the distinctions between cultures are beginning to melt as we move into a new global civilization. It could be a vastly rich period of human cultivation.

A first important observation about Buddhist ethics is that it contains various more or less detailed accounts of what virtue has to overcome. These obstacles are most simply described as greed (*rāga*), hatred (*dosa*), and delusion (*moha*). While the list of the deadly sins in Christianity covers varieties of the first two problems, it does not include delusion as such. Yet Buddhism has consistently considered lack of insight, ignorance, delusion, etc., as being crucial to the human condition. In fact the chain of dependent origination ends as the root cause of our being immersed unsatisfactorily and even painfully in the round of existence in ignorance (*avijjā*).

As we shall see, the kind of knowledge which replaces ignorance is not merely intellectual; it is a kind of knowledge involving experience and a kind of vision. It is more like *gnosis* than *epistēmē*; so I like to call it "gnowing"! But it is not without its intellectual side. So clear-headedness is important. For example,

125

treating all human beings equally, and not discriminating against any one group, is something which arises from the observation that all humans belong to the same species. Moreover humans have the freedom to be better or worse and therefore have the same chance to attain spiritual enlightenment. Such intellectual arguments are not, then, irrelevant to the right attitude of looking upon all humans as equals. Hence the Buddha rejected the moral importance of the division into four classes which was customary in the society of his day, and which formed the structure of what was to develop into the caste system of classical and modern Hinduism.

This links up to an observation about Buddhist philosophy. The insight that everything is impermanent, for instance, has both an intellectual and a practical significance. We can note that the idea of a permanent substance has no real purchase on the changing world, since what is permanent or unchanging cannot account for change. That is because if S unchangingly underlies the transition from E1 to E2 it cannot be the reason for the transition. Such and other intellectual thoughts might convince one of the truth of the statement that everything is impermanent. But the statement has a practical impact too: it helps to dispel egoism, since there is no permanent soul to safeguard and pamper; and it implies the brevity of satisfactions. And so in general Buddhist doctrines have their rational basis, but they are also expected to have existential impact. One needs too to be convinced of them in a kind of experiential way, as happened to the Buddha, of course, under the Bodhi tree. From the perspective, then, of overcoming delusion, one of the three "deadly conditions," Buddhism sees conceptual clarity as being vital to virtue.

Another general feature of Buddhist ethics which for the most part distinguishes it from the Western tradition is the use made of meditation to help strengthen virtues. There is a very practical approach to self-cultivation. Thus to promote benevolence or *mettā*, which is one of the sublime states or cardinal virtues (*brahma-vihāras*), one may in imagination exercise it toward some respected person, then toward a neutral person, and finally toward a hostile person. Such modes of meditation, which I shall come back to, frequently involve the use of our imagination.

Another aspect of Buddhist methods is the emphasis upon self-awareness or *sati*. It is a vital element in the Eightfold Path.

We are constantly called upon to become self-aware and thus to clarify and then purify our motives. For instance, I may read something in the paper and feel pleased. I should pause to notice the quality of my pleasure and to ask myself what gives rise to it. Say it is the demise of still another Marxist state. It satisfies me in part, of course, because I believe that Marxism is a deluded system, built on unnecessary hatreds. But is that all? Maybe I am glad to see Western Marxists further depressed; and maybe I am thinking of some foolish academics who have slighted me in a certain way, or perhaps have scorned my field. This reveals a deeper element in my motivation. My field is *mine*, and I identify with it. In scorning it Marxists have scorned me. Now the tables are beginning to be turned. So a small sliver at least of my satisfaction with the event I read of in the paper is egoism. I should, in thinking about my feelings, be able to see this. This exercise of *sati* may enable me to begin to banish egoism in that connection, and satisfaction based on the hatred of others, even if they be Marxists.

This, then, is another aspect of the clarity which can be a means to virtue in the Buddhist perspective. I wish to explore these means of intellectual analysis, imaginative meditation, and active self-awareness in relation to the four sublime virtues in particular and to the development of moral education more generally.

It will be recalled that the four *brahmaviharās* are *mettā* ("love" or "benevolence"), *karunā* ("compassion"), *muditā* ("sympathetic joy"), and *upekkhā* ("equanimity"). The name for these four is peculiar, for it means "holy abodes" or "abodes at the Brahma level"—or again, "heavenly abodes." The point is that the one who practices them attains the moral level of God, though God is not at all an ultimate in the Buddhist schema. The word reflects a Buddhist ploy, of moralizing the whole system of concepts involving Brahmins (those who have *brahma*-power or substance), divine power, and so on. The true Brahmin is not one who is a hereditary priest but the genuinely virtuous person. It is part of the way in which early Buddhism took the ritual and sacramental religion of the Brahmins and hollowed it out within.

Because of the centrality of compassion in the Mahāyāna, there has been a tendency for Western scholars to underrate the other three holy virtues. It is, so to speak, the melancholy analogue to *muditā*, which is that sympathetic joy a person ought to feel at the joy of others. Perhaps we naturally feel this in contemplating, let us say, the birth of a baby to friends. But often we do not feel unmixed joy at the successes of others, having an element of envy in our nature. The truly self-confident person will have achieved equanimity or *upekkhā*. This is not supposed to be indifference. That is easily achieved by locking ourselves up in a circle of family and friends, and remaining indifferent to those beyond the circle. Equanimity should make us treat others equally and in a positive way, because such equanimity is controlled by love or *mettā*. While the Buddha was keen to emphasize the virtues of the household life and the benefits of friendship he was also keen that his followers should press their moral concerns outward from their social circles to embrace all humans, and beyond that all living beings. The classical definitions of the holy virtues are in *Visuddhimagga* 318, and I have drawn on Buddhaghosa's explanations.

The process of universalizing virtues is assisted by various meditations — for instance, suffusing the differing quarters of the world with love, compassion, and so on. It is important to overcome hostilities and prejudices which we may harbor. Often, though, a meditation starts with the easier tasks, such as suffusing friends and compatriots with love. But one should train oneself to feel compassion for all. In up-to-date terms it means that we should think of "hate" figures and bathe them in love: Adolf Hitler, Joseph Stalin, Saddam Hussein, Idi Amin, and so forth. One should reflect that they too are human, have or have had freedom, and are heirs to the consequences of their acts. We see in such practices the development of imagination. One should reflect that anything which hate might dictate should happen to such people ("May they rot in hell," we might think) could happen to oneself. As one should not wish pain and disaster on oneself, so one should not wish it upon another. There are many references to such an imaginative use of reciprocity, or the Golden Rule, especially applied negatively.

The meditations which develop the virtues lead to a state of mind which is limitless (*appamaññā*) and well developed (*subhā-vita*), rather than narrow or constricted and undeveloped. So the meditations are seen as a way of improving character. As a *Jātaka* verse has it:

When a person with a mind of love
Feels compassion for the whole world,
Above and below and across,
Everywhere unbounded

Filled with unlimited kindness,
Complete and developed,
Any limited actions one may have done
Do not remain loitering in the mind.
                                        (*Jātakas*, 37–38)

A person who has cruel dispositions should perform meditations based on compassion in order to reform his nature.

Both the meditations regarding the holy virtues and the use of the principle of reciprocity imply something about the imagination: it is to be used constructively to widen and deepen compassion. It was a marked feature of the accounts of the life of the Buddha that he was ascribed considerable psychological insight into the motives and feelings of others. Later this was to be woven into accounting for his skill in means or *upāya*. He could adapt his teachings to the conditions of the hearers. This doctrine was to give Buddhism quite a lot of cultural flexibility in its expansion through much of Asia. Similarly, then, the development of meditation and the virtues could give his followers something of that psychological, and therefore therapeutic, insight. There are, by the way, some modern analogues in academic studies, which I shall come to later.

While I have illustrated something of the relationship between imagination and the holy virtues, what about the conceptual clarity and intellectual insight with which I began? For there is one feature of the Buddha's teaching which has often seemed to those raised in the tangle of Western presuppositions to be in some tension with virtues such as *muditā* and *karuṇā*. This is the doctrine of non-self. Does the intellect not look upon other human (and, more widely, all living) beings as empty shells, without egos, as it were, holding them together? Can an egoless being have rights? And can I have reverence for a hollow animal? How does the doctrine fit with the whole pattern of Buddhist ethics?

In a way the non-self doctrine leaves everything in place,

though under a different description. A person still has feelings, perceptions, dispositions, states of consciousness, etc. The person is still a bundle of *khandhas*. Nevertheless, meditation on the elements of one's existence should lead to a new view of oneself as individual, and this occurs from two points of view. First, as meditation gives a strong sense of the impersonal and instantaneous nature of psychic and bodily events, the idea of a self which possesses anything disappears. The notion that one has no substantial locus as an ego becomes lively and real; this is the function of meditation, deepening reflection. And so in a genuine way the metaphysical doctrine of *anattā* becomes transformed into a moral attitude. Another mode of understanding oneself is as a bunch of ongoing, causatively connected events. One thus begins to see the connections between this bunch of events and neighboring bunches (that is, other people). Second, in dissolving one's own ego one in effect dissolves the boundary between oneself and others. Meditation helps to strengthen the sense of connectedness of differing beings in the universe.

There is maybe a certain paradox anyway in our modes for understanding ourselves and others. The idea of the human soul, of that divine spark which resides in each one of us, is excellent in underlying such notions as the human rights of others. Exalting humans is morally good from this angle. But in regard to ourselves, is it so good? It might be held to encourage egoism, to celebrate one's own eternal soul. From this perspective it might be best to think that I have no soul but all others do. Such an asymmetry of the imagination does not work, however. Similarly, in regard to freedom, it is important that I should recognize my own freedom, but determinism in others would conduce to a more forgiving and understanding attitude. Again the imaginative asymmetry does not work.

In looking upon oneself as a complex chain of events, or rather a mass of chains, both parallel and intertwined, one is encouraged imaginatively to see oneself in the total pattern of interdependent origination (*paṭiccasamuppāda*). The most striking image of this interconnectedness was to await the Mahāyāna, through the picture of Indra's jewel net, in which every jewel in the net reflects every other one. This was of course splendidly worked out in the Chinese tradition through the Hua-yen philosophy.

Positions in Buddhism can be expressed both negatively and positively. Negatively every entity is relative to others and so lacks its "own-existence" or *svabhāva*. The doctrine of dependent or relative origination can testify to that negative appraisal. But positively this means that ultimately every event is connected to every other, as in the great jewel net of Indra.

This position is not emphasized in the Theravāda in ontological terms, but rather through the practice of meditation. Meditation on relativity connects one to other living beings and so one sees oneself as inevitably enmeshed in the lives of other living beings. The imagination is thus directed outward to all those other bundles of causation and impermanence which are the loci of living biographies. Essentially the only difference between my actions and those of others is that this stream of causation here has more effects on my future than do other streams. But in fact other streams do enter powerfully into my stream: my mother and father, friends, enemies, and so on all have some effects upon my stream. The person of perfect equanimity will thus take other streams as seriously as her own. We note in this a rather different attitude from that of Kant, who advised us to treat another never merely as a means but always at the same time as an end-in-herself.

This Buddhist understanding of non-self relates to the ideal of *nibbāna* or nirvana. It is notable that the Buddha treated the notion of the self in a functional way. That is, in so far as the notion has any use at all it somehow seems to guarantee liberation. The liberated soul is one which exists beyond the usual round of rebirth. This was to be the function of the *puruṣa* in Samkhya-Yoga. The ultimate salvation of the *puruṣa* was to exist in splendid isolation. But the Buddha considered that one did not need to have a substance to perform this role. Why not substitute for the soul the possibility of liberation? That liberation would have to be austerely described or indicated, of course; there is no being there. It is a transcendental event or non-event supervening upon the previous chains of events. Psychologically it can look like annihilation, though it is annihilation with a kind of heavenly glow. It is not surprising that annihilationism should have been a Buddhist heresy. But if we find the ideal of nirvana very disappointing, since it seems to signify the loss of individuality, then that attitude only shows how far we are from attaining to it. It is because we are still entangled in selfish desires that we find nirvana off-putting. Had we reached pure equanimity, then we would desire neither to continue to exist nor not to continue. Both immortality and suicide would be unattractive. Nirvana does also mean the cessation of suffering or illfare (*dukkha*), since there is no more rebirth. This gives us a picture, then, of the Buddha's substitution: he saw egoless rebirth plus the possibility of transcendental liberation as functionally the equivalent of postulating a permanent self (*puruṣa* or *ātman*). The self, to sum up, had three disadvantages. First, it was superfluous as a means of explaining liberation. Second, it was a useless substance, for in being unchanging it could not even begin to enter into the description of change. Third, it conduced to egoism.

As well as these more abstract uses of imagination, to understand egolessness and causation, there is also the imaginative use of the idea of rebirth, and of other exercises, such as looking back on the conduct of the Buddha. So in order to look upon an enemy positively, one might try to still one's anger at him by reflecting that his bad conduct will bring him to be reborn in a horrid purgatory (and such Buddhist hells are most vividly described). Alternatively one may reflect that another person may have been — or indeed very likely was — one's mother or father or brother or sister or son or daughter in some previous life. So one can mobilize attitudes through reflecting that the other, as mother, "removed from me without disgust as if it were yellow sandalwood my urine, excrement, spittle, snot, etc., and played with me in her lap" (Buddhaghosa *Visuddhimagga* pp. 305-7).

There is running through Buddhist teachings a strong idealism, if I may call it that. Strictly speaking there is a continuum from bodily events to pure conscious events, and while the texts certainly differentiate body and mind in some sense (that is, *sarīra* and *citta*) the cosmos is basically woven out of the same kind of stuff, which occurs in denser and more subtle forms. Still, there is a strong emphasis upon the mental component of reality as being formative. This is what makes contemplation so important in the Buddhist scheme of things: the purification of consciousness resolves the problem of suffering. Likewise ultimately social reform must arise from mental factors, for each sort of society is a mental creation, a projection of the values and ideas of the people who belong to a given society. Of course the texts are well aware of the importance of material factors, for instance in the drive for private property in early society. Nevertheless, Buddhism essentially teaches that it is by purifying mental factors that we reform the world and achieve ultimate liberation. The cosmos disappears in nirvana, even though it may survive the liberation of any one individual.

It is perhaps useful to consider what the Buddhist attitude, at least in the Theravāda, does not include. It is contrasted to theistic morality in a number of ways. First, the rules or precepts are not considered to be commandments. Even the Buddha's teachings have to be tested in experience and so assimilated by the individual. Second, and connectedly, ethics is not something whose nature is revealed, as in theistic revelation. On the whole, the ethical injunctions are looked on naturalistically. For instance, the person who genuinely practices love can not only reflect on the nature of other beings, in some of the ways we have described, but can also benefit here and now from rewards. They are eleven in number, according to the *Anguttara Nikāya* (v. 142): he will sleep in comfort: he will not have bad dreams; he will be dear to others; he is dear to nonhumans; he is looked after by deities; fire, poison, and weapons do not affect him; his mind is easily concentrated; the expression on his face will be serene; he will die without confusion; and he will be reborn at least in the Brahma world (or, as we might say, in heaven).

A third difference from the theistic context is that there is in the Theravāda little room for grace or supernatural help. It is true that the teaching of the Buddha will open up new vistas for the individual. Without the intervention of the Buddha in the world the upward trend of new spiritual life would not have occurred. But the lack of the idea of grace has notable advantages: the Christian message is often clothed in too much emotion without proper attention to self-cultivation. The idea is sometimes abroad that because God does the work of sanctifying we ourselves are not also engaged in that same work: God works, in Christian orthodoxy, through us and from within us. It is striking, though, how much more there is in the Buddhist canon of detailed practical advice. As I have hinted, there is no incompatibility between such practicality and theistic belief. This is where Western religious traditions could do well to take on board some Buddhist advice.

Fourth, we may note that the Theravāda, and a lot of the

Buddhist tradition, is remarkably unsacramental; we do not have such attitudes as that marriage is a sacrament. This lack of concern with the sacramental aspects of ritual translates in a pragmatic and psychological defense of Buddhist rituals, such as they are (modes of honoring the Buddha, for instance). It is also connected to the lack of the active concept of substance. Ritual is often seen as transforming or conveying substance, but not in the Theravāda. In fact Buddhist unsubstantialism accords much more closely with modern science than the substance-loaded philosophies which have often dominated the Christian tradition. Again, it is possible to have a nonsubstantialist cosmology within the ambit of theism (a cosmos perhaps sustained and created by a personal divine, though changing, substance).

We also may note that Theravādin ethics, while generally speaking predicated upon a utilitarian schema, differs from its typical Western counterparts in its conception of happiness and the means of getting there. Thus alcohol and drugs are banned because not only do they lead to quarreling and strife, but they cloud the mind; and this is particularly important because of the role played by insight and self-awareness in the Buddhist schema. But most significantly, the Buddhist view has a conception of the highest happiness (*sukha*) which is spiritual in nature. We can learn from this, because the Theravādin vision involves a critical attitude towards common-sense values, and a doctrine of humans as having a transcendental goal. We may call it therefore a critical, transcendentalist utilitarianism.

While the rebirth doctrine does not distinguish Buddhism from some kinds of theism, for instance that of Rāmānuja in the Hindu tradition, it does distinguish it from the framework of most Western ethics. Because the notions of *kamma* and rebirth enter into the calculation of the possibilities of attaining liberation, they also affect the utilitarian judgements. Obviously, too, the whole structure of thought gives Buddhism different potentialities of the use of moral imagination, using for instance, the wonderful *Jātaka* stories of previous lives of the Buddha to educate people in right conduct. Perhaps Westerners could adopt a version of rebirth doctrine which makes it merely metaphorical (though one might ask what this does to nirvana); such a doctrine would at least challenge us to think carefully about what promotes the highest human welfare.

Let me conclude by considering the relevance of some of these Buddhist ideas to academic life. I have long held that if we were to cultivate the virtues which arise from the whole enterprise of pursuing the truth, we would have a splendid ethic to present to our students and even the outside world. To this "ethic of truth" the Buddhist example has much relevance. First, it is obvious in the human and social sciences that we need among other things empathetic imagination (*anukampa*) to enter into the lives of other people and other times. Such empathy does not mean acceptance of others' values, but at least the possibility of understanding them. Thus, we would need it to enter into the thought world of Hitler. In such endeavors we suspend our judgments and use what some have called *epoche*. The Buddhist ethos in its advice on how to calm our feelings, both negative and positive, toward others is relevant to this concern. Maybe we can invent new methods of contemplation to enhance our ability to understand other people and cultures.

Second, the Buddhist ethos is critical and in a broad sense empirical. We of course acknowledge the critical character of enquiry and education in the West. But we do not necessarily cultivate the dispositions that have to go with it. We have to expect, for instance, critical reviews of books we write. But how well prepared are we to accept such criticism? The student is somewhat inured to criticism from teachers, and by creating a caste system wherein the two levels of academic society are differentiated the pain of professors' criticism can be made more bearable. But faculty easily become slightly paranoid, because so much subject to peer review. The pursuit of truth requires two values often lacking: one is equanimity, the fourth of the *brahmavihāras*. The other is recognition of the altruistic nature of our enterprise. This recognition would discourage the tendency to pursue knowledge egoistically, where my theories become my intellectual property.

The recognition of the impersonal character of truth might help to reinforce something arising from the *brahmavihāras*, namely, the extension of our imagination to the whole human race. It is especially for this reason that any form of groupism (racism, nationalism, sexism, etc.) is inappropriate in an academic setting. But this is not something which is abolished just by saying that it is wrong. Buddhist methods of using our imaginations could be invoked to better our attitudes towards others, and to lessen the groupism which is endemic, in one form or another, in global society.

These virtues—empathetic imagination, equanimity, love of all human (and other living) beings—are intrinsic to the proper pursuit of truth, and they represent a high ideal.

I have argued that clarity and imagination are vital as means to virtue in the Buddhist ethos, particularly as represented in the Theravāda. I have tried to indicate something of the divergence of atmosphere from much of the Western ethical tradition, both theistic and nontheistic. I have also suggested that in a global society we can borrow one another's insights. There is much to borrow from the Buddhist tradition.

BIBLIOGRAPHICAL NOTE

In writing this paper I have made use of ideas expressed in my *Beyond Ideology* (San Francisco: Harper and Row, 1981). I have benefited from Gunapala Dharmasiri, *Fundamentals of Buddhist Ethics* (Singapore: Buddhist Research Society, 1986); J. Dhirasekara, ed., *The Encyclopedia of Buddhism*, vol. 4 (Colombo: Government of Sri Lanka, 1984), article on "Compassion"; and Rune Johansson, *Dynamic Psychology of Early Buddhism* (Oxford: Curzon Press, 1979).

PART III

Contemporary Contexts for Teaching Virtue

Can Virtue Be Taught in a School? Ivan Illich and Mohandas Gandhi on Deschooling Society

LEROY S. ROUNER

THE QUESTION "CAN VIRTUE BE TAUGHT?" is the subject of Plato's *Protagoras.* I will sketch Socrates' approach to the problem in that dialogue, and then compare and contrast Ivan Illich and Mohandas Gandhi, both of whom are critics of modern schools. Socrates has little to say about cultural context, and nothing at all to say about academic institutions, since there were none in his day. Illich and Gandhi, on the other hand, both focus on the urban, industrial context of institutionalized education. And since our question is not whether virtue can be learned but whether it can be taught, I have some observations about the different models of teaching offered by Socrates, Illich, and Gandhi, and some tentative conclusions about the kind of teaching we need today.

The *Protagoras* begins with Socrates' being awakened before dawn by his excited young friend Hippocrates who announces that Protagoras has just come to town. He pleads with Socrates to arrange for him to become Protagoras' pupil. Like most well-to-do young men in the Athens of his day, Hippocrates yearned to be able to speak well, in order to make his mark in the Assembly, the center of power and prestige. Since speaking well required thinking well, rhetoric was regularly associated with wisdom.

Protagoras was a Sophist, one of a number of itinerant sages who took on the sons of the aristocracy as temporary pupils, and became wealthy in the process. Since education had not yet been institutionalized, these Sophists were the educational establishment. Studying with them was better than getting into Harvard. It was as though Henry Kissinger, or John Kenneth Galbraith, came to stay for a couple of months at the home of some wealthy business person with intellectual aspirations, and agreed to take on a few well-heeled local lads as pupils in a short course on meaning, truth, and success.

Socrates, of course, was an anti-establishment *enfant terrible*. He disliked the sophists for charging fees for teaching (he called it intellectual prostitution), and he disagreed with Protagoras profoundly because Protagoras was a relativist and believed that morals were shaped by various communities. Protagoras argued that "man is the measure of all things." Socrates, on the other hand, was an intellectual purist and a bit of a fundamentalist. He believed in absolutes. He argued tirelessly that, if there are plural virtues, like courage and temperance, then there must be a singular, absolute, normative reality called *virtue* in which the various virtues participate, and hence gain meaning and reality. The *Protagoras* does not deal with the metaphysical question about the nature of virtue, or how we come to have this knowledge. Later, in the *Meno*, Plato proposes his theory of reincarnation, arguing that we already know what virtue really is from a previous life, and that this knowledge has been obscured by common opinion and traditions of all sorts. So Socratic dialectic is largely deconstructive. It pulls away this veil of false assurance, leaves us naked with our ignorance, and thus readies us for a "synoptic insight" into the true nature of virtue. Here lies the connection between Socrates and Gandhi, who was much influenced by the Hindu nondualistic philosophy of Sankara. Sankara's doctrine of the world as *māyā* or "illusion" has much in common with Socrates' view that common opinion (*doxa*) is misleading when it comes to questions about the ultimate nature of things.

Without this transcendent understanding of virtue, Socrates argued, there was no point in trying to teach people specific virtues, like courage or temperance. They wouldn't get it, because one can't understand why courage is a virtue if one doesn't first understand what the word *virtue* means. Students will have a preliminary understanding of what the term *courage* represents, but it won't help them to *be* courageous, because they won't have any way to understand the reality of virtue in which the concept of courage is grounded. As my teacher John Herman Randall used to say, "They will get the words right, but miss the tune." They will be able to "talk a good game" but not play it. The head knows, but not the heart.

From Socrates' point of view, the purpose of teaching someone about courage was not just so that they could give an adequate definition of it, and defend that definition in debate, although the dialogues sometimes make it seem that way. That goal trivializes the purposes of education by aestheticizing or intellectualizing them. The purpose of teaching someone about courage is to make them courageous. The purpose of education is not to tinker with people's minds, or gild their tongues. Socrates, for all his lofty idealism and ingenious dialectic, is essentially down to earth. He reminds me of some of my friends in rural New Hampshire, where I live. They would say: "Is all this talk about courage gonna make you brave? And if it don't, it's all about nothin', ain't it?" Socrates would have agreed.

Socrates fascinates modern philosophers because he is both an analytical philosopher and an idealist. His dialectical method evolves a philosophy out of the analysis of language. But he also believes in the determinative reality of absolute ideas. And he was much beloved of the existentialist, Søren Kierkegaard, not only because he was such an individual, but because his ultimate focus was always personal, immediate, practical, and lifegiving. His transcendent ideals were not abstractions; they were those necessary structures of meaning which alone make a genuinely human life possible. So, when the young Hippocrates first comes to Socrates as a potential pupil of Protagoras, Socrates does not ask him whether Protagoras' instruction will get him into law school, or guarantee a six-figure income. He asks, "What will he make of you?" That question, I suggest, is as close to the bone as the philosophy of education gets.

The current curriculum debate tends to miss this point because the critical question after four years of college is not primarily information, but transformation. The test is less how much students know, of whatever cultural tradition, because they are going to forget most of that content in five years. The test is who a student has become in that process. In other words, "What have they made of you?"

It is this existential tension which keeps the debate going between Socrates and Protagoras, because the ultimate issue for both of them is not the analytical problem of definition, or the abstract question of ideals, both of which might have been readily resolved. The ultimate issue is a philosophy-of-life question. How can I understand who I am and what I do in a way that is coherent, and makes sense to me, and therefore has some integrity? In other words, how can I live a good life? Socrates is looking for a "synoptic intuition" into the transcendental reality which actually enables life decisions. Knowledge of this kind would be inherently transformative. If we *really* knew what virtue meant, we would *be* good.

This is where most of us get stuck, because Socrates seems too "idealistic." You and I usually know what we ought to do, but we usually don't do it, because we don't want to. Our wills are in conflict with our intellect. And modern theories of knowledge support our skepticism about Socrates' argument from a different direction, because they tend to focus on "clear and distinct" ideas as the necessary conceptual material for proper reasoning. Our idea of an idea is therefore more like a coin or a bucket than a cloud. But the ground issues of ethics — love, virtue, loyalty, and the like — are never clear and distinct. They are not hard coins, or measurable buckets. They are always cloudy. They are mysteries.

So the question can be recast: How can one know a mystery? Can mysteries be taught? For Socrates, the deepest dimension of knowledge joins heart and mind, will and understanding. The problem is not whether *ethics* can be taught. Ethics is not a mystery; it is an intellectual structure of moral principles. Ethics *per se* is only the tuneless prescription of social oughts.

Virtue is a song. One has to get the tune right in order to know virtue. Can the soul sing? And if not, how can the soul be taught to sing? So virtue is a mystery, a song, a transforming vision. Can anyone really teach that? And how do we get it, if in fact we do? Socrates finally suggested that it was a gift from the gods, which is probably right. But that didn't negate the importance for him of the educational process, the dialectical exploration of what words mean, how ideals are viable, and what actually works for us in the real world. At the very least these were a necessary prolegomenon to the vision. They constructed the most reliable platform from which to view the transformative insight. That was what dialectic was all about. Socrates, professing ignorance, sought to be a midwife of ideas in others. The truth was there, buried under a lot of intellectual confusion in their souls. Socrates relentlessly asked all the awkward questions which would clarify this confusion.

But there is a dimension to the problem which Plato never engaged, and that is cultural context. *Our* question is about teaching virtue *in context*. Is the modern school a viable context for teaching virtue? Both Illich and Gandhi answer "No."

Illich's *DeSchooling Society* is part of a larger critique of modern institutions generally, which included industry, medical practice, and so forth. In regard to schools: "The pupil is . . . schooled to confuse teaching with learning, grade advancement with education, a diploma with competence, and fluency with the ability to say something new. His imagination is 'schooled' to accept service in place of value. Medical treatment is mistaken for health care, social work for the improvement of community life, police protection for safety, military poise for national security, the rat race for productive work."[1] In other words, Illich is opposed to all the major institutions of modern life, and schools are here a paradigm case of that opposition.

Schools, he argues, blur the distinction between process and substance. They persuade you that process is meaningful, that "going through" school produces something substantial which, in fact, it does not. He argues, rather, that modern institutionalization (of education, health care, social welfare, crime protection, national security) "inevitably leads to physical pollution, social polarization and psychological impotence."[2]

Further, we have assumed that "school" and "teaching" are necessary for learning. Illich argues, to the contrary, that most of what we need to know we learn outside "school" and that we are taught, not by paid professional instructors, but by others in our culture who have learned their particular skill outside school. School appropriates "the money, men and good will available for education and in addition discourages other institutions from assuming educational tasks. Work, leisure, politics, city living, and even family life depend on schools for the habits and knowledge they presuppose, instead of becoming themselves the means of education."[3]

Illich's argument is that if we were serious about education we would take advantage of the educative opportunities of community life. We didn't learn how to speak our mother tongue in school. Dad taught us how to drive a car, and Mom taught us how to cook, or maybe vice-versa, but the point is that these fundamental skills are all learned informally, outside institutions.

Illich is persuaded that our problem is rooted in the invention of childhood by the middle class in industrial societies. Childhood was unknown to most historical periods, and is still unknown today outside industrial societies. "Before our century neither the poor nor the rich knew of children's dress, children's games, or the child's immunity from the law. Childhood belonged to the bourgeoisie. The worker's child, the peasant's child and the nobleman's child all dressed the way their fathers dressed, played the way their fathers played, and were hanged by the neck as were their fathers."[4]

Even today, Illich notes, "In the Andes you till the soil once you have become 'useful'. Before that you watch the sheep."[5] Further, he is persuaded that, given the choice, most people would pass on childhood. "Neither Stephen Daedalus nor Alexander Portnoy enjoyed childhood, and neither, I suspect, did many of us like to be treated as children."[6]

A major criticism of schooling is the role of the teacher. Illich argues that "we have all learned most of what we know outside school. . . . We learn to speak, to think, to love, to feel, to play, to curse, to politick, and to work without interference from a teacher."[7] And teachers, in Illich's view, impede education beause they are cast in the roles of *custodian, preacher, and therapist.* The teacher as custodian is an orchestrator, guiding the pupil through labyrinthine rituals, like qualifying examinations, which Illich finds unproductive. The teacher as moralist "substitutes for parents, God, or the state. He indoctrinates the pupil about what is right or wrong, not only in school but also in society at large. He stands *in loco parentis* for each one and thus ensures that all feel themselves children of the same state."[8]

The teacher as therapist is perhaps the most dangerous model for Illich. The teacher "feels authorized to delve into the personal life of his pupil in order to help him grow as a person. When this function is exercised by a custodian and preacher, it usually means that he persuades his pupil to submit to a domestication of his vision of truth and his sense of what is right."[9]

Illich sounds radical but is, I think, a conservative, calling for less government, more freedom, and letting the good times roll. He is essentially an optimist. He thinks people are good and will learn from life experience what they need to know. We don't really need schools. Like Socrates he is a deconstructionist, albeit a modern one. Get rid of those structures which impede genuine learning, he argues, and things will take care of themselves. There are lots of people out there ready to teach us what we need to know. In this he is not unlike Protagoras, who argued not only that virtue can be taught, but that there are lots of folk out there teaching it — parents, kindergarten teachers, police officers, and others.

Illich is, however, primarily concerned with what his colleague Paolo Friere called "the pedagogy of the oppressed," emphasizing that universal education in schools is hopelessly expensive. If the poor are to be educated it will have to be outside school, in the family, the work place, and in communities of common concern. But for all his criticism of "schools," he is an academic intellectual. He works in a "think tank." Granted it is in Cuernavaca, Mexico, rather than in Stanford or Cambridge, but the intellectual ethos is much the same.

Gandhi, on the other hand, was a practitioner. From the early years in South Africa to the time of his death he was engaged in a social reform movement. He was educated in schools, both in India and England, and was profoundly influenced by a few writers like Tolstoy and Ruskin. He was also deeply influenced by traditional elements of Hindu life and thought, but his key ideas were largely generated from his life experience. Even when he seemed to be borrowing from tradition, as with his emphasis on nonviolence or *ahiṃsā* as a way of life, he was, in fact, reinventing these ideas in order to meet the needs of his own social reform movement.

Ahiṃsā, for example, had always been a principle of personal piety in Indian culture. To kill was to infect one's soul with bad *karma* and thus impede the process of *moksha*, salvific freedom from the bonds of illusion and particularity in this world. Gandhi, however, presented *ahiṃsā* as a social principle, a way of dealing with one's neighbors, whether friends or enemies. And in the course of his long life of social activism, he almost persuaded a whole nation that this was what their tradition had always meant by *ahiṃsā*. Gandhi's program of social reform involved political freedom from British colonial rule. Politics, however, was, for him, the means to a renewal of Indian society. British colonialism was detrimental to India, he believed, not primarily because it robbed India of its right to self-government (which tended to be Nehru's view) but because it corrupted the Indian spirit through the values and institutions of modernity.

Like Illich, he was opposed to urbanization and industrialization because they corrupted the good life. And like Hannah Arendt, he believed that individuals found their creative potential best fulfilled in the type of small community found in the Greek *polis* or the traditional Indian village.

And, of course, it was not hard to criticize the British educational establishment in India. The British were not concerned with an imaginative teaching of virtue; they were primarily interested in training. They needed clerks to serve in the lower echelons of colonial administration, and they needed people who spoke their cultural language. So the curriculum required Shakespeare and the metaphysical poets of people whose English was minimal at best. Rote learning thus became the order of the day, and produced a generation of people who could only hope to get the words right, and had no idea of what the tune might possibly be.

Gandhi's philosophy of education was much like Illich's in that it was opposed to this impersonal and culturally alien educational establishment, which had robbed his countrymen and countrywomen of their cultural self-confidence and spiritual power. He said, "It does not make men of us. It does not enable us to do our duty."[10]

Gandhi believed that "true education is something different. Man is made of three constituents, the body, mind and spirit. Of them, the spirit is the one permanent element in man. The body and the mind function on account of it. Hence we can call that education which reveals the qualities of spirit."[11] He goes on: "The knowledge that is being imparted today may possibly develop the mind a little, but certainly does not develop the body or spirit. I have a doubt about the development of the mind too, because it does not mean that the mind has developed if we have filled it with a lot of information."[12]

He concludes: "Education, character and religion should be regarded as convertible terms. There is no true education that does not tend to produce character, and there is no true religion which does not determine character. Education should contemplate the whole life. Mere memorizing and book learning is not education. I have no faith in the so-called system of education which produces men of learning without the backbone of character."[13]

Gandhi's role as educator took its departure from the classical Hindu model of the relation between the *guru*, the spiritual teacher, and the *adhikarin*, the qualified student. This involved continuing, intense interaction between teacher and student in all the details of daily living, until the genius, or insight, or divine reality within the guru was inexplicably transferred to the student. The student suddenly grasped a "synoptic insight" into truth.

Gandhi's project was to establish this traditional interaction between guru and student on a huge scale, which was India itself. Gandhi was the guru, and the whole of India was the student. The project's microcosm was the life of the ashram, the intimate personal community in which Gandhi lived. But the macrocosm was India. Gandhi made himself a constant presence in the life of the nation, through political action, and especially through his writing. He wrote endlessly, inconsistently, specifically about a whole host of problems. And the extent to which he regarded his own life as an experimental instrument for the transformation of a nation is vividly illustrated by his sexual experiments.

Gandhi was persuaded that colonialism had robbed Indian men of their manhood. They had been made submissive through military conquest and political control, but they had been robbed of their spiritual power through the colonialist's celebration of male sexuality as generative, having families and children and being heads of large households. This is more profound than a criticism of pornography, for example. It is a criticism of what we would call natural male sexuality. Gandhi held a traditional Hindu view that male semen is a source of inner spiritual power, and that the loss of semen was a loss of power. Therefore the practice of *Brahmacharya*, the love of Brahma, included sexual chastity, not as a means of ascetic denial, but as a means of empowerment. Semen moved through the spinal column, throughout the body, making possible those heroic feats for which yogis have long been known: the endurance of heat and cold, the ability to live creatively with only a few hours sleep a night, and freedom from depression or mood changes. Gandhi experienced all of these. He hoped for a new generation of genuinely strong men who had appropriated these powers for themselves, and were ready to use them in the service of the New India.

Gandhi used himself as an experimental project in how one's inner spirituality could be empowered by sexual discipline. And this was not just white-knuckle abstention. He wandered naked around the ashram, to make this a natural thing. Eventually he even slept naked with two naked young women, testing himself and them with the possibility of transcending what my mother used to call "bad thoughts."

But at least once Gandhi's experiment failed. He awoke with an outward and visible sign of what, for him, was an inward and spiritual disgrace. Since he had already made his experiment public, he wrote an article in *Young India* about this personal failure and, by implication, what it meant for the future of the nation. This *is* a little bizarre, and Gandhi may well have dehumanized himself in the service of spiritual renewal in the New India. But it shows how far he was willing to go in making himself an educational tool for the transformation of the Indian character. He was custodian, preacher and therapist for the whole nation, and the *nation* was his school. He wanted people to change radically, and he was ready to use himself as a transforming vehicle for that change.

What, then, can we use from these two radical educational *enfants terribles?* Like Socrates, they are both anti-establishment, anti-institutional, and thus anti-modern. So, first of all, they give us historical perspective on where we are, and some new ideas on where we ought to be going.

In the Middle Ages, the great cultural forces in the West were the church and the university. In the modern world the great cultural forces are the state and the multinational corporation. Neil Rudenstine at Harvard has just called for a new alliance among the state, the corporation, and the university if the university in America is to maintain its role as a predominant institution. But the crisis in the university is precisely that the university has *become* a corporation, and therefore gradually lost the distinctive educational vocation that Socrates articulated so well in his question to Hippocrates: "What will he make of you?"

Both Illich and Gandhi criticize schools for creating a world of ideas and interests which are not directly related to our experience of ourselves and our world outside school. They are both Utopians. They want to dismantle our present educational institutions, on the grounds that they are too expensive, essentially unproductive, and therefore unnecessary. This dismantling might be a good thing, except for those of us who would be out of work, but that's not going to happen. Schools are not even likely to be reformed, because they are such effective means of social success in our society. My father, who had been a poor boy from the wrong side of the stockyards in Omaha, Nebraska, at the turn of the century, eventually went to Harvard, and he urged me to go to Harvard because it would make connections that would serve me for the rest of my life. And of course he was right. So Utopia is a lost cause. But Josiah Royce reminds us that lost causes today are often highly influential tomorrow. And even if they are not, they keep us focused on the purpose we serve. The fact that it never happens doesn't mean it wasn't right.

My lost cause is the hope for a growing group of people within the university who seek to *personalize* education, connecting the material of their discipline in various ways to the real life-world of students. We are left with three models of teaching for doing that. One is Socrates, the midwife of ideas, who professes to know nothing except a method whereby people may hopefully come to know their own ignorance. A second is Ivan Illich who is persuaded that true education comes from those functioning in our real culture, and not in the abstract and unnecessary institutions of schooling. These people already know what we really need to know. They are our parents, friends, co-workers, and the like. The third is Gandhi, who tried to make his own spirituality a transforming vision of virtue for India.

Illich doesn't think we need a special class of people called "teachers." Gandhi and Socrates, on the other hand, were both teachers in their own way, and both believed that the transformative insight into virtue is finally discovered by individuals in their own souls, rather than imposed by someone else from outside. So you can't "teach" virtue, but you can help people get to the place where they can learn it for themselves. They differ in their method of doing this, however. Socrates focused almost entirely on rational argument, and refused to play the role of the wise one. Gandhi played the role of the virtuous wise one to the hilt. For our present purposes, Socrates did not personalize his teaching enough, whereas Gandhi personalized it too much.

By personalization I do not mean that we should spend more time with our students, by having more office hours, open doors, inviting them home, and so forth. Nor does personalization mean that teachers should consciously try to be role models for their students. A certain amount of role modeling inevitably takes place. Insofar as this imitation is well chosen and establishes good habits in the imitator it is valuable. More than that, it is the way we all begin to learn to be good at anything. As Socrates said about learning "knacks" like cooking, one should find a good cook, and watch what they do, and then go practice.

That is really Illich's populist model of education. But Socrates knew something that Illich ignores and that is that *episteme*, real knowledge, has to be prepared for by what my teacher Ernest Hocking called "the hard work of thought." It is why Socrates said one has to have a process of dialectic first. In Illich's happy world, it all happens by itself if people just get out there and live. My view is that we have to work at it. And school is the workplace.

But Socrates lived in a world where rational argument was widely trusted; and we no longer live in that world. For most of our students, a rational proof for an ethical principle no longer "proves" much of anything. Socrates knew that rational proof needed myth in order to be persuasive, even in his culture. But the myth he appealed to was the myth of a common culture, whereas our students no longer have a common culture. Their myth needs to be brought home. The myths of our culture need to make connection with the inner myth of their individual lives. As the feminists have insisted, we all need a chance to tell our own story.

Gandhi is surely right that virtue is learned from those who are virtuous, and that we become virtuous by choosing our mentors well. But his is ultimately an authoritarian model. In the individualistic West, we eschew gurus because we fear spiritual totalitarianism. If virtue is a song, it is a song sung in one's own voice, and a major purpose of higher education is to help students in both arts and sciences find their own voice as artist or scientist. Like good parents, role models can initially enable this discovery, but they soon become barriers to it. If one's first novel sounds like Ernest Hemingway, that's all right; one is learning a craft. If a second novel sounds like Ernest Hemingway, the author is well on his or her way to becoming a bad writer.

The personalization of education means paying increased attention to the "inwardness" of both teachers and learners. "Inwardness" (Kierkegaard) is not a psychological category; it is a category of spirit. Spirit is not only what characterizes one most definitively as an individual. It is also an indication of what drives that character, that is, what one cares about most deeply. Spirit serves the mind at that moment when mind reaches beyond the dialectic of empirical experience to the "synoptic insight" concerning the nature of virtue itself. It is spirit which teaches the mind to sing, in its own voice.

It is hard for us to teach virtue because our educational process excludes the element of spirit in much of our study, thus divorcing the material of study from the lively care which students instinctively have for it. And if there is no vital connection between their real lives and the material they are studying, there is no possibility that they will be taught virtue.

The teaching of religion is a case in point. John Updike's novel *Roger's Version* includes an unfair but telling critique of Harvard Divinity School for teaching theology historically and sociologically. Students thus learn that this is interesting material. But, as in most religion departments in this country, what students learn is everything they ever wanted to know about a religion except why anyone would believe it. (The analogy in my field of philosophy is everything one ever wanted to know about a philosophy except whether it is true or not.) And eventually the material is no longer interesting; it is only curious. And it is readily forgotten, because it makes no connection with one's own religious experience, whether positive or negative.

I was asked to teach the Existentialism course in the Boston University Philosophy Department a couple of years ago. We made our way through the relevant material from Dostoevsky to Sartre. But then I read them a little book of my own about the death of my son, and for a term paper assignment I said, "Don't write *about* existentialism. You will learn what existentialism is about best by *being* an existentialist philosopher. Write an existential paper. I've told you my story; now you tell me yours. Write me something with a little blood on it."

I got papers about childhood sexual abuse, and alcoholism, and deaths in the family, and all manner of tragedies. I was stunned to know what most of them were going through while trying to do their academic business. And the papers were, for the most part, excellent: well-crafted, reflective exercises in existential philosophizing. They were so good I tried to get them published. I think that many of them wrote over their heads, but they seemed grateful for a place where their education made contact with their real lives.

Now an Existentialism course is obviously a unique example, since what I am proposing, in a way, is an existentializing of education, but that connection can be made fruitfully in many different contexts, and not simply in the liberal arts.

The dangers of personalizing education are legion. To focus on the spirit-informed mind could collapse education into therapy, or make school into church, and both of these would be disastrous. It could also make teacher-student relations dangerously intimate. But why do so many of our students at Boston University want to study with Elie Wiesel? Because he tells his story. And he makes his story connect with his students' stories, and the stories of others. And those students remember everything he says.

So the dangers of personalization may be legion, but they may also be overemphasized. We already have a built-in model for this kind of education in conservatories and schools for the arts, where "finding one's own voice" is what education is all about. Students there are saved from sentimentality and overpersonalization by the rigors of the discipline. But the focus remains on who the individual is becoming — an actor, a musician, an artist. Personal transformation is obviously at the heart of conservatory education. Perhaps less obviously, it is also what education in the liberal arts and sciences is all about. The critical question is still, "What will they make of you?"

NOTES

1. Ivan Illich, *DeSchooling Society* (New York: Harper & Row, 1971), p. 1.

2. Ibid.

3. Ibid., p. 8.

4. Ibid., p. 26.

5. Ibid., p. 27.

6. Ibid.

7. Ibid., p. 31.

8. Ibid.

9. Ibid.

10. Ramashray Roy, *Self and Society: A Study in Gandhian Thought* (New Delhi and Beverly Hills: Sage Publications in collaboration with United Nations University, Tokyo, 1984), p. 44.

11. Ibid., p. 45.

12. Ibid.

13. Ibid.

Religious Learning beyond Secularism

ROBERT CUMMINGS NEVILLE

I. RELIGIOUS LEARNING

JOHN CALVIN, THE THEOLOGIAN everyone loves to hate, opened his *Institutes of the Christian Religion* with the observation that the knowledge of God and the knowledge of human nature are intimately correlated. To start with one is immediately to be led to the other. To know the glory of God is also to know the glory of human nature defined by the divine image; or, having fallen and corrupted the divine image in it, the utter wretchedness of the human condition in contrast with its inbuilt divinity reflects the divine glory. This is Calvin's first point, the principal thesis by which his theology is known.

Calvin's next point, usually neglected in popular Calvinism, is that, in the condition of fallenness, we not only have a diminished knowledge of God, wholly missing the glory and fixing on banal and unbelievable representations of divinity, but we also have a diminished sense of the human. We lose sight of the image of God in us, substitute third-rate ideals for the strenuous obligations of living before God, and forget both the bliss of divine companionship and the wretched depravity of our true condition, stupidly saying, "I'm OK, you're OK." As Calvin put it:

> For what man in all the world would not gladly remain as he is — what man does not remain as he is — so long as he does not know himself, that is while content with his own gifts, and either ignorant or unmindful of his own misery? . . . For, because all of us are inclined by nature to hypocrisy, a kind of empty image of righteousness in place of righteousness itself abundantly satisfies us. . . . As long as we do not look

beyond the earth, being quite content with our own righteousness, wisdom, and virtue, we flatter ourselves most sweetly,
and fancy ourselves all but demigods.[1]

Calvin's analysis of the human condition was that the fall resulted
in the banality of recognizing neither divine glory nor the corrupted glory of God's image in human nature, which explains his
project of preaching depravity so that we would take both ourselves and God seriously. The contrast between religious learning
and secular learning is peculiar to the modern, post-Renaissance
West and to non-Western cultures to the extent they have been affected by modernization. Writing at the verge of modernity, Calvin
saw the issue with surprising acuteness. However much we ourselves are supposed to be postmodern — and I doubt that is very
much at all — the contrast between the religious and secular lin-
gers and sets the terms of the discussion. My intent here is to focus
the topic on religious learning in higher education, although this
is obviously connected with the religious education students bring
to that stage of learning, with the problems of continuing religious
intelligence after formal schooling, and with the general cultural
situation regarding religion and secularity.

To focus the topic appropriately it is important to be as clear
as possible about "religious learning." Religious learning is not to
be reduced to learning about religion or the religious life, however important and instrumental that might be. The primary meaning of religious learning is to become learned in being religious.
This means being intellectually sophisticated, spiritually advanced,
and highly cultured, comparatively speaking, in one's religious life.
Religious learnedness applies to individuals in ways they might
learn in institutions of higher education. It also applies by simple
analogy to religious groups that can be more or less learned, and
by a more complex analogy to whole cultures insofar as they expect
and facilitate religious learning in their educational institutions.

If there were no cultural criticism and deep suspicion of religion within modern secular culture, nothing exceptional would
be seen in advocating religious learning. Just as liberal education
includes philosophy to make people more philosophically sophisticated, history to make them more historically aware, literature
and the arts to cultivate richness and diversity of imagination, the

social and physical sciences to increase theoretical understanding and a grasp of non-obvious causal factors, so liberal education includes religious learning to increase religious sophistication. Save for some forms of postmodernism, no modern secular person questions the importance of philosophy, history, literature, the arts, and the sciences, as studies that educate people in important dimensions of life. Religion, however, is suspect as a dimension of life in the modern world, and this is the sharp edge in our topic.

Religious learning is the cultivation of the religious life in sophistication and depth. This takes place in three areas whose differences I shall exaggerate for purposes of quick clarity. The areas are understanding, spiritual practice, and ritual.[2]

Religious understanding consists in sedimented layers of myth and symbol and their theological or philosophical interpretation. As sociologists of knowledge such as Peter Berger and historians of religion such as Mircea Eliade have argued, religious cosmologies articulate a sense of the boundaries and ultimate geography of the world, including representations of the ultimate grounds and purposes of life.[3] In the sophisticated development of religious understanding, all the arts and sciences have contributions to make, and comparative religious study is especially helpful for understanding the range of application of religious ideas. Although these modern university subjects can be pursued for no religious reason whatsoever, there is profound religious reason to take advantage of any available angle of understanding. So religious studies, broadly conceived, is an obvious contribution of the university to religious learning.

The advancement of learning in spiritual practices is not so obviously a university subject. Indeed, the Baconian resonance of the phrase "advancement of learning" suggests the secular exclusion of spiritual practices from the curriculum. Spiritual practices include prayer and meditation, worship, the singing of religious songs, special attention to spiritual formation, perhaps with a spiritual director, and other devices of personal and community life designed to advance people toward religious ideals of enlightened and holy living. Different religions employ different spiritual practices. Some practices are similar from one tradition to another so that the forms are easily borrowed back and forth. Korean Buddhists now sing Protestant hymn tunes, and Roman Catholics can say the Hail Mary in the lotus position. Other practices are hard to transfer; the attempt in the 1960s to bring the sexual yoga of Tantric Buddhism and esoteric Taoism into Christianity seems to have failed, even in California. Religious maturity in many respects is to be measured by adeptness at the spiritual practices of one's community or culture, as well as by understanding.

Religious ritual is the most alien kind of religious learning in the modern world, which tends to look on ritual as empty form that expresses something better expressed in propositions. This is a misunderstanding of ritual, however. Although rituals do indeed often contain representations that assert something about reality, assertions that might be wrong, the important part of ritual is that it is more performative than assertive. Exercising the ritual is itself the reality at stake. Saying "I do" in a wedding ceremony is not just describing one's state of mind — that had better have been expressed and tested beforehand — but is the very act of marrying itself. The handshake makes the deal; it does not merely describe the partners' intentions.[4]

Confucianism is the tradition that best understands ritual.[5] Actions, words, ways of dressing, making eye contact, body language, and the rest are all artifacts of human behavior that have significance. Giving birth to children does not make a family without the ritualized practices of nurture, care, and the teaching of mutual respect. Cooperative behavior is not friendship without the rituals of attention, deference, interest, and mutual concern for the other. The ancient Confucians believed that the problem with the barbarians was not that they had the wrong culture — all culture is conventional; rather the barbarian problem is that their culture is inadequate in rituals so that the civilized and truly human dimensions of life have no opportunity for exercise. Lacking rituals of filial piety, barbarians have degenerate family life; lacking rituals of friendship, their social relations are merely competitive and calculative. American society is generally barbarous by Confucian standards.

Religious ritual consists of those symbolic actions that constitute our formed responses to ultimate things, to the boundaries and geography of our world, to our ultimate grounds and goals. We are of course related to ultimate things whether or not we know it, ritualize it, or do anything about it. But without an adequate or satisfactory ritual, we simply do not exist in that dimension of human reality that consists in responding to ultimate things.

Specific rituals such as the weekly Seder, or the Eucharist, or prayer toward Mecca five times a day, are not the whole of ritual performance; the whole of those rituals requires shaping one's life around their motifs. Understanding the depth of penetration of ritual in life is one of the subtlest elements of religious understanding, requiring a profound knowledge of the interaction of resonant motifs throughout personal and cultural forms. I myself can say something about forming personal life and community around the crucifixion/resurrection motif, but would not venture far beyond Christian rituals. Not to have the performative rituals of constituting oneself in relation to ultimate things is to be spiritually dead, however alive one might be in other ways. Purely secular people, of course, would say that there is no spiritual dimension of human reality that exists in the performance of proper rituals, and they would decry the prejudicial use of language such as "spiritual death." But here is precisely the issue about religious learning beyond secularism.

II. THE CHALLENGE OF SECULARISM

Secularism, of course, means worldliness, and modernity was launched with a new sense of what "the world" means. The invention in the European renaissance of mathematical physics, and its rapid deployment as the root metaphor for understanding nearly everything, provided for the first time a clear definition of the closure of the world. Closure is the mathematical idea of a set of things that contains only members of a certain type, as the set of even numbers is closed with respect to the odd numbers. What counts as a thing in the world? What is the world's closure? For the modern period, to be a real thing in the world is to be measurable. As Descartes pointed out, mental phenomena are not measurable in the same way physical things are, being indivisible and dimensionless; yet they are determinate and can be discriminated from one another. So the modern period has generalized the idea of measure to that of determinateness. A determinate thing has an identity that is both its own and also is constituted by comparative relations with other things. A determinate thing is always determinate with respect to some other things from which it otherwise would not be different. So the world consists of all the things that are determinate and can be connected with other determinate things.[6] The problem occasioned for Western theisms by the modern understanding of the world as everything determinate is the location of God.[7] Is God outside the system of determinations? That was the answer of early Deism which claimed that God created the world and then broke off all relations. Deism was an unsatisfactory solution because it still construed the creator God as determinate even though remote, and thus not really outside the realm of determination.

Or is God indeed inside the realm of worldly determinations? Other theists, including those whose traditions became fundamentalist and thinkers such as William James and Alfred North Whitehead, argued that God is a determinate being superior to all others but still among the many things of the world.[8] These thinkers rarely say that God creates the world in any strong sense because God's determinateness requires the world with respect to which divinity can be determinate. The difficulty with this position is that such a God-with-us ought to be discoverable by tracing out the connections among things in the world, and there seems to be inadequate evidence for such a special being.

If God is neither outside nor inside the realm of determinations, perhaps divinity is the whole. A third theistic response was made by the absolute idealists and pantheists who claim that God is in some sense the whole of the determinations of the world.[9] The chief difficulty with this strategy is articulating in what the wholeness of the world consists. A rough empirical survey suggests that the world is not a whole at all, but rather a series of loosely connected pockets of order. If the whole is itself something determinate that integrates the parts, then it turns out to be just one more determinate thing among the many, and God is once again a finite determination. Yet if the whole is not determinate, by virtue of what does it integrate or form wholeness?

The result of these failures to locate God with reference to the closure of the world has led many people to define modernity as a secularist skepticism about God and religion. Secular skepticism in these religious matters has developed a deep and thickly articulated secular culture characterized by an exclusive recognition of causation and connections among the determinations of the world. For short, this can be called "cosmological causation," because it recognizes only the causal connections among the things within the cosmos. It stands in contrast with ontological causation, the causation of the very existence of the world, its ultimate ground and meaning. Secularism denies ontological causation entirely because that seems to imply the causation of the set of determinations with closure by something from the outside. But there is no outside. Or if there is, then it is determinate and is not really outside. Stated in the language of Western theism, secularism denies divine creation, the creation of the world *ex nihilo*.

Some religious thinkers have sought to accept the modern definition of the world as the set of determinations and to say that religion points to what transcends that world. Karl Rahner, for instance, follows Kant and Hegel in insisting that any recognition of a determinate object displays as well a transcendent ground of the relation between subject and object; any representation of the determinate character of the world displays as well a transcendent ground of that determinate character.[10] But because the transcendent cannot be expressed without making it determinate, the secularist position rejects appeals to transcendence.

The word *transcendence* is somewhat misleading because it suggests an asymmetrical motion in the wrong direction. It suggests that we move up to the determinate border and then go beyond it. The alleged phenomenon moves the opposite way, however: the creator originates the determinate things and us. In the motif of divine creation, the making is a move from God to the world. The better religious language is grace: God's action is what is at stake. Although we might move cognitively from its effects back into the divine causing reality, the real move is God's creating, God's gracious action in a worldward direction. Grace is unnecessitated action, action not necessitated by the world which depends on the action wholly for its own existence, and action not necessitated by any antecendent nature in God which would make God a determinate thing. Such worldward grace is what secularism denies.

Early secularism, as exemplified in David Hume's *Dialogues Concerning Natural Religion*, was excited to deny miracles, because they seemed to be interference with the cosmological causal system by an impossible external being. Secularism denies providence, because that seems to require the world to be shaped for a purpose imposed from the side, as an artifact is made for a use. In its toughest mood of all, secularism seeks to reduce all experiences of grace or the transcendent to natural phenomena to be explained by hidden causes. Religious awe, sublimity, transformed consciousness, moments of ecstasy, and life-changing encounters are all to be explained on intraworldly causal grounds as wholly secular phenomena. One thinks of Schopenhauer, Marx, or Freud. To the extent people insist on a religious understanding, the suspicion of some general delusion is aroused.

Within a developed secular culture, the religious virtues are transformed to secular versions. On their own, religious virtues are taken to be ontologically grounded in the sense that they are normatively part of what people are created to be. To be human in the religious sense is to be obligated to perfect the virtues, or to exercise them where relevant in life. That we fail them means that we fail at being human; their failure is an affront to our created status as well as the source of whatever harm comes from their failure. Consider the five primary virtues in Christianity, which have counterparts in nearly every other religious tradition: righteousness, piety, faith, hope, and love.

Righteousness as a religious virtue is the habitual pursuit of justice out of the motive to respect the normativeness of due order in the universe. Righteousness acknowledges that things are created in relation to better and worse ways in which they can be ordered, and to respect their being is to respect them in their rights to be well ordered. There is no special religious insight into the content of just order. But righteousness as a religious virtue takes the categorical imperative of morality to stem from the ontological nature of things, from their very being, and not only from their specific cosmological characters. Secular righteousness is moved by appreciation or by commitment, but not by ontological imperative. As our appreciations become jaded and our commitments self-serving, true righteousness is replaced by pretended righteousness covering a basic relativism.

Piety need not refer to the manner of outward religious forms but better describes the habit of appreciating, respecting, and deferring to each thing encountered in the universe as a creature with its own center of worth. Whereas righteousness focuses on a human order in which people are respected as infinite and equal in dignity, and other things are subordinated as means to human welfare and justice, piety takes each thing as the center of its own universe in which all other things are environment and means. For righteousness' sake, we should kill off the AIDS virus; for piety's sake, we should acknowledge it as a creature of marvelous intrinsic worth for which human and other hosts are but utilitarian contexts. Without piety, we act as if the human sphere were the ontological center of the universe, whereas in fact it is only the center of our neighborhood. With true piety we respond to the entire creation with deference and respect for the ontological worth of each part, a far vaster vision than human morality, however amoral it is. The corruption of piety is aestheticism, the enjoyment of things only so long as they contribute to our fascination without harm to our lifestyle.

Faith is the virtue of engaging our concrete situation because that is our true being. The existentialists developed entire theologies of faith, subordinating all the other virtues to this one. The corruption of faith is to engage the world where it interests us and there alone. Where the world is tough, the secular person tends to disengage by claiming the status of a victim, or by claiming no responsibility, or by escape into illusion and delusion. Religious faith is not the conviction that God or someone else is going to fix things up, but the sense that all the power one needs to live responsibly is at one's disposal. Secular faith is a measured commitment that does not engage beyond an inventory of resources, no faith at all.

Hope is the religious virtue of pursuing a spiritual or religious path, expecting that the center can be found and one's true value achieved. The more the religious person becomes sensitive to weakness, hypocrisy, and internal corruption, the less obvious reason there is for hope, and yet the greater the virtue of hope looms. The secular corruption of hope is to measure its success, with the almost inevitable conclusion of despair. The secular world, by rejecting the grace that religious people believe regularly funds the possibilities for hope, leads to quiet despair about ultimate paths. If the secular person can whistle loudly enough about the non-existence of ultimate grounds and destinies, the despair can remain below the surface. Secular existentialism such as Sartre's and Camus's has glorified the despair.

Love as a religious virtue, whether Western charity or Eastern enlightenment plus compassion, embraces righteousness, piety, faith, and hope together. Whereas separately they are incommensurate with one another and sometimes at cross purposes, in love the other virtues are balanced and joined. Like God creating the world with ideals of order, with parts of intrinsic value, with actual situations combining parts and order, and with ontological value or centered destinies for people, religious love fosters the due order, intrinsic worth, actual existence, and ultimate significance of its object. For the religious virtue of love, the point of loving is to mirror — in the way we treat other people, nature, institutions, and God — the ontological way in which God creates us with order, with components of worth, with actuality, and with harmonious value. The secular form of love is to foster what we like and seek to possess it.

The language used to describe the religious virtues is highly prejudicial, to the secular mind. Indeed, to speak of true religious virtues and their degeneration into secular forms supposes that there is something real to the religious dimension. If in fact there is nothing real to the religious dimension, then those alleged virtues should be described in terms of various delusions and projections. The secular forms should then be redescribed as morality within the limits of our security, aesthetic appreciation of the marvelous, engagement of life so far as life is acceptable, and positive thinking so long as it has the probabilities in its favor. Anything more than these "realistic" virtues would require a kind of external grace that the secular world cannot admit.

Thus we are returned to Calvin's vision. On the one hand, the secular world in its rejections conceives God according to representations that trivialize divinity as a magical external agent, or as an internal Friend and Guide for whom there is insufficient evidence, or as an encompassing super-conundrum, no creator or redeemer. On the other hand, the secular world conceives humanity as a hamper of excuses. Morality is too tough when people are oppressed, so excuse anything. Piety is too tough when it trivializes the world, so stay with the pretty. Faith is too tough when the actual situation guarantees failure by secular standards, so pass the buck. Hope is too unrealistic when possibilities close down, so set low sights. Love is too risky when it has to balance incommensurables, so stick with those who love you first and congratulate yourself for having any "relationship" at all. If secularism is true, then the banal world of television sitcoms is realism and spice comes from the supermarket tabloids we all know to be false from the beginning.

III. THE FAILURE OF SECULARISM

Surely this depiction of secularism is biased. The realism of secular culture is not soft and relativistic but tough and stoical. Sartre and Camus said this is the one life we have, so we had better live it to the full. Yet in their thought there remained the underlying religious theme of grace: in acceptance of the absurd (that is, the nonreligious) and in continued commitment to engaged life, a mysterious meaning and fulfillment is acquired. We make our own meaning, they thought, and there is nothing else. If that and only that were so, however, then most people make little meaning and even that is evanescent. A car crash killed Camus, and Sartre the antifascist died before learning that his humanistic Marxism would be repudiated by humanity as soon as they could surmount its totalitarian power.

The need here is to assess the secularist position, and the first place to attend is the question of creation. How do we account for the contingency of the world? Secularism says that the world is not contingent or, if it is, then we still do not need to account for it.

No secularist, to my knowledge, has attempted to prove that the world as a whole is necessary and not contingent, for such a proof would come too close to saying that the world as a whole is divine. Rather, secularists attempt to claim that the question of how to understand the existence of the whole world is meaningless. In nearly all cases, this argument takes the following form, perfected by Kant: a certain kind of knowledge is valid, for instance intuitive knowledge, or sense knowledge, or common sense knowledge, or scientific knowledge. This kind of knowledge could not possibly be appropriate to ontological questions about the

existence of the world. Therefore, ontological questions are meaningless and are not susceptible to being answered with any kind
of knowledge. This, of course, is an invalid argument because it
requires a premise hidden in that statement, namely, that there
is no other kind of valid knowledge than that previously identified.
It is extremely difficult to prove that some kind of alleged knowledge is not valid just because it is different from some other kind
of knowledge. A common objection to Kant, for instance, is that
his conclusions about possibly valid knowledge do not allow for
the possibility of knowing his own conclusions. In general, secularism has adopted scientific modes of knowing as the only really
good ones, and concludes from this that nothing can be known
about the existence of the world as such, and thus that the whole
issue is meaningless.

But on the contrary, we can ask just what it is that makes
a question meaningful in ordinary common sense or scientific contexts. When we observe a complex state of affairs, to understand
it is to know what is decisive in making it that way. There are several senses of decisiveness that are relevant in different contexts.
Sometimes the particular components of the state of affairs are
decisive, and understanding is driven back to what makes them
the way they are. Other times the larger patterns of the complex
state are decisive, or the even larger patterns in which the complex plays roles. Sometimes the decisive thing to understand is what
good the state of affairs is, or what evil, or what processes it in-
hibits or fulfills. Most of the time science is interested in understanding the surrounding conditions under which happenings of
a certain sort give rise to states of affairs of the sort under analysis. In historical contexts, understanding consists in identifying a
whole story of decisive events, coming from many directions, that
in timely fashion are decisive for making the state of affairs what
it is. Some decisive events are historically unique. Some establish
enduring conditions that environ what is to be explained. Some
establish regularities and laws that make for habitual behaviors.
Some decisive events are insignificant unless massed with other
decisive events; others stand out in their singular importance. To
understand something is to identify and grasp the connections
among the decisive factors that make it be the complex state of
affairs it is. Complexity is what wants an explanation, and the

explanation consists in identifying the decisive points that cumulatively account for the complexity.

Now the realm of determinate things, however they condition one another, constitutes a vast complex state of affairs. That vast complex includes whatever physical or metaphysical conditions there are for complex determinateness itself. What accounts for the vast complex of the world? What are the decisive events by which the existence of the vast complex is to be understood? Part of the answer, of course, consists in how the determinate things are decisive for one another. But that deals only with their mutual definition. What about their very existence as mutually conditioning one another? Religion answers, to use theistic language, that the vast complex of determinate things is created *ex nihilo*.

Secularists and some theists will respond immediately that this is impossible because meaningless. If the physical and metaphysical principles of the world are really *first* principles, then nothing can lie behind them to explain them. But on the contrary, the first principles are complex, else they would not themselves explain anything, and therefore need to be understood in terms of what is decisive for making them what they are. Besides, what really explains are not principles but decisive points; principles or ordering elements are the result of creatively decisive events. To understand is to get the decisive points. What is decisive about the fundamental ontological structures of the world is that they are created to be what they are, so argues the creation *ex nihilo* position.

To this the secularist objects that creation *ex nihilo* is unintelligible. We must answer this objection directly. The answer obviously has to do with intelligibility, and behind the objection is the supposition that intelligibility consists in principles that show how one arrangement becomes another. Creation *ex nihilo* is supposed to be unintelligible because it is not a rearrangement according to some principle but rather a sheer making. The answer to the objection is to show that decisive making is the heart of intelligibility, and that principles of rearrangement are derivative from making. Principles help understanding precisely because their complex determinate structure, which is decisive for the complex state to be explained, is itself what it is for decisive reasons. To grasp this point, reconsider what it means to be determinate.

Determinate identity requires two kinds of features in a thing. It requires conditional features that constitute its connections with other things, conditioning and being conditioned by them; if there were no conditional features, the thing could not be determinate with respect to some other things, and hence could not be different from them or determinate at all. Determinate identity also requires essential features by virtue of which things take possession of their conditions, order them, and have their own being; without essential features, a thing would reduce to nothing but its relations to other things, and ultimately just to those other things.

The question of the existence of determinate things can now be reformulated as understanding how things with conditional and essential features can be together. They must be together if they are to be determinate with respect to each other. They condition one another with their conditional features, and hence are cosmologically together in ways science and other modes of understanding reveal. But they must also be together with their essential features, so that as really different things they maintain their essential integrity while in conditional relations. What accounts for their togetherness? It cannot be another determinate thing, either a cause within the world or a determinate Deistic God, for the relation of that determinate thing to its effects would itself need an ontological ground. Nor can it simply be the whole of things together; for that whole is either determinate, and thus subject to the previous refutation, or indeterminate and thus no whole at all, just the distributive collection which is the thing to be accounted for.

Rather, the only thing that can account for the ontological togetherness of essentially different and mutually conditioning things is a creative act that just makes them be together. This act creates all things together in their very differences; it creates time itself, and thus temporally distinct things: without the ontological togetherness, things could not be related as vastly separated in time. The creative act is not in time or space, but creates time and space. It does not take place in an eternal now or an aboriginal past but in sheer nontemporal eternity.

Unlike most decisive events, which themselves are selective rearrangements of previously given material, creation *ex nihilo* is sheer making and has no character of its own except what results from the creation. To understand that the world is requires science and other modes of knowing to tell us what the world is. But no amount of understanding what the world is will help us understand the decisive factor that makes it exist. The decisive factor is creation *ex nihilo*.

The argument about creation *ex nihilo* is far more complex than has been indicated here.[11] It has metaphysical, cosmological, anthropological, and religious dimensions that have not even been hinted at in this brief defense, and each is controversial. But enough has been said to show that the hypothesis of creation *ex nihilo*, which stands behind a host of fundamental themes in religions East as well as West, has a plausibility in the late modern age.

In answer to the question, Where is God relative to the closure of a world of all determinate things?, the creation *ex nihilo* hypothesis says that God is neither inside nor outside but simply the creator. Apart from creating, God is indeterminate, indistinguishable from nothing. In creating, God's only character results from the creating itself.

Science and other forms of secular knowledge can know everything there is to know about determinate things without threat that religion will insert God as a special determinate causal factor. Religion need deny nothing for which science has evidence, nor need it depend upon the truth of a particular scientific claim. In this sense, religion is perfectly compatible with modernity's definition of the world's closure in terms of determinateness.

Yet religion legitimates, and provides subtle symbols for, all those aspects of human experience that have to do with relating to the ultimacy of existence itself. In contrast secularism must say in the end that everything is relative only to its conditions. Religion articulates the pervasive sense of wonder and contingency, of joy at existence and anxiety at nonbeing. At best secularism admits surprise at the unexpected and nervousness about stability, satisfaction at life's pleasures, and fear of the unknown. Religion articulates the sense that in addition to the specific characters of our lives, this life is the real and only identity we have, and that true judgment upon it and its justification are ultimately serious, not only conditionally so. Secularism must agree that this is the only life and identity we have, but can say that judgment on our lives is only conventional and justification is in the eye of the beholder. Religion acknowledges and praises the movement of the divine creative force of the universe into, through, and out from our lives, blessing us with ultimate grace and giving us the responsibility to bless, just as Calvin said. Secularism must admit that we are the victims of worldly forces against which we can struggle with only feeble resources, and that in the end this does not matter much. The cultural force of secularism has been to turn our sights inward to the self, to the subjectivizing of what had been public life and responsibility, and finally in some postmodernism to the systematic deconstruction of any structures of priority, even subjective ones. Religion by contrast opens us to what is ontologically deeper than ourselves and to what extends far beyond ourselves, and it focuses the conjunction of these in our own personal and social responsibility.

IV. HIGHER EDUCATION AND RELIGIOUS LEARNING

The rather philosophical, even technical, remarks of the last section are intended to respond to the secular claim that there is no religious dimension of life that needs sophisticated learning in institutions of higher education. The argument has been that secularism is just wrong about ultimate matters and that religion is right to call for their investigation and for the cultivation of worthy human responses. Although expressed in the language of accounting for the existence of the contingent world, the argument has made the old-fashioned point that God the creator is real and that we had better pay attention. With respect to higher education, the following four points require attention.

First, with respect to its cosmologies and mythologies, religion needs to be understood, and people need to learn this understanding. Study is required of the beliefs and practices of all religions, and most especially of what is valuable, true, generalizable, and decisive for contemporary life concerning ultimate matters. On the one hand, the study of religion is comparative, and on the other hand it is theological in that it is concerned with the truth contained in or hidden by symbolic religious representations and practices. All this is to say that academic religious studies is a vital ingredient of higher education.

Second, institutions of higher education need to foster sophistication in spiritual practice. This by no means is to suggest that universities should become churches, synagogues, temples, or mosques. Those are the institutions that shape and exercise spiritual practices; educational institutions would do a terrible job if they tried to supplant them, and horrendous confusion would be wrought on the educational job appropriate for universities. Nevertheless, institutions of higher education should send people to religious institutions, legitimating religious practice rather than scorning it. Furthermore, educational institutions are those that enshrine public and free critical discussion, activities that are vital for religious institutions but often cannot take place there. In this instance, institutions of higher education have an obligation to be critics and constructive inspirers of religious formation. This task of promoting learned spiritual practice should be a crucial element in universities' self-understanding.

Third, institutions of higher education have a specific responsibility to contribute to the formation of public rituals that give cultural existence to the religious dimension of human life. Particular religious traditions and institutions have primary responsibility for the development of adequate rituals. But in our time religious traditions and institutions have become largely privatized. Their rituals have scope only within the narrow publics of their followers. Truly public ritual needs a true public, and institutions of higher education are the closest we have to public arenas in the modern world that are not unacceptably captive to political or economic interests. The university therefore needs to develop rituals to define genuine righteousness regarding truth and justice, genuine piety regarding respect for all the elements of life, genuine faith to engage life in its actual particularity, genuine hope for ultimate value, and genuine love for others, for nature, for institutions, and for God. These are heavy demands to lay upon the ritual dimension of matriculation and commencement, of assignments and study, of evaluation and grading, of choosing majors and making vocational life choices, of apprenticeship, friendship, and teaching. But there are religious dimensions of life that will not find ritual enactment anywhere except here.

Finally, institutions of higher education need to train professional leaders in religious life. Although universities find themselves as quasi-religious organizations, as has just been argued, they also need to pay attention to their specific calling, to educate people for life outside the university. This includes people who organize religious institutions. Thus it is entirely appropriate that universities include theological schools along with those of law, medicine, business, other professions, and the liberal arts. Theological schools have their own internal task to combine training in particular religious traditions, the only kind there are, with sophistication about other religions and about religion in general. The importance of that task lies in the fact that theological schools are the educational institutions for religious leadership.

Learnedness or sophistication in religion is culturally important because religion addresses a real and important dimension of human life, that dimension having to do with the construction of intellectual, formative, and ritual responses to the fact of existence and other ultimate matters. The secular rejection of the reality of the religious dimensions leads to what Calvin abjured: a trivialization of representations of divinity and a descent to the utterly banal in conceptions of human life. Institutions of higher education have a special responsibility now to attend to the cultivation of learned religion. Without specific attention, the universities' ritual will only reinforce the secular mistake about ultimate things.

NOTES

1. John Calvin, *Institutes of the Christian Religion*, ed. John T. McNeill and trans. Ford Lewis Battles, 2 vols. (vol. 20 in *Library of Christian Classics* [Philadelphia: Westminster Press, 1960]); pp. 37–38.

2. I have discussed these three — understanding (myth, cosmology, theology), spiritual practices (prayer and other ascetic activities and postures), and ritual (liturgies, ceremonies, and public commemorations and blessings) — in *Soldier, Sage, Saint* (New York: Fordham University Press, 1978), pp. 12–20; *The Tao and the Daimon* (Albany: State University of New York Press, 1982), pp. 32–39; and *Behind the Masks of God* (Albany: State University of New York Press, 1991), pp. 156–63.

3. See Peter L. Berger, *The Sacred Canopy* (Garden City, N.Y.: Doubleday Anchor, 1969); and Mircea Eliade, *The Sacred and the Profane*, trans. Willard R. Trask (New York: Harper & Row, 1961).

4. See John R. Searle, *Speech Acts* (Cambridge: At the University Press, 1969).

5. See Herbert Fingarette, *Confucius: The Secular as Sacred* (New York: Harper Torchbooks, 1972).

6. See my *Reconstruction of Thinking* (Albany: State University of New York Press, 1981), chap. 1; *Recovery of the Measure* (Albany: State University of New York Press, 1989), chaps. 5–6; and *God the Creator* (2d printing with a new Preface, Albany: State University of New York Press, 1992), chaps. 2–3.

7. See my *Theology Primer* (Albany: State University of New York Press, 1992), chap. 3.

8. See, for instance, William James, *The Will To Believe, Human Immortality, and Other Essays* (New York: Dover, 1956); and Nancy Frankenberry, *Religion and Radical Empiricalism* (Albany: State University of New York Press, 1987). See Alfred North Whitehead, *Religion in the Making* (New York: MacMillan, 1926); and *Process and Reality*, (1929; corrected edition by David Ray Griffin and Donald W. Sherburne, New York: Free Press, 1978), pt. 5. See also Charles Hartshorne, *The Divine Relativity* (New Haven, Conn.: Yale University Press, 1948); David Wayne Viney, *Charles Hartshorne and the Existence of God* (Albany: State University of New York Press, 1985); Marjorie Hewitt Suchocki, *God, Christ, Church* (New York: Crossroad, 1986); David Basinger, *Divine Power in Process Theism: A Philosophical Critique* (Albany: State University of New York Press, 1988); Alvin Plantinga and Nicholas Wolterstorff, eds., *Faith and Rationality* (Notre Dame, Ind.: University of Notre Dame Press, 1983).

9. See all of Hegel's books which deal with the topic. See also Josiah Royce, *The World and the Individual*, (1899–1901; reprinted with a new introduction by John E. Smith, New York: Dover, 1959); and *The Problem of Christianity* (new edition with an introduction by John E. Smith, Chicago: University of Chicago Press, 1968); see also William Ernest Hocking, *The Meaning of God in Human Experience* (New Haven: Yale University Press, 1912).

10. See Karl Rahner, *Foundations of the Christian Faith*, trans. William V. Dych (New York: Crossroad, 1989), pts. 1–2.

11. See my *God the Creator*, chaps. 3–4.

Professional Ethics, Moral Courage, and the Limits of Personal Virtue

SHARON DALOZ PARKS

IN A PORTION OF HER POEM, "North American Time," Adrienne Rich reflects upon the meaning of verbal privilege:

> Try sitting at a typewriter
> one calm summer evening
> at a table by a window
> in the country, try pretending
> your time does not exist
> that you are simply you
> that the imagination simply strays
> like a great moth, unintentional
> try telling yourself
> you are not accountable
> to the life of your tribe
> the breath of your planet
>
> It doesn't matter what you think.
> Words are found responsible
> all you can do is choose them
> or choose
> to remain silent. Or, you never had a choice,
> which is why the words that do stand
> are responsible
>
> and this is verbal privilege[1]

All of us, students, faculty, administrators, friends, and guests of the university are — at least to some degree — wordsmiths. We dwell in positions of verbal privilege. When at our best, we know we cannot pretend that we are not accountable to the life of our tribe, the breath of our planet. We know we bear responsibility for our actions and their consequences.

The need for accountability in our common, public life is a primary prompt behind the question, Can virtue be taught? The need for public accountability likewise orients the themes of this essay: professional ethics, moral courage, and the limits of personal virtue.

In the fall of 1988, I was invited, as a researcher, to join the Harvard Business School in the effort to readdress the issues of leadership, ethics, and corporate responsibility. Subsequently, I was invited to a similar appointment at the Kennedy School of Government. Thus I have the privilege and challenge of working with the issues of leadership and ethics in the context of two professional schools. Both leadership and ethics are often described as unteachables, and both are also regarded by many as matters of deep concern — even crises — in our contemporary cultural life. The linking of ethics and leadership joins the question of the good with the question of how we may act effectively in response to our understanding of the good. This linkage of ethics and leadership is another way of speaking of virtue and accountability. The importance of this linkage is vivid in the findings of ongoing study at Harvard Business School

This present study follows from my earlier work in psychology, theology, and human development, published primarily under the title *The Critical Years: Young Adults and the Search for Meaning, Faith and Commitment.*[2] This work is rooted in constructive-developmental and imagination theories, and in its attention to young adulthood, is informed also by the insights of Kenneth Kenniston.[3] This theoretical lens reveals what might be described as a new era opening in the life cycle. In the face of both the extension of the human life span and an increasingly complex world requiring extended formal education, human development, and specifically the formation of responsible adulthood, are taking new forms.

In earlier times, the development of "Identity," the central task of adolescence as described by Erikson, could be accomplished in combination with the choice of a role in adult life. Now, for many, these are two separate tasks. In contemporary society, the young adult (in contrast to the adolescent) has achieved the formation of an adult identity in the sense of having a self-aware self and the capacity for critical thought. But the search for an adult place in society — a place to stand and serve with informed integrity in the context of full adult life — this search is increasingly a complex, distinct task. The young adult may appropriately still be in a process of initiation into a profession, assessing what the available societal roles will ask and allow. This is a vital and strategic perspective from which to engage the question of the formation of professional ethics in young adults.

What does it mean for a young adult to become a professional? Burton Bledstein in *The Culture of Professionalism* describes how *professional* has come to signify a narrow and intimidating specialized knowledge and expertise, often merely legitimating one's standing in a social class, barely masking an underlying arrogant egoism. It is useful, therefore, to recall that the words *professor* and *profession* are rooted in the notion of "church member"— that is, one who has something to profess, openly declaring, avowing, or publicly claiming a belief, faith, or opinion. The word *professional*, according to *Websters' New Collegiate Dictionary* (1981) connotes that one is "characterized by or conforming to the technical or ethical standards of a profession," suggesting, at least, accountability. To have a profession is to have a stance, a way of perceiving and acting, held in common with and accountable to a community of others who bear like responsibility.

It is difficult to have such a stance when we are all losing our balance. In this historical era, the young adult task of becoming an effective, responsible professional is dramatically more difficult because we live in a time of pervasive paradigmatic shift. The practice of trustworthy relationships — accountability — has become fraught with the tension between assumed patterns and emerging demands.

This tension is signaled, in part, by the renewed activity around the issues of ethics and the professions over the past half dozen years. With reference to business ethics, as an example, many assume that the present attention paid to ethics in the MBA and executive curriculums is a necessary response to the misconduct of the 1980s. But it is important to recognize that the renewed interest in business ethics does not arise merely from recent scandals and abuses nor from a simple hope that we can return to a former civility. The renewed attention to ethics in managerial decision making is most appropriately grounded in the fact that we now live in a more profoundly interdependent world and specifically in an emerging global economy. We all now stand on a new ethical frontier, buffeted by a multiplicity of new relationships and conflicting values, some of them unprecedented — all demanding the composing of more adequate wisdom.

Across all professions, the ethical norms of the past are now called under review. We are having to re-ask fundamental questions: What can be professed in a dramatically changing world? What is our ethical stance in the face of unprecedented problems and possibilities? Can virtue be taught? (meaning, Can the distilled wisdom of the present adult generation and its traditions be made usefully accessible?) and What virtues will need to be taught? (meaning, What will constitute virtue in a dramatically changing environment?).

In the effort to name the character of this shifting set of conditions, I have been informed, in part, by my colleague George Lodge. In his prophetic book, *The New American Ideology,* he argued that we are of necessity having to rebalance the values of the individual and the communal. We are having to learn to acknowledge more adequately the individual's necessary interdependence with the whole earth community. Though we are resistant to it, we are moving, he says, from individualism toward the incorporation of a more communal, interdependent conviction. He delineates how from this basic, critical shift flow four consequent shifts: the shift from property rights toward the rights of membership, from competition-consumer desire toward the recognition of community need, from the limited state toward the state as planner and coordinator, and from scientific specialization toward holism.[4]

Indeed, this society places enormous value upon the individual, particularly on individual freedom. This is not a mistake. But we have fallen into the trap of individual*ism* as an ideology, and thus sanctified, it distorts the necessary balance between the values of the individual and the individual's dependence upon the group. The artist, writer, and critic Suzi Gablik has observed, "Individuality and freedom are undoubtedly the greatest achievements of modern culture. They have been crucial steps in the development of human consciousness: we have emerged from simple instinctive or reactive consciousness and have the capacity to transcend the tribal mind."[5] Now, however, the deep human yearnings for both agency and communion, both self-fulfillment and belonging, are being reordered, as the insights from modern physics and the development of global communications each reveal a more dynamic and interdependent universe than we have heretofore imagined. This emerging awareness presents itself in ecumenical-ethnic, economic, and ecological dynamics which now constitute a new global, interdependent reality that is both threatening and promising.

This economic, ecological, and ecumenical interdependence is well captured in an important article by John Tirman. While the tensions of the Cold War dissipate, Tirman traces the scenarios by which future wars might be formed. In sum, he delineates the broad outlines of potential economic rivalries and their intimate interdependence with resurgent ethnic and ideological-religious nationalisms, the legacy of increasingly uncontrolled nuclear arsenals, the emerging technological apartheid. He also cites "the mounting pressures of population growth, deforestation, climate change and plummeting food production" leading to the dislocation of millions of the world's poorest people and environmental degradation which will inexorably "ratchet up" the level of stress within national and international society. The sense of gloom that is generated by this interdependent ecological, economic, and ethnic-ecumenical awareness is wedded to the prevailing idea that we are locked into cycles of military conflict leading to peacetime stasis anchored in a military and economic balance maintained by the victorious powers. Tirman reports that as "fresh challenges, mainly economic, are 'delegitimizing' the U.S. hegemony" formed after World War II, many analysts believe that we are doomed to repeat the violent patterns of history.

Tirman reports, however, that others argue that "the picture is not all bleak. For example, Jerry Sanders of the University of California at Berkeley observes that 'there is some learning going on, [and the development of] new institutions and attitudes that can mitigate the patterns that lead to conflict. . . . War is not inevitable; it's a matter of political choice.' Then Sanders says, 'An *interdependent* world can build regimes that transcend the cycles.'"[6]

Thus the implications of the potential of a paradigmatic shift from individualism to a more interdependent, more cooperative, and more accountable conviction are enormous. Yet we are increasingly having to recognize that we live in an interdependent world without the institutional structures we need to function interdependently.

From this perspective, consider the fact that it is now argued that "the economy is the dominant institution in modern society."[7] Further, as Leroy Rouner has well stated, "the large corporation . . . has become the definitive institution of modern Western culture. The large corporation dominates the modern world in much the same way that the church and the university dominated the medieval world."[8] Business managers play key roles in these dominant institutions, and are increasingly and necessarily expected to exercise public leadership on behalf of the common good across a wide spectrum of issues — including employment and income security, health care development and delivery, the use and protection of the world's natural environment, the distribution of military technology, the role of espionage agencies, and the ongoing creation and management of financial structures and instruments for both global and domestic economies.

In this broad context of increasing awareness of the limits of individualism and the enlarged power and accountability of business-economic institutions, the business school faculty must now re-address the ethical dimensions of the curriculum. As they do so, I have been asked to assist in answering the question, Who are our students? Who are the young adults who are now preparing for positions of significant leadership in our economic institutions?

Every educational institution develops a shared myth about the character of its student body, and if this question is not regularly re-engaged in systematic and timely forms, the gap between that myth and the current reality becomes enlarged and debilitating for faculty, students, and administrators. Throughout the history of the Harvard Business School, members of the faculty and administration have from time to time studied aspects of the experience of the student body both during and after their two years of MBA study. In light of the changes in the cultural climate just described, it has become appropriate to do so again.

Because the purpose of this effort has been not so much to

study the students of a particular school as to study the young adult business students of this generation, I have directed a modest, qualitative study of MBA students across three schools. The other two schools are the Darden School of Business at the University of Virginia and the Amos Tuck School of Business at Dartmouth.[9] Because this study is still in progress and the subject of this essay is necessarily limited, we will consider here only a few of the preliminary findings from Harvard Business School, though initial indicators suggest that the correlations across the three schools are strong. More, these findings appear significant, not because they are specific to a particular school or schools, but because I believe they are emblematic of some of the important dynamics in contemporary American society and our educational institutions.[10]

To step into an MBA classroom to observe ninety talented students between the ages of twenty-four and thirty-two is to become immediately aware that it is not difficult to teach ethics — understood as philosophical ethical systems theory — to bright young minds. Yet as important as that is, if we are concerned with the teaching of ethics understood as the practice of accountability to a profession vital to the common good, the underlying and more profound challenge before all professional schools is located in the question, How do we foster the formation of leadership characterized, in part, by practice of moral courage?

To speak of moral courage is to be concerned not only with the capacity to know, but also with the capacity to respond, to do, to act. As Winston Churchill so rightly saw, courage is the most important of all virtues, for it guarantees the rest. Thus I have begun to think a good deal about the nature of courage.

A part of our attraction to war is our hunger for courage. War always seems to yield stories — profiles — of courage. We want to be courageous. Yet in listening to interviews with military people, the nature of courage becomes ambiguous. Is courage a mere matter of adrenalin, a psychological-biological response to threat? Is it just doing what one has been ordered to do? No one is fully satisfied with such definitions.

Courage is the joining of thought with feeling. Courage is speaking and acting from one's heart, from one's core, where spirit, mind, and disposition are one. Courage signals the presence of spirit, liveliness, lustiness, vigor, vitality, energy, confidence, boldness, love, and passion — which may include anger and wrath. Courage manifests a quality of mind and being which shows itself in facing danger, even when fear is present. Courage happens when one is able to move beyond fear because one can see a more adequate and compelling truth than the truth of the danger and can act, therefore, in response to the truth beyond the fear.

For example: Two decades ago, when I was a young member of the faculty and administration at a small college in the Pacific Northwest, I worked with a student named Scott. When Scott graduated, his parents came to the college for the commencement celebrations, and I was surprised to see that his father bore severe burn scars on his hands, arms, and lower face. A few days after graduation, I saw Scott and asked him how his father had been burned. He responded, "I never told you about the helicopter accident?" He then recounted how when Scott was sixteen, his father, an insurance man, was heading out with his best friend, a rancher, in the rancher's helicopter, to look at the land. Did Scott want to come along? Scott chose to pass the opportunity by. Later when the two men in the helicopter decided to land on a small knoll, the copter descended, then hovered a few feet off the ground, refusing to land. The rancher forced the stick, and the helicopter landed, bursting into flames. Scott's dad was thrown free, the sleeve of his jacket on fire but easily snuffed out. Then he realized that his friend was still inside. He went back into the flames and hauled his friend out. Both men were seriously burned and were flown to Mayo Clinic, where the rancher died. After months of painful treatment, Scott's father recovered.

In such a situation it becomes vividly clear that courage is predicated on purpose, image, imagination. It was the image of a friend, still in the burning copter, which enabled Scott's dad to act in the presence of fear, to move beyond his fear of the flames because he could see a more adequate and compelling truth. Courage depends upon the images we live by. Courage is predicated on faith — the meaning that we make, the truth we hold by means of images. Courage is an act of the imagination, understood not as mere fantasy, but, as Samuel Taylor Coleridge recognized, the highest power of the knowing mind. The moral life depends on the quality of the images held at the heart's core.

Therefore, when I embarked on the work of interviewing

young adult MBA students and a colleague from another context said, "Oh, you're going to get to ask them what their ethics are!" I responded, "No, I want to understand by what imagination they make meaning." We all know that we may or may not act in a manner consistent with what we say our ethics are or what we say we believe. We human beings, will, however, act in a manner consistent with how we make meaning, how we think things are really, what we perceive to be ultimately true and dependable in the most comprehensive dimensions we can conceive—and we make meaning by means of the imagination. We act on the basis of our images of self, world, and cosmos. As H. Richard Niebuhr saw so well, the moral life is the search for right images. [11]

Thus this study is concerned with the imagination by which entering MBA students make meaning, because this is our best clue as to how they will ground their day-to-day decision making and its moral, ethical ramifications. To this end, we have been curious about such matters as their images of success, how they perceive their world, and what issues seem important as they anticipate the future. To illustrate, if it was found that—like some practicing managers—students believe that responsible business decision making is best detached from our wider political life and oriented primarily to quarterly earnings and shareholder returns, we know that those values will significantly influence their ethical imagination—their workaday "faith." Such assumptions about reality will determine the nature and scope of their sense of accountability.

In the effort to understand who students are when they initially come to the school, forty-two first-year students in the class of 1991 were interviewed during the first six weeks of the academic year in the fall of 1989. Thirty-four of these same students were interviewed again in the spring. Throughout the process, I consulted with a number of key faculty and administrators to solicit input in formulating hypotheses, questions, and interpretations. [12]

The average age of these students was twenty-six. As a group, they are highly motivated and talented. They are graduates of some of our best secondary and undergraduate schools. Many, upon graduation from college, were trained in some of our most prestigious commercial and financial institutions or by the military. Many do not expect to return to the particular organization they have been with, not out of any specific complaint so much as some intuition that there is something better for them elsewhere. They do not come primarily from elite families, but predominantly from upwardly mobile middle- or upper-middle-class backgrounds. Our society seems to work for them.

What have we heard? We have heard a great deal about how these students understand their own experience of growing up and the ambitions that others have had for them and that they have for themselves. We have gained insight into the influences that have brought them to business school and how their initial experience of the school has met or differed from their expectations. We also believe that we are gaining a more complex understanding of how they perceive their world and their role within it.[13] I want to focus attention here on three related phenomena that have been salient in the majority of the interviews (though, I hasten to make clear, not in all of them).

Vacuous Credos

The first of these phenomena I have described as "vacuous credos." For example, when we ask students how they define success, typically their response is something like, "I am successful if I do my personal best," or "I would be successful if I achieved the goals I had set for myself." However, when then asked, "What might some of those goals be?" they tend to respond with something like, "Well, it would depend on what company I was with." When asked what company he or she would like to be with, the response is often to indicate some preference but conclude with, "It wouldn't really matter." On the surface, such responses sound amazingly empty, lacking any grounded value content.

Over the course of both rounds of interviews, however, we became increasingly persuaded that these "vacuous credos" do not, in fact, reveal a total absence of substantive values. To be sure, in some cases, we must conclude that the primary values are those of achieving success, however it is defined by the prevailing culture, with little self-reflective choice. Yet in response to most of the interviews, we must conclude that these "vacuous credos" signal primarily that these young adults have been upwardly mobile in a culture that is both individualistic and pluralistic. Therefore, "doing one's personal best" or "achieving one's own goals" are individually oriented values which are both socially confirmed and socially inoffensive in a pluralistic context, while articulating the full substance of one's value commitments might create tensions which would inhibit the upward flow of success.

Many of these young adults, in fact, seem to hold values such as the importance of integrity or a commitment to working on behalf of a specific social issue. Some of these students not only hold such values; they have acted in specific situations in ways that are dramatically congruent with those commitments. But like many in our society, they do not yet appear to have at hand a publicly legitimized imagination, a comfortable language, whereby they might forthrightly and gracefully articulate those commitments. The implication here is that without an adequate public language, ethical commitments tend to remain a matter of personal (or privatized) morality and are thus rendered impotent for social and corporate transformation. People become vulnerable to "splitting."[14] The public world becomes shaped by an ideology of competitive individualism and a superficial pragmatism and sheared off from a private, personal domain of care and responsibility. At a time when our society seeks a fresh, bold, and credible articulation of a compelling and grounding ethical imagination, many of these students are well motivated but are not yet adequately prepared to offer leadership that sees the far-reaching web of interdependent relationships and systems of which they and their organizations are a part. They are not yet prepared to practice the virtues of professionals who are accountable to a wider public life.

A Desire Not to Hurt

The dominance of an individual or privatized sense of morality (in contrast to a more public, systemic ethical imagination) is evident also in a second finding, most vividly portrayed in a response to one of the last questions in the first interview: "You have commented on some of the things you would like to accomplish and some of the contributions you would like to make; as you think across all of the years ahead," we asked, "who do you think you may hurt?" Because we presumed that most students would not have thought about this question previously, they were given ample time to consider it. After a pause, the typical response was, "I hope I won't hurt anybody." When the interviewer, with a questioning look, provided more time, the student might add, "I might hurt my family." If the interviewer provided yet more time, the student might then say, "Well, I might have to fire somebody." The sense conveyed by this last response is that the student might be faced with the unhappy prospect of terminating the employment of a single individual — an interpersonal situation. Yet these students generally expect to have positions of significant responsibility in very major companies, or to head their own large and successful businesses, in which they will be called upon to make decisions that will affect lives and environments that they may never see.

There are two important implications that may be drawn from this data. First, these students perceive themselves as good — neither expecting nor intending to hurt anybody or anything. There is a clear sense of personal, *individual* virtue. Indeed, these young adult students tend to have a strong sense of interpersonal accountability in immediate face-to-face situations with colleagues and superiors. But typically these students do not yet seem to have a correspondingly robust consciousness of the *systemic* reach of their own personal and collective agency, both actual and potential. They are as yet limited in their apprehension of the role of the individual, even the good individual, in systemic hurt and injustice. They do not yet recognize the scope of their power in a profoundly interdependent world. While this conclusion requires further study, it does appear that they do not yet readily discern that some of them have already made, and many of them will make, complex decisions that may affect hundreds or even thousands of lives and/or aspects of the ecosystem not immediately accessible to their analysis. Thus when a student says, "No one can teach me ethics; I know what is right and wrong," it appears that often he or she speaks primarily with reference to an individually oriented, interpersonal ethical frame.

An individual-interpersonal ethic of trustworthiness and mutual accountability in face to face relationships is essential but not sufficient for ethical managerial practice. The moral imagination of young adults moving into corporations, if constrained by the limitations of the individual-interpersonal model, is rendered vulnerable to the potential traps of personal ambition and "company loyalty" narrowly defined. It is unable to ground the moral courage required to engage the complex and interdependent relationships among competing claims within a vision of the common good.

Balance

A third and unexpected phenomenon we discovered emerged in relationship to the first two. This third phenomenon the students refer to as "balance." When asked how they would define success, the majority of students expressed concern about achieving career success and "balance." For example, when asked, "What is your sense of what constitutes success?" a student responded: "I think it's balance. I think it's having a very successful business life . . . without sacrificing everything else — friends and family, leisure, and life outside of work." While this sort of response might be expected to come particularly from women, even more men than women, in our sample, expressed this concern. Typically "balance" meant a desire for equilibrium between values marking career success such as a stimulating job, job status, money, visibility, power, and challenging-creative responsibility on the one hand, and on the other, values signifying a quality of personal life such as friendship, marriage, family, time for leisure and/or sports-fitness activities, music, travel, and vacations.

These students are deeply concerned about how to avoid the imbalance they have witnessed in the generation before them in the forms of divorce, parental neglect, early heart attacks and other stress illnesses, as well as meaninglessness after the crash of 1987. Yet while the desire for "balance" was strong, confidence that it could be achieved was somewhat more ambiguous. As noted earlier, when asked whom they might hurt, the most likely candidate was "my family."

Further conversation reveals that this expectation of the defeat of one's hope for balance is rooted in the imagination of isolated individualism. The need for balance is conceived primarily as an individual, personal challenge with which the individual student and perhaps his or her spouse must somehow cope. There is little recognition that what is experienced as a point of personal anxiety is a matter of systemic, public pain.

Yet the systemic dimensions of this issue are increasingly

evident. In an important book published in 1991 entitled *The Overworked American: The Unexpected Decline of Leisure,* Juliet Schor informs us that while for a hundred years the number of work hours had been declining, this began to reverse itself in the 1940s. Americans are spending increasingly more time at their jobs. If trends continue, we will be spending as much time at work as people did in the 1920s. U.S. manufacturing employees currently work 320 hours (per year) more than their counterparts in West Germany or France. Further, the rise of work is not confined to women entering the work force and doing a double shift, nor is it confined to a few selective groups. Rather, it has affected the great majority of working Americans. Hours have risen for men as well as women, for those in the working class as well as professionals. They have grown for all marital statuses and income groups. Nationwide, people report that their leisure time has declined by as much as one third since the 1970s.[15] Why?

Schor's thesis goes something like this. Since 1948 American productivity has more than doubled. We can now produce the same amount in half the time. We then have a choice between more leisure — or making more money. Yet the American worker has rarely had real choice in the form of the productivity dividend. Consumer-oriented capitalism has preferred longer hours for more money which has doubled our standard of living.

The American market has become a consumer's paradise, offering a vast array of products that are aggressively and artfully marketed. Americans now spend more time shopping and a higher fraction of the money we earn than any other people. We have a standard of living and level of material comfort unprecedented in human history. On a per-person basis, yearly income is sixty-five times the average income of half the world's population. Yet nearly one-fifth of all participants in the labor force are unable to secure as many hours as they want or need to make ends meet. In other words, the incentives of our present economic system have a bias toward long-hour jobs. Some of the products that result surely enhance our lives. But as Schor observes: "Once our basic human needs are taken care of, the effect of consumption on well-being gets tricky."[16] Further, she observes, "time poverty is stressing our social fabric."[17]

The ironies are large. While the business school students

express more explicit, active concern about "balance" than any other single issue, and while they invest considerable energy in coping with this issue in heroic, individual forms, balance is not merely an individual issue. While they experience themselves as vulnerable to structures which most of them seem to assume are impervious to any modification, nevertheless, business students have been and/or will be the managers who set the work hours. They will be the marketers who determine the strategies by which the consumer choices that shape public and private life will be informed and manipulated. To put it more sharply, business students are on their way to becoming architects of the economic and social structures to which they feel they will be so uncomfortably vulnerable. Constrained by the limits of an imagination dominated by individual, interpersonal virtue, they are unprepared to recognize systemic stress. Nor do they perceive their collective potential to compose and practice public virtues by means of which their own personal lives as well as the lives of others could be emancipated.

This set of conditions will obtain as long as the imagination of individualism perdures. In the complexity of modern society, no individual can expect to address such conditions as an individual and effect positive change. The attempt to do so is fostering what Walter Brueggemann has described as "a surplus of powerlessness."[18] A primary manifestation of this powerlessness is cynicism. The growing cynicism in our society — especially among the younger generations — has been documented in a study published by Kanter and Mervis of Boston University and entitled *The Cynical Americans: Living and Working in an Age of Discontent and Disillusion*.[19] Despite the pervasive cynicism in society at large, the business school students we studied do not generally identify themselves as cynical because they have a positive sense of hope about their personal futures. Nevertheless, it is clear that many of them do tend to be cynical about government, universities, and other large institutions, including business corporations. Again, the individual imagination is robust, while the interdependent, systemic imagination is limited and impoverished. As a consequence, it is in relationship to our connected-collective-common-public life, in contrast to their individual lives, that these students seem to have the least hope and feel the least sense of potential competence and efficacy.

Can virtue be taught in young adulthood? What do these phenomena of vacuous credos, a desire not to hurt, and the yearning for balance suggest to educators concerned with the ethical dimensions of professional life?

In sum, they suggest that our young adults — even some of those most talented — are coping with only half of what they need. They do have a vigorous vision of freedom to pursue individual achievement and contentment — and many are committed to personal volunteerism. But most do not yet have a connective, interdependent imagination by which they can creatively address the intensifying complexity of an interdependent global economy and ecology.[20] They can see the individual, the individual corporation, the individual nation. But they do not as readily recognize the social-ecological-political fabric within and upon which individual organisms and organizations must dwell and depend. They do not recognize the dynamic relationships among all sectors of society that constitute the rich interdependence that they are subject to and that they will shape. They do not yet recognize the interdependent complexity that, when seriously considered, confounds their too-narrowly framed interpersonal ethical resolve.

What do these findings mean in the light of what we now know about human development? While to be sure early habituation is powerful in the formation of the moral life, and the imagination of individualism is long since planted deep in the American psyche, young adulthood is, as I have elaborated elsewhere, a time of extraordinary educational potential and vulnerability.[21] The potential of the young adult lies in his or her capacity for critical thought — the capacity to critique both self and world and to imagine what self and world might become. This is the time of an adult formation of a life "dream." On the other hand, the vulnerability of young adults lies in their yet appropriate dependence upon the imaginations of the future that are available in their environment.

Accordingly, we are finding that when young adults are being initiated into the norms of their profession, there is a particular readiness for a positive confounding of a too narrowly framed moral resolve. If "good enough" early habituation has taken place, and if the professional curriculum offers an initiation into complexity and ambiguity, the moral imagination can be strengthened and enlarged.

Such transformation becomes possible under three conditions. First the young adult must have access to an articulate, compelling, viable vision of a positive future that recognizes complexity and ambiguity. Such a vision of possibility must be challenging, attractive, and experienced within the environment of the young adult.

Second, if visions and strategies are going to be compelling to the young adult, they must resonate with the young adult's own felt sense of dissonance and yearning. Thus for this generation, it appears that the issue of "balance" is a primary pathway into a more virtuous imagination. The problematique is keenly felt in a personal-individual frame; yet when seriously pursued, it opens into a more systemic and public horizon—providing the ground for a more adequate awareness of public responsibility.

Third, if the young adult is going to be able to appropriate a constructive, alternative imagination over against the prevailing conventions, there must be not only a sense of individual choice, but more, the conviction of a "we." This is to say that as we are all social beings, we must have the confidence that if we move into new forms of meaning and ethical practice we will not be alone—there will be a new sociality. Moral courage is not only a matter of images at the heart's core; it is also a matter of the company we keep.

To join a profession is to keep company with others. To create and to practice professional ethics is to make covenant with others in the light of our most worthy truth and on behalf of the common good. If we are to foster a positive future of ethical professional practice in service to the common good in the context of this now global society and pervasive paradigm shift, reflection upon the assumptions of entering business school students invites us to practice the moral courage by which educators and students may move together from an exclusive dependence upon the imagination of individualism into the now vital virtues of a more interdependent conviction. Our historical moment asks us to cultivate the moral courage by which decisions are made which are not only legal but just, not only defensible but compassionate. Such decisions press toward both efficacy and efficiency because they are rooted in an imagination that embraces the common good of the whole earth community — an imagination by which together we may become more adequately accountable to the life of our tribe and the breath of our planet.

NOTES

1. Stanzas III and IV from the poem, "North American Time," are excerpted from *Your Native Land, Your Life: Poems* by Adrienne Rich. Copyright 1986 by Adrienne Rich. Reprinted with permission of the publisher, W. W. Norton & Company.

2. See Sharon Parks, *The Critical Years: Young Adults and the Search for Meaning, Faith and Commitment* (San Francisco: Harper Collins, 1986).

3. See Kenneth Keniston, *Youth and Dissent: The Rise of a New Opposition* (New York: Harcourt Brace Jovanovich, 1960).

4. George C. Lodge, *The New American Ideology* (New York: Knopf, 1976). See also George C. Lodge, "The Large Corporation and the New American Ideology," in *Corporations and the Common Good*, ed. Robert B. Dickie and Leroy S. Rouner (Notre Dame, Ind.: University of Notre Dame Press, 1986), pp. 61–77.

5. Suzi Gablik, in *Lightworks*, ed. Milenko Matanovic (Issaquah, Wash.: Lorian Press, 1986), p. 10.

6. John Tirman, "Shifting Balances Point to New Spurs for War," *Boston Globe*, 22 December 1991, p. A20.

7. Willis W. Harman, "For A New Society, A New Economics, World Good Will," in *The United Nations Division for Economic and Social Information Development Forum* vol. 15, nos. 3–5 (1987), p. 10.

8. Dickie and Rouner, *Corporations and the Common Good*, p. vii. This is, of course, not necessarily a desirable condition, for as Irving Babbit wrote in *Democracy and Leadership*, "when studied with any degree of thoroughness, the economic problem will be found to run into the political problem, the political problem in turn into the philosophical problem, and the philosophical problem itself to be almost indissolubly bound up at last with the religious problem." Quoted in Douglas Steere, *On Beginning from Within* (New York: Harper & Brothers Pubs., 1943), p. 8.

9. Rosalyn Berne and R. Edward Freeman are responsible for the study at the Darden School of Business, University of Virginia, and Deborah Chapman and Leonard Greenhalgh are responsible for the study at the Amos Tuck School of Business at Dartmouth.

10. See Piper, Gentile, and Parks, *Can Ethics Be Taught?: Perspectives, Challenges, and Approaches at Harvard Business School* (Boston: Harvard Business School Press, 1993).

11. H. Richard Niebuhr, *The Meaning of Revelation* (New York: Macmillan, 1941), p. 79.

12. Research Associate Karen Thorkilsen served as second reader and assisted in the analysis.

13. See Sharon Daloz Parks, "Is It Too Late? Young Adults and the Formation of Professional Ethics," in Piper, Gentile, Parks, *Can Ethics Be Taught?*, pp. 13–72.

14. Note the concept of "doubling" and the dangers of the split between public and private values. See Robert Jay Lifton, *The Nazi Doctors: Medical Killings and the Psychology of Genocide* (New York: Basic Books, 1986), chap. 19.

15. Juliet Schor, *The Overworked American: The Unexpected Decline of Leisure* (New York: Basic Books, 1991), pp. 1–5.

16. Ibid., p. 9.

17. Ibid., p. 15.

18. Walter Brueggemann, seminar conversation, 1988.

19. Donald L. Kanter and Philip H. Mirvis, *The Cynical Americans: Living and Working in an Age of Discontent and Disillusion* (San Francisco: Jossey-Bass, 1989).

20. See George C. Lodge, *Perestroika for America* (Boston: Harvard Business School Press, 1990); and Thomas Berry, *Dream of the Earth* (San Francisco: Sierra Club Books, 1988), chap. 8.

21. See Sharon Parks, *The Critical Years*, chap. 5.

Teaching Virtue Turns Vicious: "Political Correctness" and Its Critics

GEORGE RUPP

THE AGE-OLD QUESTION "Can Virtue Be Taught?" continues to be asked in our own day. One arresting example in our current cultural life is the controversy surrounding so-called political correctness. I will focus on this controversy because I think it provides an illuminating angle of vision on the age-old question that these essays are addressing.

IRONIES AND CONFUSIONS IN USES OF THE TERM "POLITICAL CORRECTNESS"

Ironies abound in the current uses of the term "political correctness." Those who attack their opponents for allegedly attempting to impose politically correct views themselves advocate the centrality of what they present as a long-established common culture. In terms borrowed from dissension in religious communities, defenders of the faith (as defined in accordance with long-established authorities) charge heretics with imposing orthodoxy. It is as if the culturally normative were to designate the socially deviant as politically correct. Part of the explanation for such paradoxical formulations lies in the recognition that the debates about political correctness are directed at one and the same time to quite different audiences and that the debaters themselves simultaneously participate in multiple communities. Roger Kimball's *Tenured Radicals: How Politics Has Corrupted Our Higher Education*[1] already calls attention to the multiple audiences in its title, which suggests the contention elaborated in the book: counterculture critics whom the larger society repudiated after the 1960s have prevailed in colleges and universities and in the process their political agenda has corrupted higher education. Similarly, in "Curdled Politics on Campus," George Will contrasts "the campuses" with "the real-world politics of the larger society":

> The enforcers of political correctness . . . , having been trounced in the real-world politics of the larger society, are attempting to make campuses into ministates that do what the Western tradition inhibits real states from doing: imposing orthodoxies.[2]

Dinesh D'Sousa writes in the same vein — albeit with less modesty about the influence of those outside the campuses. He ends his essay (entitled "The Visigoths in Tweed") with an appeal to his readers:

> Resistance on campus to the academic revolution is outgunned and sorely needs outside reinforcements. . . . Keep abreast of what is going on and don't be afraid to raise your voice and even to close your wallet in protest. Our Western, free-market culture need not provide the rope to hang itself.[3]

Such references to "the real-world politics of the larger society" and "our Western, free-market culture" are helpful in drawing attention to the overall context for allegations of political correctness. However influential the views so characterized may be on the campuses, those who charge that they amount to an imposed orthodoxy in the academy clearly take them to reflect positions that are out of favor in the society at large. Indeed, the triumphalism in their celebration of their own dominance in the larger society and their enlisting of that larger society in their battle against this alleged new orthodoxy on campus raise questions as to how committed the critics of political correctness are to the free and unfettered inquiry that they invoke as at the heart of liberal learning.

In any case, debates about political correctness take place in a context that includes not only the multiple cultural traditions represented in the academy and its disciplines but also the further contrast between the campuses and the larger society. As a result, the debates concern such issues as the ways in which societies are fundamentally racist, the degree to which long-established patriarchal patterns define opportunities for women, alternative approaches to the study of Asian, African, and Latin American cultural traditions, and the extent to which historical relativism calls into question claims to absolute truth. But the debates also reflect and are fueled by underlying disagreements between dominant tendencies in the larger society and dissenting voices that may have a proportionately larger representation on the campuses. In sum, the charge of political correctness is at the same time an attempt to counter campus-based criticism of the prevailing consensus in the larger society.

This fact about the deployment of forces in the society as a whole does not in itself determine the merit of the opposing views. In this setting the claims of the critics of political correctness to the status of an oppressed and besieged minority do, however, ring a little hollow—the more so in view of the formidable array of media that provide amplification for their allegedly suppressed positions. Similarly, when the critics charge that political correctness amounts to "a new McCarthyism," they wield a two-edged sword. They allege that campus radicals are imposing their own orthodoxy on their students and other colleagues. At the same time, they call for pressure to bring campus-based dissent into line with the dominant views of the larger society. The question is: which of these two threats is more aptly labelled "a new McCarthyism"?

To consider how charges of a new McCarthyism cut in more than one direction requires not only awareness of the ironies in uses of the term "political correctness" but also examination of confusions in the controversies themselves. The controversies are as confusing and as confused as they are because they concern at least three interconnected and overlapping sets of issues that can and should be distinguished but all too often are more or less deliberately conflated. The three sets of issues emerge at successive levels on a continuum from the concrete to the abstract. First, there is the particular practical experience of contemporary communities that include members from diverse cultural traditions. Then there is reflection as to the role of the West or Western traditions in this multicultural context. Finally, there is the general theoretical question of the status of any claims to express or represent the truth.

These three sets of issues certainly bear on each other. The challenge that multiculturalism poses affects alternative approaches to the history of Western traditions and the continuing role of those traditions in a pluralistic world. Conversely, Western ideas and movements committed to civil rights and human freedom have deeply influenced advocates of multiculturalism, even in cases when that advocacy includes defamation of the West. Debates about the role of the West and the challenge of multiculturalism in turn also clearly have implications for attempts to assert the truth of one or another position. In short, the three sets of issues are interconnected and do overlap. The issues are, however, sufficiently distinct that examining each one in turn may clarify at least some of the confusion that the term "political correctness" has engendered.

THE CHALLENGE OF MULTICULTURALISM

In the context of the larger society and its dominant traditions, the fact of a plurality of cultural positions challenges prevailing patterns of thought and action to attend to submerged currents. More than most other institutions, colleges and universities have risen to this challenge. The result is those much maligned intellectual and social initiatives collectively scorned as "victim studies": Afro-American, Mexican American, Native American, and other ethnic studies; women's studies; gay and lesbian studies. Also implicated are attempts to broaden the almost exclusively Western focus of traditional academic disciplines so that African, Asian, and Latin American perspectives begin to be represented as well.

There is certainly much room for vigorous debate about the intellectual quality of the academic programs that have developed in response to the challenge of multiculturalism. But one role of such studies is undeniable: they serve to call into question the tendency toward uncritical celebration of established patterns that is inherent in the dominant stratum of every society. Not surprisingly, that questioning role is often less than welcome. Men prefer not to hear about how different the world looks from the perspectives of women. The majority is quite content to assume it can do justice to the views of various minorities. Euro-American traditions are already enormously complex without the limitless further variables of Asian, African, and Latin American attitudes and orientations.

The tensions that such multiple perspectives engender concern more than exclusively intellectual issues. The changing demographics both of the campus and of the larger society assure that new areas of academic inquiry are not without constituencies to encourage them. At the same time, both the areas of study and experiences on the campuses have implications for public policy.

Certainly both the campuses and the larger society would be more tranquil without the stresses of multiculturalism. Not only education but also the rest of social life would be less challenging if in fact America had a single common culture available for all to celebrate. But that is not the case. One of the great strengths of this country has been the capacity to forge a shared identity out of the differences that are integral to American life. Those differences are perhaps greater today than ever before. At least more Americans are more acutely aware of differences than at many times in the past. The challenge is to continue to incorporate new contributions into a larger shared identity rather than to presume that a common culture is simply there to be celebrated.

In the arena of international competitiveness, the multicultural character of the United States may at first seem, and may in fact initially be, a significant disadvantage over against more homogeneous societies such as Germany and Japan. After all, goals across the entire spectrum of social attainments, certainly including education and training, are more readily reached when there is a common language and culture. Yet the capacity to incorporate difference without insisting that it be harmonized, muted, even suppressed, can also be an even greater strength in the world of the future than it has been in the past. The United States certainly has a far from unblemished record on this score. But this society has developed structures that provide legal protection against discrimination on the basis of minority status, that allow considerable social mobility, and that press for cultural tolerance. While those achievements are far from perfect, they point the way to what will be required more and more in a multicultural world.

In its capacity to incorporate difference within its own society, America compares favorably with competitors. Consider, for example, the difficulties that Germany has had in accepting Greek and Turkish laborers as permanent residents or that Japan has had in treating its Korean minority equitably. In understanding and appreciating other cultural traditions on their own terms Americans have, however, been far less effective. No doubt a major reason for deficiencies in this regard is the status of English as the leading international language. But that fact only renders the global challenges of multiculturalism all the more formidable, not least for the educational institutions that will have to do far better in the teaching of language and culture.

To engage with utmost seriousness the challenge of multiculturalism is crucial not only for developing a shared identity within this country but also to allow effective interaction with other societies. To meet this challenge is critical for American society as a whole. That they have attempted to rise to this challenge is a credit to colleges and universities, even if they have fallen far short of definitively meeting it. Insofar as those who assail what they term "political correctness" target multiculturalism, they are therefore attacking a set of developments that is crucial for the health and future vitality of this society. This assault must be resisted as an exercise in nostalgia for an era in which a relatively homogeneous majority culture was unquestionably dominant and presumed to be universally shared. That era is over, and assaults on what the majority culture ironically calls "political correctness," no matter how intense or prolonged, will never bring it back even if that were desirable.

To defend the aims of multiculturalism is certainly not yet to rebuff in its entirety the attack on political correctness. While multiculturalism has been one of the labels pinned on developments that critics of political correctness oppose, some of its goals have nonetheless been defended. Even so vigorous a critic of political correctness as Dinesh D'Souza, in the most sharply worded of his recent pieces, namely the April 1991 essay in *Forbes*, allows for "benign goals such as pluralism and diversity":

> No controversy, of course, about benign goals such as pluralism or diversity, but there is plenty of controversy about how these goals are being pursued.[4]

The "of course" is more than a little disingenuous, at least for many of the critics of political correctness, whose tolerance for pluralism and diversity often seems quite slight. Still, insofar as the goal of accommodating pluralism and diversity is accepted, the line of attack against political correctness shifts from multicultural-ism as such to the other two sets of issues I have identified: the role of Western traditions and the status of truth claims.

THE ROLE OF WESTERN TRADITIONS

The challenges of multiculturalism and the role of Western traditions have been linked very directly in what are in any case always contentious discussions, namely, deliberations about the structure of undergraduate general education requirements. As so often happens because of the tendency of the media to pick up stories from each other and thereby to amplify their impact on pub-lic perceptions, one case has received disproportionate attention: the curriculum revision at Stanford University that moved into the spotlight beginning in early 1988. As Roger Kimball observes, it is "perhaps the most notorious case involving canon revision."[5]

I am reluctant to continue the pattern of what I think can fairly be called excessive attention to the Stanford curriculum revi-sion. But much of the discussion in the media has been so funda-mentally misinformed or even deliberately distorted that at least cursory consideration of it is unavoidable for any engagement of the criticisms levelled against political correctness. In any case, in view of its widespread use as an illustration, the Stanford case may serve to focus the issues involved in the criticism of political correctness for allegedly undermining Western traditions.

Ironically Stanford is not one of the American universities that has a long-established required sequence of courses in West-ern civilization — as have, for example, St. John's College, Colum-bia University, and the University of Chicago. Instead, since 1980 Stanford has required that freshmen select one out of eight quite different year-long sequences or tracks. The names of the tracks indicate how great the disparities among them have been and are: Conflict and Change; Great Works; Values, Technology, Science, and Society; Structured Liberal Education; Philosophy; Humani-ties; History; Literature and the Arts. In short, even before the revisions implemented in 1988, there was no single Western cul-ture course offered at Stanford.

In the fall of 1987 a Stanford faculty task force submitted

recommendations for modifying this Western culture program. The recommendations were based on a review of the program conducted over almost two years and were not, as some media stories implied, a hasty response to student demonstrations. In the spring of 1988 the Stanford Faculty Senate voted approval of the recommendations from the task force, for implementation in the 1988–89 academic year.

In terms of overall structure, the changes in the requirement are very modest. Seven of the eight tracks continue in the new program. Only one — Conflict and Change — was dropped. In the initial year of the new program, one track was added on an experimental basis. Entitled "Europe and the Americas," this track received full approval after its first year. In that first year, it enrolled fewer than fifty of the 1,500 Stanford freshmen, but it also attracted the most media attention because it marked the greatest departure from the previous Western culture program.

Despite the only modest changes in the overall structure of the requirement, the new program does register a significant shift from the courses that preceded it. For example, while there continue to be works common to all eight tracks, the number is smaller than the sixteen core readings in the predecessor program. To be specific, in the 1989–90 academic year five authors or works (the Bible, Aristotle, Shakespeare, Marx, and Freud) were assigned in all eight tracks; three more (Augustine, Rousseau, and Virginia Woolf) in seven of the eight tracks; four more (Descartes, Machiavelli, Aquinas, and Plato) in six tracks; and five more (Euripides, Dante, Luther, Montaigne, and Homer) in five tracks.

More significant than the reduction in the number of common readings is the rationale for this change. That rationale is signalled in the new name for the program: Cultures, Ideas, and Values (CIV). Not only the one new sequence — Europe and the Americas — but also the continuing tracks are required to include readings from at least one non-European culture. Each track is also expected to address issues of ethnicity and gender and to study works by women and persons of color. In sum, the traditional canon of the great works of Western culture is augmented with readings that often were not included in the predecessor program because the previous core list contained not a single entry from a non-Western thinker, a woman, or a person of color.

My purpose is not to assess the specific strengths and weaknesses of this particular curriculum revision at Stanford. It is instead to examine this revision as one of the most frequently cited instances in indictments of colleges and universities for allegedly abolishing great books curricula and repudiating teaching and learning about Western civilization. Tried on those charges the verdict on the revised Stanford program certainly is not one of guilt beyond a reasonable doubt.

An arresting calibration of how reasonable are the doubts is provided in the judgment of John Searle, a professor of philosophy at the University of California-Berkeley. In an extended review essay in the *New York Review of Books*, Searle examines the issues involved in recent curricular debates. He provides a sharp critique of trends in the humanities and is sympathetic with Kimball's journalistic attack; yet Searle offers a judgment on the revisions of the Stanford curriculum that is not only exculpatory but on balance even positive. Here is his verdict on the seven tracks that have continued to be offered in the new program:

> If anything, these seven tracks look to me like a slight improvement on the original course in Western culture, because they retain enough of the core readings so that the educational purpose of the original is not lost, and at the same time they enrich course work with readings from outside the European tradition.[6]

Even more striking is his commentary on the eighth track, Europe and the Americas. His description and evaluation of this sequence offer a refreshingly judicious assessment that acknowledges the potential for distortion in the course without resorting to the almost hysterical exaggerations featured in attacks on the revised curriculum. A fairly extended quotation is necessary to capture a sense of the balance in his views:

> In this course, the required elements of European canon remain, but they are read along with works of Spanish American, American-Indian, and African-American authors. This eighth track presents a genuinely radical change from the earlier program, and it arouses the most objections from Kimball and other commentators.

However, it seems to me one can make a fairly strong case for the new course on purely educational grounds. Of eight tracks, it is not necessarily a bad thing to have one optional track where European civilization is taught as simply one civilization among others, and it does not seem to me at all worrying that Aristotle and Tocqueville are taught along with Frantz Fanon. Of course, as with all courses it all depends on how the course is taught. Yet even if we assume that the organizers have political goals, as I suppose they do, one of the most liberating effects of "liberal education" is in coming to see one's own culture as one possible form of life and sensibility among others; and the reading lists for the new course suggest that such an outcome is likely. . . . So my general impression from observing events at Stanford is that reports of the demise of "culture," Western or otherwise, in the required Western course at Stanford are grossly exaggerated. If I were a freshman at Stanford, I might well be tempted to take "Europe and the Americas."[7]

Searle's commentary is illuminating because it helps to sharpen the focus on what most troubles thoughtful critics of developments in recent scholarship and teaching in the humanities. It does so by indicating clearly what are not the central issues. Not the central issue is inclusion of works from outside European traditions, even if the result is a smaller number of common Western readings in core courses. Indeed, this inclusion may well contribute greater awareness of the distinctive identity of Western traditions through comparison and contrast with others. Also not central as an issue in itself is the teaching of European traditions "as simply one civilization among others" or "one's own culture as one possible form of life and sensibility among others." Nor is the central issue a stance of criticism over against Western traditions. In sum, pluralism as such, even if it eventuates in criticism of established beliefs and practices, is no more the crux of the matter in considering the role of Western traditions in curricula than it is in addressing the challenges of multiculturalism. Instead of pluralism as such, the central issue is disagreement as to the very nature of the intellectual enterprise, which in turn entails quite different approaches to claims to express or represent truth.

THE QUESTION OF TRUTH

This contention — namely, that the crucial issue in debates not only about core curricula but also about multiculturalism entails disagreements as to the status of truth claims — no doubt fuels all of our apprehensions that whatever may be concrete or down-to-earth in this array of concerns is about to evaporate into a fog of abstractions. I acknowledge that danger. But I am also convinced that elucidating alternative approaches to truth claims will in turn clarify such contentious subjects as codes to regulate offensive speech and the relationship of pedagogy to advocacy.

Certainly not all of the developments packaged together with the label "political correctness" in fact constitute a single and unified movement. The internal contradictions in the ways critics characterize political correctness are at first glance nowhere more evident than on the question of access to truth. On the one hand, political correctness is charged with subscribing to an unqualified relativism, notably in such trends as deconstructionism, a relativism that collapses the very distinction between true and false. On the other hand, political correctness is alleged to be completely intolerant of deviations from proper attitudes on, for example, issues of race, gender, and class.

Yet despite initial impressions, there are significant connections among quite disparate developments and apparently contradictory positions. Deconstructionist literary theory does seem unavoidably to entail an unqualified relativism insofar as it succeeds in allowing no judgments as to adequacy from outside the interpreted texts themselves. This relativism is reinforced by attacks on so-called logocentrism, which by definition resist any appeals to rational criteria and indeed portray Western rationalism as oppressive. That line of attack is consistent with feminist and ethnic criticism of the dominance of elite white male culture. From there follows insistence on a more fairly representative curriculum. This reduction of intellectual arguments to the influence of political constituencies in turn may be hospitable to administratively mandated codes to regulate acceptable behavior and even speech.

I do not contend that all of those connections are necessary ones. But the disparate developments that the label "political correctness" packages together do coexist in contemporary campus life and do in some ways reinforce each other. They do so not only because they are all out of step with the prevailing consensus in the broader society but also because they share a critical stance toward the dominant historical patterns of interpretation of Western traditions. Insofar as that shared critical stance is based on unqualified relativism, it is, however, inadequate. Accordingly, a more robust approach to the question of truth may lead to quite different areas of both agreement and disagreement.

In reading the opinion columns and articles and books of the critics of political correctness, it is striking how consistently poststructuralist literary theory and deconstructionism are cited as indicators of the crisis in the recent trends of scholarship in the humanities. This frequent citation no doubt results in part from the tendency of the various accounts to borrow, repeat, and thereby amplify the same series of themes. It is, however, also remarkably the case that influential discussions of such questions as the status of truth claims frequently do develop from work in literary criticism or literary theory. Indeed, the rubric "theory" has become a mark of distinction for members of literature departments who thereby signal their conviction that their approach to interpreting texts has profound ramifications for all attempts to understand cultural artifacts, which of course includes any and all claims to knowledge.

There is much that is of interest in such discussions. Careful reflection on the hermeneutics of texts in fact may illuminate other forms of knowing or claims to truth. Examination of how a particular text has been read over time, how variously it has been understood, and how its institutional status and cultural influence have changed may lead to remarkable insights not only about historical developments but also about the process of interpretation.

This ongoing work in literary theory is, moreover, broadly consonant with other, for the most part earlier, developments in such fields as linguistics, cultural anthropology, the sociology of knowledge, the history of science, legal theory, and philosophy. In this range of fields there certainly are developments that reinforce each other in undermining claims to have attained disinterested, objective, and universal truth. In short, there is very widespread acceptance across such disciplines of some form of cultural relativism over against scientific positivism or other kinds of absolutist positions.

The recognition of the fact that truth claims are historically conditioned certainly opens up significant lines of inquiry. It calls attention to the ways in which knowledge that is generally accepted expresses and reinforces existing power relations, and it also questions whether and how claims to neutrality in knowing may mask vested interests. But fruitful as such lines of inquiry may be, the fact of cultural relativity that underlies them is scarcely a new discovery.

Nor does recognition of the fact of cultural relativity across an impressive range of disciplines warrant a presumption of unqualified relativism in the practice of those disciplines. Cultural anthropology strives to understand each particular community in its own terms. But the aim is, to use Clifford Geertz's term, "thick description," characterization that captures as fully as can be attained the nuances of the culture described. In short, there are more and less adequate interpretations, and the relative adequacy is not independent of the data available. Perhaps no discipline is more aware of the relativity of truth claims than the sociology of knowledge. But here too the aim is to identify the interests and power relations that shape knowledge in order more adequately to understand the processes involved in, to use the term that Peter Berger and Thomas Luckmann have popularized, "the social construction of reality."

I am acutely aware that rehearsing such points amounts to belaboring the obvious. But the claims of literary theorists and the criticisms those claims in turn elicit too often suggest that the only alternatives are unqualified relativism on the one hand and some form of absolutism on the other. This framing of the alternatives is inadequate to the practice of the fields to which literary theory appeals. It also cannot do justice to the vigorous debates within literary theory itself over which approaches are more or less illuminating. Thus the very practice of the disciplines at least tacitly denies unqualified relativism.

Such fields as the history of science and philosophy entail systematic reflection on the adjudication of truth claims and therefore address this set of issues more explicitly. But notwithstanding the references to historians of science and philosophers in the works of literary theorists, there is little support to be garnered in those fields for unqualified relativism. The history of science, for example, does demonstrate that there is over time no single objective and unchanging frame of reference accepted by every disinterested observer. There are, to use the term that has become ubiquitous since Thomas Kuhn's *The Structure of Scientific Revolutions*, "paradigm shifts." The basis for favoring one paradigm over another is not, however, arbitrary preference. It is instead precisely that one paradigm is more adequate to the data than are the alternatives.

Careful reflection on this set of issues in the history of philosophy over at least the last two hundred years also weighs heavily against posing the alternatives as a choice between absolutism and unqualified relativism. Even the most cursory survey of influential streams of modern philosophy corroborates this point. For example, the tradition of German idealist philosophy from Kant on emphasizes the crucial role of human interpretation in shaping knowledge, but it also, virtually without exception, recognizes that human apprehension depends on and strives to be adequate to what is not yet fully within the consciousness of the knower. Similarly, while the tradition of the post-positivist analytic philosophy in Great Britain and the United States rejects a correspondence theory of truth in which individual terms refer directly to independent realities, thinkers in this tradition also painstakingly demonstrate how ordinary language captures and expresses experience and how in contrast technical philosophical terms may distort that experience. Finally, to take the instance that is perhaps most congenial to relativistic claims, in the American tradition of philosophical pragmatism, claims are adjudicated by various forms of appeal to the practical consequences of taking them to be true; but such claims are still more or less viable, depending on those consequences and not simply on arbitrary personal or political preferences.

In sum, even scholarly disciplines that most emphasize the historically conditioned and culturally relative character of all truth claims do not subscribe to unqualified relativism. Instead, both in the actual practice of their disciplines and in their systematic reflection on this set of issues, they exemplify what is required as an alternative both to unqualified relativism and to scientific positivism or other absolutist positions. That third option has many forms or instances. But what they all have in common is the insistence that judgments of relative adequacy are indispensable precisely because disinterested, neutral, objective, universal, or absolute truth is not attainable.

The result should be agreement that what traditionally is referred to as the search for truth is not only appropriate but crucially significant, indeed central, to the life of the academy. This search for truth must be critical, including in particular self-criticism. It must also be comparative in that it recognizes a plurality of truth claims that must be assessed for their relative adequacy. Finally, it must be continuous or ongoing, since fully adequate comprehension is always an ideal rather than an achievement. However different it may be from absolutist claims, this critical, comparative, and continuous quest for truth stands in sharp contrast as well to those forms of unqualified relativism that reduce all positions to personal or political preferences and in principle refuse to allow judgments of relative adequacy.

IMPLICATIONS FOR THE POLITICAL
CORRECTNESS CONTROVERSY: TWO INSTANCES

To recognize and affirm this ongoing process of critical and comparative inquiry as central to the identity of academic institutions sets the appropriate context for addressing the controversies involved in the charges of political correctness. By way of conclusion, I will consider two instances of such controversies: codes to regulate offensive speech; and the relationship of pedagogy to advocacy. In so doing, I will also draw together the several lines of argument I have developed, in as much as the first instance is a concern generated from the campus experience of multiculturalism and the second is an issue in curricular debates.

Among the most disputed issues emerging from the fact of diversity on college and university campuses is the question of whether or not to regulate offensive speech directed against individuals or groups. A significant number of institutions in fact do have codes that originated in the early 1970s as a response to disruptions of speeches that were deemed insufficiently critical of, or even apologetic for, American policies in Vietnam and elsewhere. Thus the codes were designed to promote free speech, for example by prohibiting heckling or other disruptions that prevented a speaker from having his or her say. In contrast, more recent elaborations of speech codes have attempted to forbid ethnic or racial or sexual epithets that insult or stigmatize individuals or small groups and may lead to violence.

The opposite ends of a spectrum of responses are easy to adjudicate. On the indefensible end of the spectrum are codes that go so far as to forbid "inappropriately directed laughter" and "conspicuous exclusions of others from conversations," to take extreme instances of attempting to protect minority sensitivities. On the clearly appropriate end of the spectrum are proscriptions that simply restate the prohibition against "fighting words," that is, assaultive or threatening behavior that the Supreme Court has ruled is not protected by the First Amendment guarantee of free speech. But deciding the easy cases representing the ends of the spectrum still leaves the large area between them.

Insofar as academic communities are guided by their commitment to the ongoing process of critical and comparative inquiry, constraints on expression beyond those clearly sanctioned by the Supreme Court face a heavy burden of proof. Even the most offensive speech may contribute to the exchange of ideas. Accordingly, unless violence is directly threatened, the response called for is firm disagreement, vigorous rebuttal, even eloquent denunciation — but not formal prohibition. This resistance to elaborating detailed codes with punitive sanctions for violations is all the more important in view of the subtle intimidation and censorship that may already be at work in colleges and universities where the institutional culture officially and visibly provides programs to counter ethnic, racial, and sexual stereotypes. To argue against codes that regulate hate speech is certainly not to condone ethnic, racist, sexist, or other slurs. Nor should resisting detailed codes be taken to imply the position that the choice of words and other symbols is in any way a trivial or inconsequential or simple matter. To argue against such codes is, however, to maintain that freedom to express even deeply offensive ideas is so crucial for academic communities that the risk of less than desired sensitivity or even civility is a cost worth incurring for the benefit of exchanges that are unfettered, unless they degenerate into assaultive or threatening behavior.

Insistence that academic institutions are centrally committed to ongoing critical and comparative inquiry also provides an illuminating vantage point for addressing a second controversy involved in the charges of political correctness. In this case the charge is that the faculty members who are intent on dismantling the canon heretofore at the heart of the Western culture curriculum are doing so in order to indoctrinate their students with their own radical cultural and political views. Even a quite moderate critic like Donald Kagen, dean of Yale College, sounds alarmist on this issue:

> The study of Western civilization is under attack. We are told we should not give a privileged place in the curriculum to the great works of its history and literature. At the extremes of this onslaught, the civilization, and its study, is attacked because of its history of slavery, imperialism, racial prejudice, addiction to war, its exclusion of women and people not of the white race from its rights and privileges.[8]

There is no doubt that significant numbers of faculty who teach courses in Western civilization are highly critical of flaws like those Kagen notes. It is also true, as Kagen argues, that insofar as it focuses exclusively on flaws, "the assault on Western civilization badly distorts history." Here again the extreme case is easy to adjudicate: to teach with the intention of systematically defaming it as exclusively a tradition of oppression is irresponsible pedagogy that rests on indefensible scholarship.

But agreement in castigating the limiting case of highly tendentious and unbalanced representations that are exclusively negative still leaves much room for discussion. Certainly, as Kagen argues, the substantial and distinctive achievements that have shaped Western civilization should be represented not only as impressive attainments in the past but also as values to be cherished and preserved. Yet equally certainly such courses should not become uncritical celebrations of the West. As Kagen himself notes in the same opinion column, "the Western heritage" has as "one of its most telling characteristics" the "encouragement of criticism of itself and its ways." Hence even the critics of Western civilization themselves offer eloquent, if sometimes unspoken, testimony to the power of libertarian traditions nourished in the West — including feminism and the movement for civil and human rights, both of which emerged in the West to exercise worldwide influence.

In realizing this aim of critical and self-critical appreciation and even appropriation of the great range of Western traditions, recent scholarly trends in fact have substantial contributions to offer. New historiographical methods have allowed the reconstruction of how ordinary people, as distinguished from intellectual and political elites, lived in various periods. Feminist scholars have focused attention on the special situation of women in past eras. Similarly, extensive scholarship has been devoted to recovering narratives and other data about the experience of slaves and other repressed or minority groups. Such studies provide arresting data and intriguing hypotheses that may indeed be more critical than traditional accounts. At the same time, the recognition that all claims to knowledge are registered from particular locations and that therefore there is no completely objective or disinterested or neutral standpoint appropriately leads to questioning any and every established pattern of interpretation. All in all, there are excellent prospects for lively interaction among quite different perspectives — interaction that almost certainly will lead to a critical and self-critical appreciation of the powerful traditions that have shaped the West.

This lively interaction is, of course, precisely what a community committed to ongoing critical and comparative inquiry should welcome. That teachers and scholars are engaged vigorously in their subjects and even advocate definite positions can be entirely consistent with responsible pedagogy. Such advocacy is more likely to be responsible if it is acknowledged rather than disguised; proponents of definite views can then be held accountable to the requirement that the expression of other positions be allowed and that countervailing data not be suppressed. As importantly, the academic community itself must execute its responsibility to assure that a range of interpretations is represented.

In executing this larger responsibility, colleges and universities face the two quite different pressures that I referred to in my initial sketch of the ironies in uses of the term "political correctness." One is the tendency that critics of political correctness characterize as an assault on the West by disenchanted radicals who have lost out in the politics of the larger society and now seek to impose their views on the campus community. The other is the threat to marshall resources in order to press for acceptance on the campus and in particular among the faculty of the prevailing wisdom of the society at large. Those two quite different pressures recall the phrase "a new McCarthyism" that has been deployed in discussions of political correctness to designate the enemy to be attacked, the danger to be averted. The question remains: which of the two dangers is more accurately captured in that phrase?

NOTES

1. Roger Kimball, *Tenured Radicals: How Politics Has Corrupted Our Higher Education* (New York: Harper & Row, 1990).

2. George Will, "Curdled Politics on Campus," *Newsweek*, 6 May 1991, p. 72.

3. Dinesh D'Sousa, "The Visigoths in Tweed," *Forbes*, 1 April 1991, p. 86.

4. Ibid., p. 82.

5. Kimball, *Tenured Radicals*, p. 27.

6. John Searle, "Review Essay on Multiculturalism," *New York Review of Books*, 6 December 1990, p. 39.

7. Ibid.

8. Donald Kagen, "The Western Heritage," *New York Times*, 4 May 1991, p. 15.

Author Index

Subject Index

Darling-Smith, Barbara (ed.)

AUTHOR

Can Virtue Be Taught?

TITLE